The winds of reform and renewal sweeping through the Church have left untouched no major portion of her life. The Second Vatican Council has ushered in a process of self-scrutiny of a breadth and depth without parallel in the long history of the Church.

No one either expected or hoped that the seminary would be exempt from the necessary stage of re-examination, for much of the ultimate success of *aggiornamento* will depend upon the priest and the effectiveness of his preparation for the tasks of the "new" Church.

Granted the strategic importance of the seminary, however, it becomes clear that criticism of it must be constructive and not carping; it is absolutely necessary that the critic be both responsible and knowledgeable, for only harm could come if the seminary were regarded as fair game for the amateur marksman.

By every criterion *The Genius of the Apostolate* is a significant book about a significant subject: the pre-seminarian, the seminarian and the priest. Its authors live and work with priests and seminarians, and write with that special clarity that comes when one's knowledge of a subject is illumined by one's reverence for that subject.

The result of the authors' empathy is a book of greater honesty, not less. Nothing could be more trenchant than their indictment of certain "recruiting" methods to interest candidates in the priesthood; a Voltaire could not be more forceful in emphasizing the need for mature seminary professors if the seminarian is to reach the psychological maturity necessary for the priestly apostolate today.

This is a book which will be welcomed not only by those who staff seminaries but by seminarians themselves, as well as by those priests who might feel that their own training had not fully prepared them for either the rigors or the glories of their priestly vocation. In its frankness and fullness, in its awareness of the real and insistence on the ideal, *The Genius of the Apostolate* is an invaluable contribution to the renewed understanding of the mystery and meaning of the priestly life.

EUGENE C. KENNEDY, M.M., a native of Syracuse, New York, received both his Masters and Doctorate Degrees from The Catholic University of America. He is currently Professor of Psychology and Psychological Counselor, Maryknoll Seminary, Glen Ellyn, Illinois.

He also serves as a consultant to a number of dioceses and religious orders, and conducts Maryknoll's pre-seminary testing and counseling program. He is a supervisor of priest-counselors for the Archdiocese of Chicago and Lecturer in Pastoral Counseling at Loyola University (Chicago).

PAUL F. D'ARCY, M.M., a native of New York City, also received his advance degrees in psychology, including a Doctorate, from The Catholic University of America. He is the Director of Education for the Maryknoll Fathers and teaches Pastoral Counseling at the Maryknoll Major Seminary.

Father D'Arcy is a member of the staff of the Iona Institute of Pastoral Counseling and of the Committee for the Study of Methods in the Psychological Assessment of Candidates for the Religious Life of the American Catholic Psychological Association. He has delivered papers at numerous meetings of counseling, educational and vocational organizations.

The Genius of the Apostolate

The GENIUS
of the APOSTOLATE

PERSONAL GROWTH IN THE CANDIDATE,
THE SEMINARIAN AND THE PRIEST

by PAUL F. D'ARCY, M.M.
and EUGENE C. KENNEDY, M.M.
Foreword by BISHOP O'DONNELL

SHEED AND WARD : : NEW YORK

Library of Congress Catalog Card Number: 65–24690 *

Nihil obstat:
    Thomas J. Beary
    Censor Librorum
Imprimatur:
    † Robert F. Joyce
    Bishop of Burlington
July 10, 1965

The nihil obstat and imprimatur are official declarations that a book or pamphlet is free of doctrinal or moral error. No implication is contained therein that those who have granted the nihil obstat and imprimatur agree with the contents, opinions or statements expressed.

Manufactured in the United States of America

Foreword

I am happy to take up a task to which Albert Cardinal Meyer would have turned if he had lived longer. No Churchman was more concerned about the priesthood and no greater priest ever served the Church than he. A healthy and growing priesthood was at the center of the Cardinal's vision of the Church, and that is the subject of this book.

Current comment on the priesthood underscores the humanity of the men who have been called to it. The proffered categories of our fallibility are endless and, while honest men are never afraid of the truth, some contemporary criticism is bitter and empty. Fathers D'Arcy and Kennedy look at the priesthood from a positive and hopeful viewpoint. As the vocation of the Church is to grow, so each priest is called to "the full measure of manhood in Christ Jesus." Priests are men, and they can make mistakes. We cannot, however, settle for cynicism in a world that needs hope. It is not just a question of proclaiming and analyzing the "irrelevance" of the priesthood; the more difficult and urgent task is to reveal the priesthood in everything it can mean when fully grown men exercise it in a darkened world. Manly priests bring light and life, brighter and fuller, to mankind, and it is through this ministry to human need that they are themselves redeemed.

There is no doubt that we must re-examine our attitudes toward vocational recruitment, seminary training, and the structure of priestly life itself. Unwilling to do this, we have already failed the human family at its hour of maximum need. Our hearts must be ready for change, but for the change that is the concomitant of healthy growth, not the change of disintegration that leads to death. The authors of this book have made this the basis for their reflections and suggestions for positive growth in vocational development, seminary training, and priestly life.

This is not a regret-filled reappraisal but an honest effort to understand deeply the priesthood and the men who are priests. This understanding attitude gives rise to sympathetic insights into the immense problem of making it possible for priests, and through them the Church, to "have life and have it to the full." This book aims at understanding the priest as a man related to all men just as Christ Himself was. It is not an effort to alleviate the symptomatic complaints of the disaffected or restless. The answers to whatever problems the priesthood faces are not in fringe benefits or fads. Neither does this book advocate slick or superficial campaigns to get men into the priesthood or to keep them there. Through psychological insights the authors illumine the possibilities for a full and fulfilling life within the essential aspects of the priest's work with people.

Love is not soft or sentimental; neither is it the super-mystical and supercharged experience that some writers would make of it. Love must fill a priest's life, a strong, free and respectful love that brings other people to life. "He loved me," St. Paul wrote of Christ, "and gave himself up for me." This will be a good epitaph for any priest who sees that people are the real prize in his apostolate. He is called, not to be remote from them nor to generate an esoteric mystique for his own satisfaction with them, but to love them all for their sake, to "give his life as a ransom for many," to be "poured out like water," as he translates God's love by his own life into a message men cannot misunderstand.

This takes healthy men who are fully mature, because only such men can lead the life of faith the priesthood is meant to be. The priesthood is not something for posturing enthusiasts; it is truly the vocation that asks most, because it asks for everything that a strong man can give.

The authors deal with these fundamental terms of life and growth and health. It is part of the fresh air that Pope John's open window has let into the Church. It is also a stirring of the Spirit that blows where it will, the Spirit of Love that is the source of priestly growth and effectiveness, the Spirit that, through fully grown priests, will renew the face of the earth.

† CLETUS F. O'DONNELL J.C.D.
Auxiliary Bishop and Administrator of the
Archdiocese of Chicago

June 10, 1965

Dedicated to
Bishop James Edward Walsh
of Maryknoll
*The last American Missioner
in China, now serving a
twenty-year prison term in
Shanghai*

Contents

Introduction

We have written this book as two priests who are also psychologists who have worked for a number of years teaching, testing and counseling seminarians, priests, and religious Brothers and Sisters. As priest-psychologists we have had an unusually rich opportunity to study and try to understand the process of full personal growth in men and women who have sensed Christ's invitation to follow Him. The most important issue of the day, as far as our seminaries and other houses of training are concerned, is a deep and lively grasp of the conditions of healthy growth in Christ. This book sees religious vocations as necessarily dynamic and growing and tries to apply the insights of psychological training to the various phases of religious vocational development. The theme, then, is growth—that they may have life and have it more abundantly—and the direction is, as it must be for all growing things, positive and forward.

The book is written for vocation directors, seminary professors, novice masters and mistresses, and others who are responsible for the growth of vocations in any way. It is also directed to seminarians and religious aspirants who are still growing in the process of understanding themselves and their own vocations, and to priests and professed religious who are pursuing fuller growth in their vocations.

It is in no sense a book of formulas for success for recruiters or rectors. It will not tell you, in carefully measured steps, "how to do it." Growth, if it comes at all, comes from within; so too it must be for the reader of these pages. Too often, in the field of vocational recruitment and development, the discussions and programs presume that growth comes from without. This is why vocational work, in any phase, can be filled with hidden but painful frustrations. It is like the man who decides to open a clam that does not want to be opened. At first he feels confident that the task is under his control. Then he finds that the clam's shells do not part when he exerts pressure. Mildly irritated, the man gets a knife or some other instrument and begins to pry and scrape at the shell; still there is no success. He is really frustrated now, and, in his anxiety to succeed, gouges a bit of flesh from his own hand. The man is sweating and muttering as he makes the peculiarly disproportionate vow, "I'll open this if it kills me." Now the man and the clam are as one thing locked in mortal combat. Incredibly, the man seems to be emotionally involved with the clam. Then, in a burst of self-defeating anger, the man tosses the clam away, covering his loss by rationalizing, "I never really wanted to open it anyway."

It is quite a spectacle: the man is perspiring, his hand is cut, he is frustrated and angry; perhaps he now vows never to eat clams again. But the clam is lying quietly in the sand and the sun and, in a few minutes, it opens by itself, just the way God made it to do. The frustrated and truly self-defeated man did not understand either clams or himself, and so it can be with the vocation director, the seminary professor or postulant mistress, who tries to force things to grow from the outside alone. Only those who have suffered it can understand the frustration and discouragement that can arise in religious vocational work. Only those who have bitterly tossed them aside can understand the sterility of approaches to vocations through advertising, cajolery, manipulation or other purely external means. At least some of this distress, as in the analogy, is self-inflicted injury, pains reaped from a seeding of our own ignorance about ourselves and about the persons with whom we work. When we understand these personal dimensions of vocational work more thoroughly, when we grasp the notion that healthy growth comes from within, then we will truly be freeing our candidate's God-given potential for real growth. We may plant, Apollo may water, but God gives the increase. There is, then, no way that you can learn from this book unless it encourages and frees you to grow from within, just the way God made you to do.

Our special thanks go to Mr. Philip Scharper for his encouragement and understanding as we prepared this manuscript. We are grateful to Father Charles A. Curran, Ph.D., for his longtime friendship and encouragement. We are indebted to all our friends in the worlds of psychology and seminary and vocational work for their suggestions and encouragement. We are especially grateful to all Maryknollers, priests, Sisters, Brothers and students, all over the world. Our deepest debt is surely to all American priests and religious men and women whose lives of growth in Christ inspired us to write in the first place.

PAUL F. D'ARCY, M.M.
EUGENE C. KENNEDY, M.M.

I *The Candidate*

1 Characteristics of Growth

This book about vocation emphasizes both person and growth. A healthy person is one who is "in process," who grows, who matures. Vocation is a part of a person, not a thing in itself. It is what a person wants to do and what he does with his life. Vocation grows as the person grows, it shares in the growth of the person, and so it too matures. This opening chapter presents some reflections, of a general sort, on how a person grows.

Growth and change have never been experienced more than by the man of today. Modern history has been accelerating so fast that change in one's way of life due to scientific and industrial developments is an accustomed part of our experience of living. The intellectual world has focused its genius on the domains of growth. The biologists have opened to us their theory of evolution contributing insights into growth of cosmic scope. From the psychologists have come searching studies of what it means to mature. Philosophers now look on life, and even existence, as a process. Such currents have had vital impact on the Church and are partial causes of the great renewal now in progress there. Theologians explore the development of doctrine and of morality; the biblical scholar writes of the emerging consciousness of Christ. Particularly relevant to this

1

book are the researches going on, especially in secular centers of learning, into the vast and intricately complex question of how a person comes to settle on his life work and how a vocation grows.

Growth comes from within. It is not like a garment which can be put on; it is more like a seed. The ground in which a seed is placed can be cultivated and watered, but the growth itself comes from within. We can only provide an environment in which growth is made possible or easier. The principle of growth is not something that we cause. A person does not grow the way a building does, although some who are responsible for the training of men may work on this premise. A building is put together by someone else out of many small parts. A living thing grows from within; it cannot be basically directed from outside without great risk of interfering with healthy growth. What a man makes, i.e., a building, a rocket, or a car has a unity only in the mind of the man who draws up the plans.

Many insights into personal growth occur in counseling or therapy. Growth implies reorganization, and to an untrained observer a person who is growing may look worse for a while rather than better. He may look worse than he did when he was not growing. One learns not to confuse controlled calm with health or to confuse upset with sickness and decline. An example of this is the person who, for the first time, is beginning to assert himself, which is a very healthy step, but who looks rebellious. Or the individual who has been withdrawn and now has his first relationship with another person, which strikes others as immature; but it is a step forward from his previous isolation.

Growth has a habit of coming where it is least expected. This is because it comes from within; the organism does the planning instinctively, with the mind often not knowing what it is up to. We are hoping to grow intellectually in school and have paid costly tuition; instead interpersonal growth problems interfere with our studies. So often we are frustrated by growth opportunities appearing on one side of us, when we have counted on them appearing on another side. Sooner or later we see these rude obstacles as disguised opportunities for growth. The organism often has a greater sense of where growth is needed than can be known from our own analysis of the situation. Growth is full of surprises.

One comes to trust the innate wisdom of the organism, to respect it and learn how to listen to it and not fight it. The way to listen to one's organism is first to become *aware* of one's feelings, inclinations and reactions. These are the spontaneous responses of our organism. Secondly, we must gradually accept what our organism thus tells us about ourself and incorporate it into our image of ourself. But that does not mean that everything we accept ourselves as being satisfies our ideal of what we want to be. We have the task of distinguishing those reactions in ourselves with which we are satisfied from those which do not harmonize with our values. Finally, we have the process of patiently modifying those reactions and feelings in ourselves which do not mesh with our ideal. This is the deep growth process of integration of feeling and value which leads to inner peace and maturity.

Growth is full of uncertainty and risk too. One who is growing does not always know that he is. For all he knows he may be on the wrong track. It is not secure—it is a voyage of exploration. We recognize our rigidities and defenses and let them go. We substitute for these crutches the support of a person who has faith and confidence in us, until we are able to walk alone again. We cannot do this alone. Growth occurs in any relationship in which one finds sincerity, acceptance and understanding. Growth is an unfolding, an opening up, not a repressing. Growth occurs in the warmth more than in the cold. Furthermore, growth is not as steady a thing as we might imagine. It is not a constantly rising slope but a series of ups and downs which have an overall growth direction. When we are down, there is no sense of growth; when we are up, the confidence and assurance of progress returns. A proof of this is the fact that whatever appears to have been lost in a slump returns immediately when one gets back out of the slump.

Growth occurs when there is hope; it is slowed down by discouragement; it ceases with despair. Teilhard de Chardin wrote in his book *The Future of Man:*

First, the hope. This must spring to life spontaneously in every generous spirit faced by the task that awaits us; and it is also the essential *impulse* without which nothing can be done. A passionate longing to grow, to be, is what we need. There can be no place for the poor in spirit, the sceptics, the pessimists, the sad of heart, the weary and the immobilists. Life is ceaseless discovery. Life is movement.[1]

To feel oneself growing is to feel the pulse of life itself, to get a glimpse of its beauty. It is thrilling and invigorating. It alone gives one the feel of the value of living. We thrill to music because we feel the life in it. By sensing our inner growth we experience life's worth despite its pains. "Is not beauty created at every encounter between a man and life? . . ."[2]

Growth has many facets. Deep growth and strengthening of the self can occur in ways we are not conscious of at the time, but realize only later, when we are confronted with a situation

---

[1] New York: Harper, 1964, pp. 72 ff.
[2] Dag Hammarskjold, *Markings* (New York: Alfred A. Knopf, 1964), p. 57.

which would once have been too much for us but which now, to our surprise, we can handle comfortably.

The process of growth is deeply connected with the uniqueness of the individual. Each individual has his own temperament and his own unique life history. He must grow in terms of these and find goals appropriate for one with his capacities and background. He has to be guided from within and find the sense of his own inner direction. Learning spontaneously to trust those inner inclinations of ours which we know from experience are to be trusted is nothing other than learning to listen to the voice of the Holy Spirit guiding us from our inmost depths. The attempt to produce growth by putting men into a mold or demanding conformity is based on a total misunderstanding of man, of his nature and the indwelling of the Holy Spirit. It is sacrificing the person for the convenience of system; it is the mechanizing of man. It is a basic lack of respect for the mystery of the human person.

This book looks at the priestly vocation from the point of view of growth and develops this perspective at three levels; one, the early years of life; two, the years of training for the vocation; and three, the years after the person has entered upon the full living-out of that vocation.

2 The Mature Priest—
The Goal of Vocational Growth

Experience as a therapist makes one aware of how deeply weakness is rooted in man. When the therapist is a priest, he realizes how closely weakness and despair are linked. If a man is to grow, he must have hope that he can cope with those weaknesses deeply rooted within himself which appear to be beyond his own unaided capacity. He needs support from outside himself; and for this help he more frequently turns to the Church than to any other agency.

The Church is a mother to the poor, to those in need, for those who are weak. They need the pastoral ministry of the Church. They need to be consoled in their misery, to be healed in their weaknesses, and to be guided. Sometimes the Church appears to have room only for a psychologically adjusted elite, for the strong, for those who are emotionally mature.

Emotional maturity is a grace which is largely unearned, bestowed on the individual in the early years of his life by mature and devoted parents. Too frequently the weak find no place for themselves within the Church. Those who are immature, those with character problems, those with weak psychic structures do not feel welcome and do not find the pastoral solace they require.

Who within the Church is responsible for the ministry to the weak? Who is to help those who are unable to help themselves? Who is to feed those who are hungry? Traditionally, this is the role of the pastor, of the priest. It is his mission to feed rather than to be fed.

The work of a priest is to minister to the needs of God's people. In contemporary theology it is the people of God who make up the Church, and the role of the priesthood is to minister to them. This is in opposition to a view in which the priest is on a pedestal to be admired by the people. His role is the active one of feeding them rather than the passive one of having his vanity and self-esteem fed.

The heart of the vocation to the priesthood is to minister to the deepest needs of man: man's need for meaning in life, man's need for encouragement in despair, for support in crisis, for forgiveness of guilt and return to God.

To minister perseveringly to the needs of others requires maturity. Immaturity is based on an unsureness of the self which keeps a person trapped inside himself, unable to give himself to the service of others. Such a person has to protect himself, to seek security; he is not able to give himself.

It is for this reason that the priestly vocation calls for a mature man. Directives from the Holy See and the Congregation of Seminaries, as well as the things set down in the Code of Canon Law as the impediments to Orders, have constantly emphasized that a candidate for the priesthood must come from a sound family background, must have mental health, must have been blessed with those inner strengths which free him to perform the pastoral duties of the priesthood and to minister to others. The strong among God's people are thus called to minister to the weak.

This is not to say that we are not all weak. True humility, which is a strength, is an acceptance of one's weakness and a turning toward those sources of strength which will heal the weakness. No one is perfect. It is a question of degree. A priest must have sufficient strength to meet the demands of his calling, which is the ministry to others. In order to accomplish this ministry, he must be able to establish relationships with his people. His people must be personally important to him. To the extent that he can respond to them individually, he can meet their needs. This, then, is what it means to be a priest. To be able to know and care for others, to be sufficiently sure of oneself that one's inner needs do not, in a notable way, interfere with this work.

A study in Belgium investigated what adolescent girls looked for most in a priest. This study has been repeated since with other populations; the same result always emerges. What is looked for most is understanding, and next to that sincerity. These are deeply personal qualities, the capacity for empathy and the capacity for genuineness. They are recognized correlates of maturity.

It is important to understand what a mature priest is, for this helps us to understand what qualities to look for in a candidate for the priesthood. We look for someone who is capable of realizing this goal. It is not that a candidate must already have attained it; rather, he must show signs that he wants to attain it, and, with the helps and programs available, has some likelihood of doing so.

It is not enough that a priest should perform the liturgical duties in a routine way. His task is a deeply personal and human one of reaching the hearts of men. It is not a formalistic role. There is no other vocation which demands, of its very essence, such maturity, because there is no other vocation that must deal so deeply, intimately and importantly with men.

When those who are incapable of functioning in the priesthood find themselves in the priesthood they can turn the

Church upside down and inside out. Instead of ministering to the people who need their help, they have the people ministering to them. Instead of respecting the deep inner worth of the people, they manipulate them like slaves. History is full of examples of the evils that befall the Church when its clergy are immature as persons. Anticlericalism is the hostile, suspicious reaction of the people of the Church against such men.

3 Vocation—Personal and Dynamic

A vocation is something deeply personal; it is in fact one of the most vitally important portions of one's self. It is not an entity in itself, a separate thing, but it is a part of a person. It is what gives meaning and purpose to his life. This is true whether he consciously realizes it or not. Those with no sense of vocation find life empty and without meaning; those who do not yet know and who are searching for their role in life are unsettled and can be described as floundering or drifting. They lack the moorings and stability that a sense of direction gives. It is a very painful experience not to know what we want to do with our lives.

Two trends within modern thought which are relevant here are:

(1) The emphasis on "person" as the greatest of values, who is not to be treated as an object or as a thing;
(2) The dynamic outlook that sees life as a process, a flow, a development, an expansion, a growth, a fulfillment.

The implications of this are that since vocation is such an intimate part of a person, it is to be treated with the respect due a person and primarily at least in the most personal of ways. It is not to be manipulated or treated as a number, a case or a thing. It is best cultivated by relationships, not by techniques. Further, since a person, at least one who is truly alive, is in process of growth, his vocation can also be viewed as part of a process, as something dynamic, evolving and maturing. It is not a static all-or-nothing thing which at one moment we do not have and at another emerges full-blown. A vocation grows from its remote and subtle beginnings in our earliest years to its mellow maturity in the autumn of life. A vocation is a part of our life which grows as we grow.

Recent psychological research has emphasized both the relation of vocation to the self-concept of the individual and its dynamic aspect. This research has not, of course, concerned itself with vocation in the religious sense; but it can shed light on the natural human aspects of this process. There is no reason to believe that grace does not build on nature in calling an individual to the service of God. Research that illumines the natural process of vocational development can cast light on vital aspects of religious vocation.

In harmony with what has been said above about vocation being personal, recent vocational theory stresses the relation of vocation to the self:

In expressing a vocational preference, a person puts into occupational terminology his idea of the kind of person he is; that in entering an occupation, he seeks to implement a concept of himself; that in getting established in an occupation he achieves self-actualization. The occupation thus makes possible the playing of a role appropriate to the self-concept.[1]

It also shows how vocational growth is self growth:

[1] Donald E. Super, Reuben Starishevsky, Norman Matlin, and Jean P. Jordaan, *Career Development: Self-Concept Theory;* Self-concepts in vocational development (New York: College Entrance Examination Board, 1963), p. 1.

Career development then is self-development viewed in relation
with choice, entry, and progress in educational and vocational pur-
suits. It is an evolving conception of self-in-situation which is
occurring over *time* in man who is capable of anticipation, experience, evaluation, and memory.[2]

And it illuminates the importance of vocation in achieving
one's sense of identity:

We have so far set forth the premise that a person more or less
continuously develops an attitude or posture toward himself and
his situation in life. This attitude toward self-in-situation is ego-
identity. Such attitudes are one source of intentions which are
guides of action. Work is one of the accomplishments of human
action. Hence, the locus of career development is in this presumably continuously differentiating ego-identity.[3]

One of the most striking insights from current psychological
research is the dynamic notion of vocation. This implies that
it is a process patient of growth and that this growth may be
at varying rates among individuals. A vocation does not come
full-blown, as one may be led to expect if it is considered a
static entity. Vocational development through time is not a
new notion, surely, to anyone who has experienced it from its
first vague stirrings all the way to full-hearted conviction. A
little introspection reveals to a priest, Brother, or Sister that
his or her own vocation grew through time; and is, in fact, still
growing. Ordination and religious profession set a certain seal
on the presence of a vocation in an individual. This does not
mean, however, that the vocation is perfected. A dynamic

[2] David V. Tiedeman, Robert P. O'Hara, *Career Development: Choice
and Adjustment;* Dependent decisions and career development (New York:
College Entrance Examination Board, 1963), p. 46.
[3] *Ibid.,* Time and occupation: A frame for career development, pp. 57 f.

notion of vocation suggests that the individual continues to seek to fulfill his vocation even after these significant milestones. A religious vocation, viewed as a dynamic entity, is never over and done with. It speaks a challenge that is lifelong. A priest, as an example, accepts the full responsibility on the day of his ordination to grow, all the days of his priestly life, more fully in his vocation.

A major study of vocational development, known as the Career Pattern Study, is being conducted by Professor Donald E. Super of Teachers College, Columbia University. This is what is known as a longitudinal study, i.e., one which studies the same individuals over a span of years—in this case, twenty-five years. The basic field work was begun in 1951–52 with a study of boys in late junior high school. The study, with frequent follow-ups, will continue until 1975, when the subjects will have reached the age of thirty-five, and will presumably have achieved a substantial degree of occupational stability. The primary purpose of this study is to formulate and verify a theory of vocational development—something which does not as yet exist. Their tentative theory, which the research is designed to test, looks on vocation basically as a process, and the first three postulates of their theory expound the nature of vocational development and give some glimpse of the dynamic, evolving way in which the specialists in the psychology of vocation look upon it today:

Proposition 1. Vocational development is an ongoing, continuous, and generally irreversible process.
Proposition 2. Vocational development is an orderly, patterned process and thus predictable.
Proposition 3. Vocational development is a dynamic process of compromise or synthesis.

The first volume of their research findings has already been published, *Vocational Maturity of Ninth Grade Boys*.[4] In it vocational maturity is defined as:

The maturity of an individual's vocationally related behavior in his actual life stage . . . as shown by his behavior in dealing with vocational developmental tasks as compared with the behavior of others dealing with the same developmental tasks. (P. 141.)

Super has been able to isolate the relevant variables on the basis of which he can rank boys who are only fourteen years of age in terms of their vocational maturity. This means that fourteen-year-old boys differ measurably from each other in their overall ability to make realistic life choices at this stage in their lives. Certain background factors were found to correlate with vocational maturity. They are summarized by Super:

Vocational maturity in the ninth-grade boys studied was associated with (1) living in an intellectually stimulating environment (2) having the mental ability essential to respond to that environment (3) responding to these stimuli by aspiring to occupations at higher rather than lower socio-economic levels, and (4) achieving in one's activities. (P. 147.)

In general, vocational maturity at the age of fourteen means that a boy is able to perceive his vocational goals in a very general way and take the realistic steps to attain them. Already, decisive vocational steps must be taken on entering high school if one is to attain long-range vocational goals. It makes a difference whether one goes to an academic high school or

[4] Columbia University Teachers College; Horace Mann-Lincoln Institute of School Experimentation; Career Pattern Study: Monograph 2 (New York: Teachers College, 1960).

to a trade school. For a boy considering the priesthood, one test of his maturity would be whether he is realistic enough to take the appropriate programs available to him in the beginning of high school.

One important finding that emerges from this study is that neither the boys who are vocationally mature nor those who are vocationally immature have as yet attained one of the important ingredients which will eventually be necessary for a settled vocational decision. This ingredient is self-knowledge, which is not yet present in an appreciable degree in the fourteen-year-old. This is a development which occurs during the high school years.

These findings have important implications for those counseling youth in the area of religious vocation. One is the importance of "the self" in the growth of a vocation. The task is to open a youth to himself, so that he can find his own way rather than to overpower "the self" of a candidate and talk him into a vocation.

The guidance counselor can be of benefit to a young man who is considering the priesthood by helping him make correct preliminary decisions. The greatest role that a guidance counselor can play during the high school years is in helping the young man with a potential vocation grow in self-knowledge so that he can determine better whether this vocation is one which is appropriate for him.

The study also makes it clear that there are vast differences in vocational maturity, that one candidate differs from another and each must be dealt with personally and uniquely. Different individuals, though of the same age, are likely to be at quite different levels of vocational growth. We can detect the vocational maturity of a boy considering the priesthood by seeing whether he has made realistic choices early in high school.

The study also gives credence to the fact that some individuals have sufficient vocational maturity to enter a minor seminary knowing what they want to become and that the seminary provides a realistic way to get there. It also emphasizes the fact that in a minor seminary, one of the most important aspects of vocational growth will be in the area of self-knowledge. This makes it important to have very competent counselors at this stage of the training.

4 Recognizing a Religious Vocation

There are many difficulties involved in accurately determining the presence of a religious vocation. Anyone attempting to evaluate candidates eventually realizes that what constitutes the essence of a vocation is impossible to assess directly; what one has to base one's decision on, like it or not, are other qualities of the individual which are not of the essence but bear some relation to it. It is like determining the IQ of a two-year-old child, which is best done by ignoring the child and averaging the IQ's of the parents. This is perhaps why psychologists involved in the practical task of assessment of candidates are suspected of neglecting the role of a divine call in a religious vocation and making the whole business completely natural. Theological discourse on the nature of a religious vocation is one thing; determining whether I myself have a vocation, or whether someone who comes to me for advice has one, or whether this seminarian should be promoted to orders—these are very different problems. The following considerations are aimed at clarifying these complex issues.

A religious vocation is like the two sides of a coin. Let us call one the subjective side, the inner urge to devote one's life to God's service. And the other is the objective side, acceptance of this individual by the Church, signified by ordination or religious profession.

Subjectively, a religious vocation is the desire to devote one's life to the work of God and the Church. In today's theological perspective, the Church is nothing else than the people of God with Christ as its head. A religious vocation thus implies a relationship to God, to Christ and to one's fellow men. Such a response can only emanate from the heart of a man who believes, and to believe is the unearned gift of faith. Vocation to the priesthood, therefore, is a response to God to serve him as He is known through faith and to bring the people of God closer to Him. A person is called in the sense that he has the grace of faith and the further inner grace of desiring to respond to it totally with a life of service. In this respect it differs profoundly from other professions such as law, medicine or engineering into which religious motivations may enter but in which the vocation itself is not grounded in faith in the same way.

The person who experiences within himself this appeal of total dedication to the work of God is still free to commit himself to it or not. The choice comes in agreeing to go along with this response even though it may mean the denial of other appeals in oneself. Thus a religious vocation in a very important respect is not something of our own doing; yet in another vital respect it is a personal responsibility requiring our own initiative.

An authentic vocation is a response to a value existentially perceived as something one wants for oneself. It is not just an abstract value; it is one related to the self. Many value the priesthood and religious life who would not care to live it. Many a mother who has chosen married life for herself would see the importance of the priesthood and wish it for her son. Every candidate who seeks the priesthood perceives this vocation as an intellectual value, i.e., as something important in itself. This is uniformly true even of those who decide that this vocation is not meant for them. It is especially in the high school years that many young men learn to make the distinction that the priestly vocation, while good in itself, is not good for them. This is the distinction between what is a value abstractly considered and a value concretely good for me.

It is not enough that the vocation should be valued. What is required over and above this is that one finds a personal inner response, not only of the will, but of one's whole self to this value. That is why a candidate must be free and not coerced with regard to his vocation. It has to be a value that strikes responsive chords within the individual, and not merely an extrinsic, cultural value passed on by his parents or the Church to him. It has to be something he wants for himself and is attracted to, not something which others say is good and he feels he should aspire to, even though it has no positive appeal and may even repel.

One cannot help noticing how a vocation to the priesthood or religious life is distinguished from other vocations by a far deeper involvement of conscience. It has an important aspect of renunciation. For many there is a struggle to choose God over other appeals or in the face of other tendencies. If the vocation is denied, there is a growing guilt. It is a sense of letting God down, of betraying Him, of being selfish, of putting one's own pleasure before God. It is a choice between God and self, and raises the personal question of generosity versus selfishness. God is involved in a vocation to the priesthood, then, in a very special way, and though a candidate can be reassured by the knowledge that sin is not involved in his choice of vocation, guilt can still be deeply experienced unless the question is basically resolved. Some men and women are haunted for life by such guilt feelings.

We have just examined the subjective personal aspect of vocation—the inner appeal; now we must turn the coin and examine the objective social aspect of vocation. A vocation to the priesthood is more than personal; it is social as well. It requires serving within the structure and organization of the visible Church. This social aspect is characteristic of all the professions. One must not only choose them—one must also meet their standards and be accepted by them. There are no free-lance doctors or lawyers—one must, as a minimum, pass the State Boards or be admitted to the bar.

Because of this necessity of being admitted to a group, which is the objective aspect of a priestly vocation, those in authority in the Church have to assess the qualifications of each aspirant. This is an unavoidable and difficult responsibility. What makes this exceptionally arduous is that it is impossible to assess directly the authenticity of the subjective inner response which brings a man knocking on the door of the priesthood.

Subjectively a vocation is the response of an individual who feels he is called. Every individual who enters into the religious life has reason to think he may be called. Many, later, come to realize that what appeared to be a call from God had some other source. The desire to be a priest or religious is not an infallible subjective sign of a vocation, for there can be other roots of this desire, other motivations than the authentic and enduring one of total dedication of one's life to the service of God and Church. Many who enter the religious life with great assurance and with deep attraction to it will say later on, openly and with conviction, that they never had a vocation in the first place.

It is, therefore, a problem, both for the individual embarking on this vocation and for the community or diocese sponsoring him, to discriminate between an authentic and a pseudo desire for this life. This, as was said above, is impossible, or at least very difficult, to assess directly.

In general, it could be said that the more emotionally healthy a candidate is, the more likely it is that his motivation for the priesthood will be of a healthy, essential, and enduring kind. The less emotionally healthy an individual is, the more likely it is that the roots of his attraction for the life will be unconscious and hence unknown to him, and will be bound up with the roots of his unhealthiness.

A candidate with promise is growth-oriented. He is looking forward to the realistic challenge of his vocation and is ready and free to grow and develop to meet these goals. He does not have to be perfect. He goes to the seminary to learn and to develop into a priest, but not to find out whether he wants to be one in the first place. The development to which he is open has many facets: moral, social, intellectual, vocational, emotional and religious. Such a person is reaching out toward life, not backing off or retreating or escaping. He responds to challenge. He is not security-oriented. A person who is security-oriented is looking for a setting in which it will be safe to stay as he is, in which he will not have to grow, in which he can make use of a variety of defenses which protect him from the anxiety of meeting life. A person who is growing is secure enough in his relationships to be able to abandon rigid defenses and launch out into the adventure of life. A promising candidate, then, is one who is ready to grow.

While it is difficult to determine whether a candidate has a direct calling from God, there are a number of indicators by which we can identify a candidate with growth potential. Many will not have all the signs, but the greater the number of signs which are present, the more promising the candidate, and vice versa. These include the kind of family setting from which he comes, his own life history, his vocational motivation and his relationships with others.

ORIGINS

Probably the best prognosis of future growth can be made on the basis of the home environment, and it is here, as well, that the main barriers lie. A healthy candidate for the religious life comes from a family setting within which growth is possible. The most important source of growth is exposure to mature people. The mother and father should themselves have attained a level of maturity appropriate to their years. They need to be sure enough of themselves and close enough to their children to provide an environment in which their children can develop. Some of the ingredients of such a home are a spirit of trust and mutual affection, consistent discipline without undue severity and a democratic rather than authoritarian approach. These enable the children to grow in ego strength and to form healthy identifications with the parent of the same sex. Parents play such a fundamental role in a child's development that when they themselves have not been able to mature, their interaction with the children is bound to leave scars which inhibit the child's capacity for growth. Typical signs of immaturity or lack of growth in the parents are a history of mental disorder, alcoholism, instability in work, separation, divorce, illegitimacy, non-practice of the faith, chronic family strife and the like.

While each child in a family has his unique experiences with his parents, we get clues to the healthiness of the family atmosphere of the candidate from the success and healthiness of the other children. In cases where they have run away from home, or been expelled from school, or had problems of delinquency, or left the faith, or had marriage difficulties, there is reason for questioning whether the candidate himself has not encountered serious home problems which will interfere with his growth.

For minor seminary candidates the home and the record of

academic performance are the best indicators. The minor seminary is not the place for those who come from poor home environments; it should be only for those from clearly wholesome homes.

PERSONAL HISTORY

A healthy candidate has a productive personal history. His record of performance shows a growing capacity to face up to, and cope with, the challenges of life effectively, and in a way appropriate to his age.

Academically

He has been effective in the whole area of school and learning in general. Obvious as this may seem, it is often lost sight of, in accepting candidates at the lower levels of training, that he must from the start have sufficient ability to succeed at the higher levels of training. The average IQ for college students is about 118 and for high school graduates is about 108. A candidate for first-year high school in the minor seminary must have sufficient ability to do college and professional level scholastic work when the time comes.

1. The healthy candidate's record of achievement, as reflected in his grades and rank in class, is proportionate to his ability. Studies of underachievement show that, more often than not, this is a chronic pattern, not easily changed. The fact that it is a chronic pattern means that the individual has not been growing academically, but is in a rut he has not been able to get out of. Where there is a chronic history of underachievement, there is very likely to be maladjustment. For some reason, perhaps the illusion of automatic unearned success, the religious life attracts many nonproducers. They have a charac-

teristic optimism, the feeling that now that they have a goal in life, they will be able to devote themselves to their studies. More often than not the same old pattern continues. Skilled personal counseling may be helpful here in unearthing the roots of the problem and remedying it before application is made to a diocese or community. Postponement of entry into religious life until there is evidence of mastery of this problem is a wise course.

2. A vocationally mature candidate is also one who has taken realistic steps toward achieving his vocational goals. In the Career Pattern Study at Columbia University the vocational maturity of ninth-grade boys was investigated. Even at this early age the vocationally mature youth can be discriminated from the vocationally immature one. This has relevance for those who think that no boy is mature enough for the decision required to go away to a minor seminary. The vocationally mature youth knows what he wants to be, at least in a general way, and has taken the appropriate steps at his age to achieve these long-range goals. The vocationally immature youth either does not have any idea of what he wants to be or neglects to take the appropriate steps to get there. Examples of not taking appropriate steps would be the young man who wants to be a priest but who has not studied Latin when it was available, or has gone to a trade school, or who has not bothered to take college preparatory courses or has quit high school to go into one of the Services.

Morally

He should have a productive moral history as well. Many young people, as they mature, encounter emerging feelings within themselves or new environmental situations which provoke moral struggles to which they succumb. This is not at all unusual in the history of candidates for the religious life. However, when the individual has never, over an extended period of time, realistically come to grips with these problems and eliminated them or brought them under control, he has demonstrated a lack of maturity and growth. He has not been able to cope with life appropriately for his age. Scrupulosity is an emotional problem in the moral area. Episodes of scruples are, again, familiar to most candidates. Prolonged, intense scrupulosity over a period of several years is a very negative indication for success in the priesthood or religious life. Often the vocation itself is a part of the scrupulous complex and tends to disappear as the scrupulous condition subsides through therapy.

Religiously

A candidate for the religious life should also have a productive religious history. This means a continuous practice of the faith without lapses. Signs of religious maturity are that the values of faith mean more than the cultural tradition passed on to him by his parents and teachers, that they are personally important to him. His vocation is not a conversion experience from a basically irreligious way of life.

VOCATIONAL MOTIVATION

The dominant motivation of such healthy candidates lies in helping others. The appeal is to a way of life which is outgoing and altruistic, in which they see themselves as serving the needs of others rather than as basically gratifying themselves. Studies of the interest test scores of candidates for the priesthood and religious life show interests of the Social Service type as most characteristic.

RELATIONSHIPS WITH OTHERS

Another sign of growth potential, and a very important one, is that the individual has shown himself capable of establishing healthy relationships with others. This will be especially true if he has come from a home which has had within it healthy relationships between the parents, between the parents and children, and between the children themselves. Such a person then has a history of working cooperatively and effectively with others. Some can get along well with authority but not with their peers. Some get along with their own age group but not with their elders or with those much younger. Some are withdrawn and have had no effective relationships with anyone. Healthy candidates have had effective relationships both with authority and with their own age group. Two recognizable symptoms of lack of health are chronic withdrawal or chronic conflict. Withdrawal is more characteristic of the timid, insecure person, and conflict of the aggressively insecure person. A healthy candidate has a confidence in himself which enables him to be sincerely and securely himself in his relationships. This is the basis for his capacity to be understanding of others. He then has the basic personal ingredients for effectiveness in the priesthood, which is deeply related to effectiveness in one's relationships.

5   The Image of the Priesthood

Why are so many whose endowments are less than adequate attracted to the priesthood and religious life? As a corollary to this, why do so few of those who are adequately qualified experience the call of a vocation? It is puzzling. Is it that God uses the weak things of this earth to confound the strong? Is this what is to be expected, and is it the way that a man of faith looks at vocation to the priesthood or religious life? On the other hand, is, perhaps, something going wrong?

It seems clear that there is a vast difference between having a desire, however strong, for the priesthood and religious life and having the capacity to be effective in it. Many with the capacity do not have the inclination; many with the inclination do not have the capacity. Why? This is the question to which this chapter is addressed.

The image of the priest as perceived by youth and the image of the training required to reach the priesthood are both deeply involved in this question. A recent study of the relative social status of occupations shows that the priesthood has slipped to a lower position than it formerly held.

Eagerness on the part of vocational recruiters to attract candidates in what is, after all, a highly competitive market has led to an appeal to the kind of motives through which the best of our youth can only be repelled, while the less adequate sort of candidate is attracted. If the underachiever is moved to choose the priesthood or religious life because it can mean success and security without effort, then any appeal which would stress these elements should be avoided. Yet when one consults vocational brochures and advertisements one finds that sometimes this is the very dimension of religious life emphasized. For example, one community ran an advertisement which proclaimed, in large letters, "SECURITY, HERE AND HEREAFTER." If that community wonders why it is getting applicants who do not seem to be very adequate, the answer is quite simple. They have asked for them. A healthy person wants more than security, and any kind of meaningful Christianity is filled with risk. But the healthy person, the one who is not afraid of life, passes up the profession that can offer womb-like protection. He wants to live, and the only successful way to do that is by not being afraid to die.

Another current appeal is to stress some abstract theme such as "challenge." This sounds fine, but it is all too often unspecified. The more abstract an idea, the more attractive it is to the dreamer. The more vague and general a notion, even if it is a stirring contemporary concept like "challenge," the less it will move the mature young man or woman. It is the cold abstraction, the grandiose ideal, that the immature youth can aim for because he does not have to change himself in the process. He can commit the age-old mistake of believing that because he has thought about an idea he has really done something about it. But vague and dreamy appeals make an impact on the immature and inadequate; if they come applying, it is probably because they have been given a direct invitation through publicity.

Another serious distortion of the meaning of the priesthood may arise from the way the work of the priest is presented. For example, the priest, in photographs and sketches, is usually shown working with a group of men or boys. He is pictured as though his ministry were to an all-male society. It is apparently not considered good taste to show the priest working with women. Sometimes the other side of the coin is shown in the pictures of nuns constantly surrounded by girls. But the priest is chosen for all mankind, and the candidate who aspires to the priesthood must be ready to adjust successfully to all mankind. If the priesthood is presented as an exclusive masculine haven, should one be surprised if this appeals to sexually maladjusted candidates? There is such inordinate fear of the dangers of women that they are eliminated entirely. This serious distortion of the world of priestly activity can hardly appeal to most mature youths. If there is one quality that is necessary in a priest or religious, it is the elementary one of being normal. Make the seminary or the priesthood look like a fraternity of bachelors whose attitude toward women is immature and undeveloped, and you will assuredly gain the interest of the ill-adjusted.

The image of priestly training which many of our youth have is of a very monastic, restricted, highly disciplined type of education which is very different from any other type of training found on the American scene. It is not at all characteristic of the training found in the other professions. The other professions have gradually, over a period of decades, incorporated into their training more and more existential experience in which the problems of the profession are encountered. In this way, a young man begins to test the realistic stresses and satisfactions of the vocation itself upon which he is entering, and through his association with active and prominent members of this vocation he develops his identification with it.

He also has the benefit of skilled supervision while he is being initiated into his vocation. This supervision is not so much over his personal life as over his functioning in his work. This is the way an American man expects to be dealt with. To him the discipline of a supervised and regulated work experience is much more meaningful and acceptable than a rigidly disciplined personal life. Professional training for the priesthood has changed little over the years and has a character all its own. It has little in common with the patiently evolved approaches to training of other, allied professions, or even with the training for the ministry in other faiths.

The facts show that (1) the image of seminary training is not an attractive one for candidates who are growth-oriented and who are looking for personal fulfillment, and (2) the priesthood itself does not present the attractive image it could. The image of training and the image of priestly life to which young American boys are exposed appeal more than seems necessary to the weak, and less than we would hope to the strong. Unless this is remedied, we can look forward to grave future difficulties with vocations. Improved methods of screening and "Madison Avenue" public relations techniques do not come to grips with this fundamental problem.

Vocation work can with great profit be specialized, but the continued flow of healthy candidates cannot be separated from the whole climate of religion in society, from the state of the Church and from the image of the priesthood. Attitudes toward the priesthood based on youth's experience with priests do exist, as well as attitudes toward the program of seminary training of which they have heard reports and rumors.

The vocational recruiter is not selling a theoretical product based solely on speculative theoretical values such as a theology of vocation. Such an appeal to values might well work with a semi-scrupulous applicant with a strong superego and a somewhat weak ego, of whom there are so many. This approach would, however, leave untouched many other healthy young men who sense the far greater "de facto" opportunities and challenges and the broader scope of other vocations. The recruiter is promoting an actual vocation situated temporally in the "here and now" of this culture, one which the prospective candidate has had an opportunity to observe for himself. He already has had a chance to develop attitudes about the priesthood quite independently of any contact with the recruiter. Mission societies depend for their vocations on a double image—the image of the work their men are doing in the field, which is presented to youth second-hand, and the image of the parish priest at home, with whom youth has immediate contact.

Vocations depend on the whole Church and not just on the vocational specialist. Those vitally interested in vocations must come to see the relation of the success of their work to factors normally outside their direct concern. The vocational recruiter's normal concern is in attracting candidates, meeting with them and evaluating their vocations. He is apt to overlook the fact, or not consider it his business, that vocations, first and foremost, depend on the image of the priesthood as a vocation which is in competition with the images of other vocations a young man or woman considers in the teenage years.

In a business corporation, if the sales department find that they are selling an inferior product, they do not just try to improve their salesmen's techniques. They go to the engineering department, the research department and the production department, so that they will have a better product to sell. The principles of good salesmanship show that one has to be sincere about what one is selling, to believe in it and to give an accurate picture of its qualities. Some vocation directors hesitate and experience internal conflicts about encouraging youth to dedicate their lives in certain sectors of the priesthood, brotherhood and sisterhood. If we are to continue to attract vocations, the two related questions of the updating of clerical training and the conditions of the priesthood after ordination must be faced squarely. The image of the priesthood depends on the impact of truly mature priests who are effective in their work and happy about their choice of vocation. There are too many unhappy, frustrated men not ministering to the needs of the people. A frustrated priest is not as appealing as a fulfilled priest. Many young men are attracted to the missionary priesthood because they would like to be priests—but not like the parish priests at home.

The blame for the frustrations of the priesthood cannot all be placed on the shoulders of individual priests. There are antiquated aspects of the system of priestly life itself which clamor for updating. The very structure of the life of diocesan priests builds in needless frustrations. These problems must be confronted and certain traditional structures reorganized. There is a great hope that the present Ecumenical Council will address itself to such questions. For one example, the growth of vast urban dioceses combined with the extended life-span of pastors due to medical progress creates a very difficult situation in flourishing city dioceses, and one which is quite new. There, only men past their prime have responsibility, while younger men spend the first thirty years of their priesthood in very subordinate positions. The Church takes on a conservative cast. It is inhumanly frustrating to be still a curate in one's mid-fifties. These chronic frustrations of priestly life do not pass unnoticed, and they have their effect on the image of the priest.

In summary, there is too much appeal of the priestly vocation to the less adequate candidate and not enough to the better-qualified. It is proposed that this is due in part to the candidates' image both of the priesthood and of the training leading to it. Moreover, this image of a training out of step with other professional training and of priests who are not fulfilled as persons is at least in part true to the facts. The solution is not a "Madison Avenue" type refurbishing of the image through public relations techniques. What is required to assure the flow of competent candidates is that the Church should address itself deeply to the questions of priestly training and the conditions of priestly life, so that this vocation will regain the appealing image which should reflect its profound value.

6 Developing Vocations

One of the core themes of this book is that a vocation is deeply personal and that it grows as the person grows in his contacts with other mature individuals. The real answer to whatever vocational crisis exists lies not in campaign literature, elaborate files, or I.B.M. machines but within each person. Valuable as research can be in illumining vocational work, the work itself is accomplished only through genuine personal intercommunication. The priesthood means something because of what living priests are like; the sisterhood, the brotherhood are not summed up in a pamphlet; they mean whatever the lives of the Sister or Brother in the classroom mean. There are many relationships with others which can have positive value in the growth of a religious vocation— such as that with parent, teachers, guidance counselor, vocational director and confessor.

Parents can exert various influences on a vocation to the priesthood. In both obvious and subtle ways they can put pressure on their children toward or away from a religious calling. A vocation is something so deeply personal that it must be treated with the greatest respect. Pressure means a lack of respect. Monsignor Knox writes, in one of his books, that there is real wisdom in learning that we must allow young people to develop in the way God wants them to and not necessarily in the way we want them to. This may demand a hard look at ourselves, but it can be immensely rewarding. The personal element is crucial in vocational work, but this will surely suffer, as the Church will eventually, if we place our own feelings and our own goals first and miss the fact that the emphasis must be on the feelings and goals of those with whom our work is done.

Genuine vocations appear to come from intact, undisturbed home environments in which there is a love of the Church and a respect for the priesthood, and a freedom for the child to work out his place in life. However, there are many stable Catholic homes from which no religious vocations come. Vocations seem to run in some families or clans and to be nonexistent in others. There is no doubt that vocations are greatly encouraged if, along with the parents' love for the Church, there is an accompanying love and respect for those who have devoted their lives to its service:

One peculiar and important phenomenon stands out in the religious background of these prospective candidates, and that is the fact that "vocations run in families." . . . The reason for this may be partially the personal example and influence of the individual who is following the vocation; but it seems also to be the fact that an attitude, or frame of mind, toward the concept of vocation is built up among the members of a family in which some are already in the Church vocation.[1]

Parents need not abdicate all their rights over the children as soon as the question of a religious vocation is presented. They may have many genuine and legitimate concerns about whether their child's choice of a religious vocation is mature

[1] Joseph H. Fichter, S.J., *Religion as an Occupation* (Notre Dame: University of Notre Dame Press, 1961), pp. 49–50.

enough, about whether at this stage of his life it is better for him to remain at home with the family, about whether the child has been unduly influenced, about whether he has the capacity and qualities for the life, or about whether he is making the right choice of communities and of work within the priesthood. An uneasiness in the parents perennially centers around the very young candidate who is considering entering the boarding minor seminary for high school. They wonder if the boy is mature enough to make such a decision, as well as whether he will develop in a rounded way at this stage of his life away from his family and the normal activities and associations with those his own age.

Candidates for the priesthood start preparing for it at various stages. Most begin either in the first year of high school or in the first year of college. Some come after college or after they have worked for a few years. When is the best time to come? Most priests seem to advocate the way they did it themselves. There are many mature and fully functioning priests who started their preparation for the priesthood after the eighth grade. It is a misconception that a young man could not possibly mature in the minor seminary. What is clear is that there are varying states of readiness for this vocational decision. It is unfortunate if a person is forced to make the decision too soon, just as it is unfortunate if a person who is ready to make a solid vocational choice is delayed.

When to come to the seminary is a very personal question, to be decided on its individual merits. Many factors enter in, such as available educational opportunities, location of the seminary, family circumstances. In general, candidates start preparing for the priesthood and enter the seminary once it is clear in their own minds that this is what they want to be. Usually they are no longer content where they are and prefer to start "full speed ahead" on the program which will directly prepare them for their goal. The dissatisfaction they feel is not because of anything going wrong but rather because they are not working at what they want. One young man left the college he was attending at the end of his third year, although he was very happy there and would have been delighted to graduate. But he knew what he wanted to do with his life and did not wish to procrastinate about working toward it. This was his own decision and was made against much contrary advice to finish up at the school he was attending, where he was so near to graduation.

The most promising candidates are the ones who have been doing well at the activities in which they have been involved, have been successful and effective, but who still want more from life. It is a difficult question when the individual has been failing with his life, and suddenly the urge to be a priest occurs. This is very apt to indicate a desperate search for security and safe moorings by someone who is conscious of floundering.

There is something motherly about the Church, and many who feel the need for her support begin to wonder whether they have a religious vocation. It is surprisingly common for individuals with emotional problems to be attracted to the religious life. They have a real need for personal help, and the pastoral ministry of the Church should be extended to them. The first priest to whom many of them have turned has been a vocation director. It is important that he is able to distinguish such disguised calls to the Church for help from the genuine religious vocation, which is a desire and capacity to lead a life of giving help. He should know how to go about referring such individuals to the proper sources of assistance. Some make the mistake of trying to rehabilitate those individuals so that they can go on for the religious life. This is a waste of time. Vocational directors have more than enough

to do in finding and working with candidates of good potential
to challenge all their available energies.

In evaluating candidates we must remember that in the
long run what is important is not the number sent to the
seminary, for the majority drop out before ordination, or
even the number ordained, for some of these will not find
fulfillment in their vocation or be effective in it. The Church
needs candidates capable of developing into mature, effective
servants of God and of His beloved people. It is the projected
maturity of their later functioning in the priesthood which we
try to forecast. For this great growth is needed in all candidates. That is why it is helpful in evaluation to see which are
truly ready to grow, which with some help can be made ready,
and which are already fixated at some immature level of development and will find it very difficult to grow.

The priesthood in general and the priests with whom the
young man comes into personal contact in either the parish
or school are some of the potent sources of his image of
the priesthood. Candidates for the priesthood say that the
strongest influence on their vocation came from a priest they
knew. Presumably, if such a priest is a fulfilled man and personally interested in them, his influence is likely to be positive.
The priesthood is a rich and full life, but it must be lived this
way if anybody is ever going to be convinced that this is so.
The priesthood can seem a dull and dusty road, a long and
lonely one too, if we picture it in terms of security, safety and
seclusion. The failure to reveal the fully human nature of the
priest's life is one of the most crucially damaging factors in
vocation work.

Teachers in Catholic high schools play a prominent role in
vocational development. Most vocations come from Catholic
schools, and there is furthermore some evidence that more
candidates persevering to the priesthood come from schools in

which priests teach. There are many reasons for this. Usually such schools are more selective and hence include more students with potential vocations, but it is also clear that the boy identifies with the teacher who is himself a religious and absorbs a better understanding of the priesthood during these important years. This is especially true when the teacher is young and still in training himself. Many a boy is attracted to joining the Jesuits because of the young scholastics who taught him in high school. The Deacon who goes out from the seminary to preach in a parish on Sunday has a special fascination for youth.

People crave understanding, and adolescents perhaps more so than any other group. It is a great risk, the first time one approaches another person to let him into one's inner world. For most, this first sharing, if it occurs, will be during the high school years. These young people are looking for someone with whom they can grow through their problems. If they find such a person, the experience can be a very constructive help in the process of removing barriers to the growth of a vocation. But for some reason people react more strongly to the news of someone having a religious vocation than to that of other choices. This probably accounts for the reluctance of some young people to discuss this question with anyone until they are quite settled about it. They are afraid to bring it into the open because they will be immediately subjected to pressures. One fear is that they will be steamrollered into coming to the seminary by parents or religious personnel before they have had a chance to think the question through. Another fear is that they will no longer be free to be themselves, because they will be expected to conform to some stereotype of what a candidate should be like.

The teacher would do well to re-examine his own attitude in working with vocations. For one thing, it is obvious that each vocation must be treated separately, that the rate of development may be different in different individuals, that the same answers cannot be given to everyone who speaks of a vocation. Nor can the same advice be given to all. All our words, and more importantly, the attitude underlying them, must be directed to the needs of the individual with whom we are dealing. It is necessary for the worker to develop what might be termed a "counseling" attitude. This means an openness to the other individual, a willingness to explore his own world with him, and a readiness to abandon preconceived notions that may interfere with the kind of understanding help that will further the personal growth of the individual. In order to assist the individual with his vocational decision, the one who helps must be in process himself: he must himself be growth-oriented and capable of forming an effective relationship. This is in itself healthy for the candidate, and if the counselor is a priest or religious it also provides an attractive image of the religious life.

It is almost fatal advice, to judge possible future vocations by our own experiences. It is not unusual for a priest or a Sister to feel that because he or she experienced certain things when they were contemplating their life choice, these must be experienced by everybody contemplating a similar choice. Another bias that sometimes appears in teachers' attitudes toward potential vocations among their students is the tendency to exaggerate the importance of authority conflicts and underestimate the seriousness of passivity, docility and withdrawal. Some teachers favor the docile, who cause no trouble and may even relate well to them, but who may carry very little weight among their peers. Teachers have been known to select whole groups for vocational weekends who have had no inclinations toward religious life, and to have totally ignored others who later indicated that this was their vocation.

All things being equal, it is easier to evaluate someone of the same sex and easier to establish rapport with someone of the opposite sex. A Sister can have a discriminating eye for the girl who is considering entering the convent, but be a little biased in favor of boys with potential vocations. This is often compensated for by the extensive knowledge gained from multiple contacts which a teacher has with a student. A priest, on the other hand, is more apt to be favorably impressed by the girl who wishes to enter the convent and to be more down-to-earth in his judgment about the boy.

Most boys think of being a priest in grammar school, but very few have this ideal by the fourth year of high school. Something has gone on during this time to change their minds. What happens, especially during the high school years, is that a young man's understanding of himself grows considerably. It is also during these adolescent years that he becomes aware of the sexual currents within himself and of his attractions to the married life. Counseling of the vocational prospect should have the development of his self-knowledge as a primary aim. This is often not the case. Self-knowledge implies a clear perception of motivation. A young person should not be urged to enter until he has a good grasp of the fundamental motivation for doing it. This is precisely where counseling can be of great service. The individual will develop real insights into himself and his capabilities and will be able to make a more informed and realistic decision.

In some cases, the teacher is not in a position to help a young man of this age with personal problems, but he can refer him to others. A school spiritual director, guidance counselor or confessor with real empathy, understanding and skill can work very constructively with young men in their personal maturing.

Guidance counselors who are not themselves priests or

religious often feel insecure when it comes to dealing with individuals who are considering religious vocations. Their first tendency is to keep hands off and refer the lad to a priest. To stand aside is a big mistake, for guidance counselors with their specialized training can play an important role in the discerning of such a calling and in helping those who appear to have one to take further steps toward this goal. They can refer the individual to a priest and still continue to help in their own way.

In many high schools special tests are given to determine the vocational interest pattern of the students, so that the guidance counselor can use these in helping the student clarify his vocational goals. By research it has been found that there is a pattern of interests, as measured by these tests, characteristic of the majority of candidates for the priesthood. About eighty percent of seminarians would have this characteristic pattern, which is found only in one out of six high school boys. It is helpful to realize that only a fraction of boys have this interest pattern, and it is almost entirely from this group that vocations come. There is a great deal of technical information available on this problem. On the most widely used Vocation Interest Inventories—the Kuder Preference Record —seminarians score above average in social service, literary and musical interest; below average in mechanical, scientific and clerical interests, and average in artistic interests. On outdoor, computational and persuasive interests, there are different norms for different seminary groups.

The guidance counselor, who is at home with these tools, when he sees these indicators can at least raise the question of a religious vocation for consideration. He can also discuss alternate areas of vocational aspiration and give the individual information on the basis of which he can make a more intelligent vocational decision.

In many cases individuals considering entering the seminary could profit from special help in the years preceding their coming. Some may have problems in the academic area, such as underachievement, which may require either personal counseling or remedial work. Others may have social difficulties, difficulties with authority, or any other of a host of problems with which help would be extremely beneficial at this stage. There is no more accessible source of aid than the school counselor. It would be most beneficial to vocations if the lay guidance counselor were less reluctant to function within his competence for these areas.

One of the most helpful experiences is for a candidate to meet and talk with others preparing for the same vocation. Many are apprehensive about what the others will be like— whether they will be normal red-blooded Americans or ethereal spiritual "creeps." In pre-seminary counseling interviews a topic which often comes up is an uneasiness on the part of the candidate about what kind of young men he will be living with in the seminary, and spending his priestly life with. He wonders whether he will be happy in their company and be accepted by them. One of the best pre-seminary experiences is the chance to spend a weekend at a seminary. This is ideal for those who are already seriously considering the vocation. The highlight of such weekends is not the exposure to seminary routine or the talks with the priests, but invariably the same thing—the opportunity to meet and talk with the seminarians. The candidate has a chance to pose questions he would hesitate to ask an adult and get answers from someone who has already embarked on the vocation he himself is considering.

In vocational recruitment as in anything else, one must strike a happy balance. Students complain, on the one hand, of being bombarded with propaganda for religious vocations until it no longer registers, or even until it becomes distasteful. On the other hand, one hears the opposite complaint that no one ever personally suggested to an individual that he might have a religious vocation. This touches on the crux of the vocation problem. In an effort to promote religious vocation there is an exaggerated reliance on the mass media, to the point of oversaturation, and a corresponding lack of intimate personal contact with the individual. Some confessors, in an effort to make some personal vocational contact, make it a practice to suggest at least the consideration of such a calling to likely penitents. Occasionally, it is reported, they mistake the voice and present the ideal of the sisterhood to a seventy-year-old grandmother. However, it appears to be a good practice because it does not put external social pressures on the individual, owing to the anonymity and the confidential nature of the confessional.

The Peace Corps has had great success in captivating the idealism of youth. Their radio advertisements are in the spirit of the late President John F. Kennedy's "Ask not what your country can do for you, but what you can do for your country." The call has been for those who want to work long hours *without* pay, *far* from home, in *under*developed locales, where there is *risk* and *danger* but where there is also something of importance that needs to be done. They will have a real share in the responsibility for doing what has to be done.

The office of director of vocations with the special responsibility for the recruiting and processing of candidates is a recent development in religious communities and dioceses. The value of this new role specialization in the Church is that it provides someone dedicated to vocations who has a greater understanding of what is involved. The dangers of such specialization are twofold: that others will leave the work of vocations to the vocation specialist and that the vocation specialist will think that the entire problem of vocations can be coped with exclusively by improving methods of publicity and processing.

The vocational recruiter is not selling a theoretical product based solely on speculative theoretical values, such as a theology of vocation. Such an appeal to values might well work with a semi-scrupulous applicant with a strong superego and a somewhat weak ego, of whom there are so many. This approach would, however, leave untouched many other healthy young men who sense the far greater "de facto" opportunities, challenges and scope of other vocations. The task of the vocational director or recruiter is to present the priesthood to groups so that this vocation will be called to the attention of those who will respond. How is this best accomplished? He wants to present through films, talks or literature, a picture of the priestly vocation which will awaken the spark in those youths who have the capacity to become mature priests. Evidence shows that it is very easy to get a vocational response from youths who have no capacity for the vocation. In other words, it is very easy to arouse a pseudo-vocational response. What appeals most to those candidates who are best capable of fulfilling the requirements of the priesthood? Such candidates are reaching out and looking for fulfillment. What appeal to them most are the vital pastoral functions of the priesthood itself and a program of training that realistically leads to these goals. They are interested in serving others, and in growing and transforming themselves to be capable of doing this. This is the appeal which is important. As Bishop Ford said, "A missioner is a man with a message who mixes with men." Our appeal must be to the young men of faith who are capable of dedicating their lives to the service of their fellow man.

The personality of the vocational recruiter is in itself an

important instrument in the cultivation of a vocation to the priesthood. One might ask just what kind of relationship vocation recruiters establish with the young men whose lives they try to influence. How deep and genuine is it? What kind of values do they try to give them? Can real vocational development take place in the context of a superficial, salesman-like relationship? Can we expect depth on the part of a candidate if only shallows exist on the recruiter's side? Since a vocation is such an intimate part of a person, it is to be handled personally. The whole purpose of talks, films and literature is to initiate a response in the young man that leads to personal contact. It is an easy thing to do, but deeply fallacious, to place too much emphasis on the mechanical aspects of vocational work, to the neglect of the more personal parts. When a young man has made contact with a diocese or religious community by mail, it is important to let him know that a personal meeting can be arranged if he desires it. One has to be careful not to put pressure on a youth in this regard, for it is easy to frighten him off. In the course of one's personal association with a candidate, one has the opportunity of explaining the vocation to him. Here, it is important not to put so much emphasis on the ideal of the priesthood that one makes it impossible for the young man to discover whether he himself has a genuine inner response to this ideal. We do not want a young man coming to the seminary merely because he would be afraid of the guilt of not coming or of disappointing someone. We want to help the young man explore his own feelings about the vocation, which are often full of doubts.

There is a great deal of sentimentality about religious vocations, and some are reluctant ever to discourage any but the grossest misfits from giving the life a try. One must often be firm in giving advice against a religious vocation. There is a need for being objective and recognizing those who have little realistic hope of persevering to the priesthood. This can save many a young man from an unnecessary life detour, from heartache, discouragement, and an increased sense of failure, and help him to formulate more realistic life plans. In the long run more is done for vocations by honest evaluation, since it preserves houses of training from becoming diluted with numerous unsatisfactory candidates and from the discouraging effect on morale of large numbers of drop-outs. There is no use in "stringing someone along" who does not have the ability or the other qualifications. It is good to evaluate prospects early, so that they will not be falsely encouraged and led on, only to discover later that they do not meet the requirements. This holds for regular mailing lists of vocational literature, which should be periodically screened and pruned. Major obstacles to acceptance are easily brought to light by a good interview form. This prevents the embarrassment of having strongly encouraged a candidate only to discover at the last minute some serious obstacle to acceptance.

An excellent practice in the processing of candidates is to visit the home. It gives the parents an opportunity to meet a representative of the community or diocese and form their impressions of the one with whom their child has been in contact and of the group he hopes to join. They can express their feelings about his vocational plans and ask questions that are on their minds. Finally, it affords an opportunity to assess the family atmosphere in which, as we have already seen, a vocation is so deeply rooted.

Evaluation of a home is no simple task; it calls for skill, experience and technique. The religious maturity of the home is far too subtle a thing to be evaluated in terms of whether or not there is a crucifix on the wall or Catholic magazines on the table. The spirit of religion is not the only factor that is important in the home. Where this is strong and other things are missing in the emotional climate, there is fertile soil for the development of a pseudo-vocation.

It is especially relationships in the home that are important—that between the parents themselves, between mother and child, father and child, between the children and between the child and others who may form the household. Is the mother warm or cold? How dominating is she, how possessive? Is the father a part of the picture or is he withdrawn? It is a mistake to say that because a boy has had a rough life and been exposed to many strains others have missed, and has had to survive many struggles in the home, this will be an asset to him and make him more understanding in his priesthood of those with similar problems. The boy who will be better able to meet stress in later life is not the one who has grown up in it but the one whose sense of self-value has been solidly constructed in an atmosphere of strength and warmth. One must have had a warm affectional start to be secure enough to forget about one's self and minister to the needs of others. One must have been loved in order to love.

The profession of social work has developed approaches to home evaluation to meet its task of placing children for adoption. The open-ended interview has been found very effective. The skill comes in providing an atmosphere in which the parents can talk freely and easily and the interviewer, by skilled response to their feelings, keeps the conversation moving along. Unfortunately, on such scheduled visits all are apt to be stiff and on their best behavior, much as they would be on the first visit of prospective in-laws. When the sincerity and reality of the family comes through on such occasions one can usually trust what he feels about the family. If not, a further visit may be warranted.

God blesses only a chosen few with a priestly vocation, not even enough to fill the need, but He asks many others to help such vocations grow. Parents are asked to provide the right soil. To the teacher or the vocation director He entrusts the sowing of the seed. He inspires the counselor to tend the seedling. Many relationships are important in the growth of a vocation. A person and a vocation cannot help growing when in personal contact with another mature person—and there is no substitute.

7 Vocational Doubt

Doubt is a characteristic of man. The Cartesian *"Cogito, ergo sum"* has been translated, "I doubt, therefore I am." There is very little about which we do not have doubts; we doubt our values, our friends, our families, our abilities and our faith. Doubt is part of the process of growth by which we relinquish old beliefs and acquire new ones. There is nothing strange or surprising in the fact that vocational decision should have its share of doubt.

Some people are afraid to doubt—they must be sure and definite about everything—the social scientist has noted this quirk in men and has labeled it "the intolerance of ambiguity." Others are excessively prone to doubt and are indecisive to a fault. Chronic generalized indecisiveness is a symptom of personality difficulties centering around lack of strength in the "self." This is a problem of those who have no mind of their own on any subject. They are so used to meeting expectations that they have no sense of their own preferences, inclinations and convictions. It is very hard for such people, in youth, to discover what they really want to do with their lives. Occasionally, the problem hits them later in life when they finally realize that they have chosen their life work not because of its appeal to them but because of its appeal to someone important to them, such as their mother.

Doubts are found at all stages of vocational growth. A few can look back after years in the priesthood and say that they have never had a doubt about the priesthood being their life, but most could not. For the majority, doubts, conflict and indecision are part of the process of deciding whether they have a vocation and whether they are ready to go away to a seminary or a religious community. Many experience these doubts again in the course of their training periods, especially at times of Vows or Ordination, or such natural times of decision as the end of a semester, year or stage of transition. A number feel the conflict after the final commitment has been formally made.

Some guides, directors and superiors look on vocational doubt as a temptation of the devil, to be put aside like a bad thought. They encourage its repression. On the other hand, doubts can be looked on as an opportunity, since they are a sign that one is experiencing conflicting motivations, and if the sources of these ambivalent feelings can be brought to awareness, accepted and understood, the doubts can be fundamentally resolved at the roots. This cannot be said of the case in which repression is resorted to. The sources of doubts are contrary feelings or responses which the individual experiences but usually cannot identify or understand. Skilled counseling can turn times of doubt into very profitable opportunities for growth.

In general, it is good if a candidate can postpone entrance into the seminary or religious life until the doubts he has at that time are resolved, or are on the way to being so. The man who goes to the seminary not even knowing whether or not he wants to be a priest interprets all the ups and downs in terms of his vocation and is unable to enter into the program in an effective way. The candidate who is not plagued by doubts and knows that he wants to be a priest gets off to a much better start in the seminary, because he has come there prepared to profit from the program and to grow toward the priesthood. It is well to realize, however, that most candidates go through an intense period of decision about their vocation characterized by considerable vacillation, which lasts somewhat less than a year. The early part of this process is full of doubt and uncertainty for those youths, but as they work through it, it ends up in a stable decision either to go to the seminary or to stay at home. One should not, because of his manifest indecision, discourage a candidate who is in this normal early stage of the decision process. He will usually be well settled several months later. It is here that a priest can be very helpful; but it is also here, as a matter of fact, that many priests fail. They should not encourage boys to go and give it a try. This is unfair both to the candidate and to the seminary, and it is not necessary. With some skillful counseling help, a candidate can be enabled to resolve his doubts in advance.

Doubts which are suppressed can recur in the same way on a later occasion; doubts which are fundamentally resolved will never occur again. This does not mean that new doubts based on further experience in the vocation and deeper understanding of one's own self will not later occur. There is a big difference between making a decision to go on, as one does at the end of a Novitiate or at a time of Orders, and being fully settled. An individual may put aside his doubts and make a deliberate commitment, only to discover later, to his amazement and to the concern of his superiors, that these doubts have never been fully settled. If one faces doubts, there is always the risk that one will have to take a step one is hesitant to take. There is equally the possibility that a doubt looked at squarely will vanish of itself. A doubt is only permanently resolved by an understanding of its roots.

Vocational doubt can arise even though one has made what

appear to be ultimate commitments. This is due to conflicting currents of motivation which have always been present but have never previously been strong enough to demand resolution. New circumstances expose these conflicts and make them sharply felt. Some people discover, to their dismay, that the question of their basic vocational commitment arises again late in life, long after the time of their formal lifetime commitment, which had appeared very easy. Then they realize how naive their original decision was.

Psychological studies of conflict cast interesting light on the problem of vocational doubt. Three varieties of conflict within the individual are described. The conflict of having to choose between two positive incentives is called approach-approach conflict. The conflict involved in deciding between two alternatives, both of which are unpleasant, is known as avoidance-avoidance conflict. The conflict involved in commiting oneself to a course of action which has both pleasant and unpleasant aspects to it is called approach-avoidance conflict. Each of these types of conflict has different characteristics.

A young man who is faced with the problem of deciding between the priesthood and marriage, both of which are attractive to him, is faced with an approach-approach conflict. In such conflicts there is an initial period of vacillation which is more acute the more important the decision and the more equally appealing the alternatives. As one gets closer to one of the goals, a decision is accelerated because of the positive attraction.

An example of an avoidance-avoidance vocational conflict would be found in the candidate who experiences strong parental disapproval for his desire to be a priest and great anxiety of conscience and guilt at the prospect of deciding for another vocation. Avoidance-avoidance conflicts are characterized by great vacillation. The nearer one gets to either of the unpleasant alternatives, the greater the pain, and the tendency is to retreat from decision, to avoid it and to procrastinate.

An approach-avoidance vocational problem would be exemplified by the young man who wants to go to the seminary, but who is very insecure about his own body image and his athletic abilities and who knows that in the seminary there will be an active athletic program. Positive attractions are more strongly felt the further away we are from the decision. Negative reactions to a decision increase rapidly as we get closer. A young man like this will find that he is attracted to seminary life, but as he gets closer to the time of decision, the time of entering the seminary, his anxiety rises sharply. As he backs off, the anxiety wanes and the vocation becomes attractive again. The tendency here is to find that safe distance from the decisions which balances out both the negative and positive reactions. What is needed in situations such as this is personal counseling which enables a young man to face and grapple with the experiences and responses within himself that account for the ambivalent, conflicting feelings he is experiencing in regard to his vocation.

One can try to resolve doubts and ambivalences about vocation by intellectual means, such as more and more reading about the priesthood and the community. It is an attempt to plan out the future and know all the eventualities. While such investigations are helpful within normal limits, when exaggerated they are a compulsive way of dealing with one's own insecurity and are incompatible with the nature of a religious commitment, which is to the unknown. We cannot know fully to what we are committing ourselves in a religious vocation any more than we can in marriage. It is a commitment to many unknowns which will emerge in the future. It is for better or for worse. It is a commitment to grow toward the goal of being a shepherd and giving mature service to the flock, come what may. Like growth, it is a voyage of exploration. That is why it is exciting, and not for the faint of heart.

II *The Seminarian*

8 The Seminary

The seminary years are the background for the second stage of personal growth in the candidate for the priesthood. He begins a special course of training, in special circumstances which are designed to prepare him for the third phase of development, his life in the priesthood. The signs of a growth process are clearly found in the traditional seminary program. Tonsure and minor orders represent intermediate goals and presumably proofs of growth in the seminarian. The steps of major orders, with their increment of responsibilities and rights, bring him gradually to ordination. While this is truly a goal for this stage of vocational growth, it is not the capstone of "having a vocation." One aspect of growth ends on ordination day, but another immediately begins. The newly ordained priest is still in pursuit of his vocation, and the pain of continued growth will be a part of all his days.

The seminary, as a stage in the lifelong vocational development, should provide the conditions that will maximize the growth of each seminarian as a person. This involves his physical, academic, spiritual, and psychological growth. A true atmosphere of growth embraces all these phases of personality at the same time. The human person grows in unitary fashion; he grows altogether or he does not grow at all. A vision of the human being in the existential reality of his unique personality is essential for any real educator of future priests. In other words, he must understand the human person as he is found in the flesh. This person is not merely an intellect and not just a body. Nor is he a disembodied will to be exercised like a muscle, nor a set of sentiments to be stirred by rhetoric. The person is one, and any approach to facilitate his growth must flow from a real grasp of this unity of function.

Just as basic in understanding the mystery of man is the fact that the human person is a social product. From the first moments of life he needs other people in the right kind of relationship to him. His growth at every stage is linked inseparably to the persons with whom he is in contact. The process of becoming a mature man has been described by one psychiatrist as passing from the state of "being loved to loving." That is to say, the growth of the individual begins in, and is furthered by, the real love he experiences from his parents or from those who take their place. Whether the infant in the crib will wax or wane as a person depends on the depth and healthy quality of his relationships with others. Human growth is accomplished only in this eminently personal manner. Nothing is more imperilled by technology and organization than this truly personal component of human growth, the key component of seminary education.

When for the first time infants were born in hospitals rather than at home, American culture was proud of this major advance, allowing as it did for greater hygiene and the other benefits of institutional care. With "antisepsis" as the very byword of this medical development, a new, wasting illness in the newborn babies suddenly appeared. It was called *marasmus* or *infant debility*. The infants showed a daily loss of weight, and they were less active. Even the crying of the infants was muted and nurseries, ghostly by their silence, attested to the presence of a new and puzzling difficulty. The puzzle did not survive long, as the realization dawned that in the hospital's highly organized passion for cleanliness, the infants were being denied physical contact with other human beings. It turned out that the deep need for others and their message, so vital to the initiation of life and communicated in unspoken ways, was more important than hygiene. So today it is hospital routine, whenever a nurse has to care for a baby in any way, that she also pick him up and caress him. This deeply personal and human interchange cannot be supplanted even by the best advances in hygiene and administration. The human dependence on others to take, or even to be interested in taking, the first few steps in life reflects profoundly the social needs of the growing human being.

Man can be understood by looking at his relationships through the advancing periods of his life. His early relationship with his parents, his position with his brothers and sisters, his moving out of the family into the world of his age-mates; all these are powerful factors in freeing the individual to grow in a wholesome manner. These relationships can be equally powerful in preventing or distorting his growth if they are inadequate or unhealthy. Perhaps the best expression of that elusive term "mental health" is found in the man who is functioning wholesomely in his interpersonal relationships. Ordinarily the selection of and life with a marriage partner is the source and atmosphere of adult growth. The drama of any man's life is acted out before a complex of constantly shifting settings. So the father and mother must grow if their marriage is to have meaning; they must develop with their child if he is to become a man. As a famous psychologist, reflecting on the factors that affect the deep relationship of psychotherapy, has said, ". . . if I am to facilitate the personal growth of others in relation to me, then I must grow, and while this is often painful it is also enriching."[1] The good father of the five-month-old baby is a different man to be a good father to the five-year-old child or to the fifteen-year-old adolescent. He must be even more mature to be in relationship to a son who has grown to share the status of being an adult with him. The conditions of true growth and development for human beings are very demanding. They escape static systematization and are always *in the process of being fulfilled,* at best. It is never over and done with or all figured out. Risky and wonder-laden at the same time, it is far too real to be comprehended or planned very successfully on the theoretical plane. Human beings are not characters in a play prompted by wiser elders to speak lines written long before and in another place. Theirs is the script to write, the life to choose and live out. Dynamism is of life's very essence, and each day the road seems to take a new turn, a turn which reveals a new obstacle to be overcome or a new height to be scaled.

[1] Carl Rogers, *On Becoming a Person* (Boston: Houghton, 1961), p. 51.

9 The Conditions of Growth

"The greatest good we can do for others is not
to give them of our wealth, but to show them
their own."—Quoted by Cardinal Suenens in
The Gospel to Every Creature.[1]

The Oxford Dictionary, in giving us the meanings of the word
"discipline," gives us also a history of seminary training. The
word, related to the Latin word *discipulus,* originally meant
the instruction of disciples. From an emphasis on teaching it
has come to mean a system of rules for conduct or a system
by which order is maintained in the Church. It has a religious
meaning of correction or chastisement. So a word that originally signified "to educate" or "to train" has come to mean
"to bring under control." These meanings catch the attitudes
that many seminary professors have experienced toward training future priests. They would like to make disciples of them,
but sometimes the problem seems to be just to keep them
under control.

The task, however, has never really changed; it is mature
disciples that the Church needs. It is this task with which we
have been charged and, although it is currently fashionable
to criticize seminary educators, American priests can be proud

[1] Westminster: Newman, 1957, p. 75.

of the progressive tradition of American seminary education. Critics abound, however, as just a few recent examples indicate.

In the February 1964 issue of *Jubilee* Magazine, an interviewed priest says this: "Seminaries in general, I think, are too tightly disciplined. There is a stifling of initiative; and almost complete separation from life; a hothouse environment which delays maturity and the development of natural and social virtues . . . it's hard for a seminarian to know exactly what a seminary is supposed to be. Mostly he just conforms to the wishes of the Rector."[2]

There is hardly any doubt that the layman has emerged when one reads Daniel Callahan's criticism of seminaries:

But it is not at all clear that this systematic erasing of many important and normally laudable human traits—initiative, self-direction and psychological independence—is actually the best way to produce a clergy capable of understanding the contemporary spiritual needs or the modern world.[3]

In the updating of the Church, these voices seem to plead, the seminary should not be left behind. We would like to discuss the psychological conditions for the growth and development of our seminarians into a generation of disciples truly attuned to the needs of their times. There is one basic hypothesis about growth that is essential to the viewpoint of this book. It is this: we should try to make conditions in seminaries, convents, rectories and other houses of training and religious life as *normal* as possible. The word "normal" is used in the sense of *healthy,* not in the sense of *average.* The

[2] "Father John," quoted in an interview conducted by Ned O'Gorman and Oona Sullivan, "Whose Parish Is It?" *Jubilee,* vol. 11, no. 10, pp. 6–13.

[3] Daniel J. Callahan, *The Mind of the Catholic Layman* (New York: Scribner's, 1963), p. 132.

reasons are clear: first of all, healthy people thrive in normal conditions and, secondly, abnormal people stand out clearly as ill-fitting in a normal setting. This plea is not without many echoes in the world today. The efforts to modernize religious habits, the struggle to make real schools out of seminaries, the repeated papal theme that our task is to become a part of our age; all these say that we may have gone too far in many ways in being different from the world around us. "Worldly" has suddenly taken on a refurbished meaning. Where it used to connote evil and weakness, it has suddenly come to describe that part of the universe we are meant to transform, "becoming like man in all things except sin."

We know that grace builds on nature, and, in our pursuit of perfection, we must surely discover the favorable conditions for natural growth and maturity. Supernatural perfection can never be rooted in abnormal and unnatural environments. To say that something is supernatural is not to say that it is not natural. We do not contrast the healthy with the supernatural. We see them related as a building to its foundations. Unfortunately, however, and for rather involved historical reasons, many practices that can only be described as unhealthy have been baptized and are found in ecclesiastical and religious training houses. These practices or values are often preserved under the guise of tradition and people hesitate to question them. This creates a peculiar situation. Quite often the normal person in religion is made to feel guilty because he cannot lead an abnormal life perfectly. On the other hand, abnormal people are not only tolerated but are often rewarded because they can lead such an abnormal life almost perfectly.

What this hypothesis suggests is not that everything seminary educators have been doing is wrong but that they might profitably inspect some of the things in which they have had a rather absolute faith as means to develop men. Normal people just do not grow in a healthy way in abnormal atmospheres any more than flowers grow in a closet. Abnormal things develop and occur in abnormal institutions, such as prisons and other places where the pattern of life is necessarily distorted. Families that are broken produce children who are crippled emotionally. Some examples may be instructive.

If one has ever seen a Sister or a seminarian, or perhaps even a seminary professor, visit the home of his brother or sister who is married and has small children, one can understand something of the way values in religious can operate. A youngster tumbles through the front door, home from school again, brimming with the sense of rich surprise that fills the life of the very young. Perhaps his shoe comes off, or his glove, or he drops a book on the floor. The Sister or the seminarian becomes very uneasy until that shoe or that glove or that book is picked up; in other words, until the good order of the room has been restored. That would be the first thing that some professional religious would see, and they would feel very restless until things could be made neat again. But the mother of the family does not value these things in quite the same way. Cleanliness, she understands, is only next to godliness, and she emphasizes her relationship with the child, a child who needs her attention, her love and her greeting in this daily encounter. And she gets the glove or the book or the shoe picked up too, but first things have come first.

That mother, in being so personally a mother with her child, fulfills her vocation in a wonderful way and also helps to create the conditions in that home in which her child will grow to healthy maturity. She knows how to love that child, just as she knows how to get the house cleaned up, and just as she knows how to correct him when that is necessary. But she puts the emphasis on him, not on the furniture, or merely, to quote a familiar ecclesiastical phrase, on "the good order of the house." This is not a secret or a great psychological discovery on the mother's part. She is just an example of how healthy families live when they have a basic sense of values. It is the vision of real values that seminary educators must have if the process of making disciples is going to be successful. Perhaps it is abnormal, after all, for some religious houses to look as though nobody lived in them, a little antiseptically inhuman.

Seminary education, like the raising of a good family or the meaning of a real marriage, has to be a personal enterprise. Reliance cannot be placed on schedules and rules, no matter how skillfully they are devised or how efficiently they allow us to run our institution. The main value is the development of the persons of the seminarians; everything else must be seen in relationship to that. This is only to say again that what we have to try to do is what is normal and healthy. It is no wonder at times that people in the world can only shake their heads at us when we explain some piece of procedure or some intricacy of rule or regulation. What kind of distortion of life is it, for example, in the religious community where the Sisters are never allowed to speak at meals, though they are allowed to take their meals in the recreation room in order to get around the Rule? What could be farther removed from the real-life world than this manipulation of regulations and this rationalization of behavior? What of the priest, forbidden by Rule to own books, who spent much time and energy ripping the bindings off hundreds of volumes and putting them in ring binders so he could possess what were no longer "books"? It is not enough to say that it is supernatural. God must be weary of our heaping our inadequacies at His door. He must be tired of our explaining every failure or inexcusable

abnormality as part of Providential preparation for life. It is
unhealthy to have a built-in guarantee that we are never really
wrong.

Let us consider some other examples. A great mass of
psychological testing has revealed a curious truth about the
typical American seminarian. While he has a great desire to
help other people, he has a built-in difficulty in making easy
relationships with them. While part of his basic motivation
for the priestly life is to reach out to others, he finds that this
is difficult to do because he is shyer and more self-conscious
than his peers. The seminarian, however, rates highly on
characteristics like self-control or self-discipline. It is clear
that the seminarian, whose priesthood should be marked by
fruitful communication with other men, needs some development of his social self. Sometimes, however, seminaries
merely reinforce what the seminarian is already good at (self-
control) by insisting on practices which further inhibit the
very kind of social development he most needs. It is common,
for example, to insist on a great deal of silence in seminaries.
But this is an easy kind of discipline for the shy person and
may, in fact, protect him from a healthier social development.
Silence is undoubtedly a condition for meditation and real
thought, but making rules against speaking guarantees neither
of these. A normal, reflective person will seek out periods of
quiet as a part of his healthy adjustment to life. He does this
while retaining the freedom to communicate and without having to feel guilty about it. Seminaries often seem to propound
the idea that large periods of silence are productive in themselves of mature growth. Psychological counseling offers an
insight into silence and human communication. During effective counseling interviews periods of silence may frequently
occur. These silences are not uncomfortable but are very
fruitful times in which both client and counselor are deeply

involved. It is the period in which the client, having communicated deeply with another person, looks deeply and contemplatively at himself. It is a vital part of the personal growth process, but there is nothing awkward or embarrassing about these reflective silences. The contemplation, in other words, flows from the experience of real personal communication. The silence is the natural and appropriate condition for deeper self-discovery. It blends with the periods of spoken interpersonal exchange to constitute one experience. Speaking and not speaking are not in an antagonistic but a cooperative relationship. In seminaries we have, at times at least, made the mistake of expecting contemplation to flow from silence in itself. We have contrasted periods of silence and talking as though we failed to see them as two aspects of the overall process of human life. Silence will neither be chosen nor used as a condition for mature contemplation unless it comes in the context of healthy interpersonal sharing.

This insistence on separation, detachment, aloofness from one's fellows, can create a distinctly abnormal atmosphere where the very values of contemplation may never be achieved. This placing of a premium on distance in human relationships goes against the very basic and Christian notion that man never grows alone. The mature man is a social product of wholesome relationships with his fellow men. Those interested in the conditions of real growth must ask a simple question: Just how wholesome are the atmospheres in our seminaries? That will be the measure of the maturity of the priests who leave them on ordination day.

In a study of one hundred hospitalized priests VanderVeldt and McAllister discuss the fifteen of the priests who were diagnosed as sociopaths. A sociopath is withdrawn and poorly related to others. A comment of the authors is interesting:

The fifteen sociopaths among the clergy group are rather striking. Seminary training and the clerical life lend themselves easily to lack of duration and depth in interpersonal relationships. For many the "spirit of detachment" becomes synonymous with "fugitive, fleeting, involvement with other people," words which Sullivan used so aptly to describe the sociopath. Sociopaths are perhaps attracted to the challenge of the clerical life, since they need to prove themselves. They are perhaps more comfortable in the impersonal relationships of seminary life, in their need to keep a distance between themselves and others.

They go on to add a significant comment:

Forty-six of the clergy were diagnosed as personality disorders, suggesting the presence of lifelong patterns of maladjustment. These patterns of maladjustment must, therefore, in most cases have preceded the clerical state.[4]

At times, seminaries provide inadequate and unhealthy models to train young men for later life. There is no guarantee that doing things that are simply hard and unreasonable will even make us better equipped to do hard and unreasonable things in the future. St. Thomas reminds us that a thing is virtuous, not because it is hard but because it is good. In the name of making men mature, we are deceiving ourselves if we think this can be accomplished by giving them immature things to do. This is sometimes illustrated in the way that we try to develop responsibility in them. We give them very limited responsibilities, and we may frequently be uneasy about giving them the trust and freedom they need truly to carry even these out successfully. Here again true growth will arise only through personal relationships. These should be

4 Robert J. McAllister and Albert VanderVeldt, "Factors in Mental Illness among Hospitalized Clergy," *The Journal of Nervous and Mental Disease,* vol. 132, no. 1 (January 1961), p. 87.

very demanding, not the soft, mothering, and somewhat sickeningly overprotective postures that some few faculty members at times adopt. To be personal does not mean to be weak, and to be understanding does not mean to be so permissive that chaos is the result. It is not enough to make a man responsible for cleaning the hallway or making his bed. Neither is it enough to direct all his responsibility to ever more exact observance. But "observance" is often the thing that is emphasized. As one author wrote of this: "Not a few books on the seminary rule and on growth in spiritual perfection seem to delight in driving the soul to more and more precise observance; there is in them little sense of enlargement, wholesomeness, freedom, and love, such as one gets in reading the Gospels."[5]

The models are frequently too intellectual and do not take into account the real unity of man, who in the Christian vision is one thing, soul and body, intellect and emotions. The seminarian is told, over and over and over again, what are the things he must do and what ideals he should make his own. Yet these ideals are often quite intellectual and far too abstract. He is presented, as President Julius Stratton of M.I.T. said, with "an anemic image of the human drama."[6] He is urged to examine his conscience, but this is in a curiously cold and intellectual way that prevents him from seeing the roots of his behavior in his feeling self. He is told that he must know how to love people. This cannot be taught like geometry or English, and it can only be learned through personal experience. He is told that he must be a priest for all men, but this is often rhetoric rather than reality. What he really has to do is experience some of these things, bump

[5] Michael Novak, "The Priest in the Modern World," *Review for Religious,* vol. 20 (1961), p. 270.
[6] *The New York Times,* May 26, 1960.

himself against real people, feel deeply the demands of life that can be so unsentimental and unforgiving. Things that are merely abstract in the realm of serving other men do not appeal to the normal and healthy person; they are, however, just what the inadequate and abnormal feast upon. They love to dream, but, as Housman said, "the house of delusions is cheap to build but drafty to live in."

In the same way, a distortion of Teresian spirituality makes an unproductive life not only safe but sacred for the immature. Perhaps, after all, there has been too much insistence that life is nothing but a succession of little things. We read over and over again quotes like this one: "Holiness is not a matter of doing great things." But in this day and age men are needed to address themselves to the *magna opera Domini*. It is doubtful that we will convert the world by spending the day looking for little scraps of paper to pick up off the floor and offer to God in secret. Such devotion may have its place, but it is not a substitute for the fundamental business of being in the middle of the world, unafraid of its fierce competition and its cruel realities. But it is all too easy to make of the spiritual life a little world that each can generate like ectoplasm and in which each can live and move and have his being. Healthy people do not want to shut themselves off with their eyes cast downward and their thoughts turned inward or to isolate themselves from the needs of suffering mankind. It is a sign of health that a man wants to do something with his life, that he wants to be somebody in the profound meaning of fulfilling his own personality. But at times we have even taught that to thwart these things is admirable and virtuous and that every desire to excel is to be suppressed. It is a curious reversal of the healthy striving that a normal person experiences in wanting to grow and go beyond himself and make the world different because he has passed through it. But the man who is afraid of the world, the man who cannot get out of himself, because of neurotic shackles, rather fancies this kind of spirituality which removes him from competition and sanctifies his weakness. He reminds one of the Mexican villager's greeting. "May God go with you and may nothing new ever happen to you."

There is a trend on the part of some right now to misunderstand the nature of the mature freedom that must be provided as the normal atmosphere for mature growth in our seminaries. Some have felt clearly the changing nature of the seminary population. This is a generation that asks questions, a "new breed" which does not seem satisfied with some of our answers and strains for changes in everything. So some of us have been conservative, like the little old lady Barzun described as saying that "The modern thunderstorm no longer clears the air." But if there is one thing that is normal it is *to change*. (An amazing number of things are normal, when you think about it for awhile. It is normal, for example, to be imperfect.) Others have been the very opposite of conservative in facing this new generation. They have taken all sense of restriction away, and let the seminarians have anything they want. This, in quite unhealthy fashion, presents reality as without limits. Neither of these viewpoints represents the mature kind of making disciples that is so much needed. Freedom is not an easy thing to bear. Erich Fromm once wrote a book suggesting that some of us truly try to escape freedom because of the inevitable cross of responsibility that it places on our shoulders. But the normal person wants to be free just as he wants to meet the demands of responsibility, arduous though they may be. We cannot abandon our standards of excellence or our demands on the very best that our students have to offer. We cannot give them license in a chaotic world of their own making from which all the adults have fled. That is something like the "teenage tyranny" that has been written about recently.

Only mature men can love other men effectively, and this Pope Paul VI says is "the genius of the apostolate." Our young men cannot grow in a vacuum; they will only grow through their interrelationships with very strong and good normal priests. There is absolutely no substitute for this. Seminary education has got to be deeply personal or it is merely an elaborate game. There is no technique, no plan, nothing outside of ourselves that can answer the needs of seminary education in this day and age.

The world is not a sandbox full of playing children. The Church cannot send out anything less than a mature and manly generation of priests to minister to the human needs of men. St. Thomas, in writing of the parable of the wise and foolish virgins, says that we must burn with our own oil, that we cannot borrow our fuel from others, and that we had better have it when we need it. Our light is not meant to be under a bushel but on the mountaintop to give light to a darkened world.

The secret of healthy growth is that it comes from within. A successful gardener must understand the nature of growing things and his own nature as well. He must know what conditions further growth, and exactly what the possibilities and limits of his own role in this wondrous process are. If he is wise, he operates on the principle of making it possible for the flower to grow for itself. He can create favorable conditions of soil, moisture, and sun, but basically he relies on the inner power of the seed. If he tries to hurry growth too much or to delay it too long, he defeats his own vocation as a gardener. If he tries to style the plant against the dictates of nature, he ends up stunting its growth or, perhaps, killing it. His success is in cooperating in a healthy way with a power for fuller life, a power that belongs to the nature of all growing things. It is perhaps no accident that seminaries have traditionally been based on the gospel notion that "the hope of the harvest is in the seed."

Nor is it an accident that the hopes of all men, but especially of young men, were enlivened by John F. Kennedy. A man can indeed measure his own stature by the light from the President's graveside flame. President Kennedy has become a model for a young generation of Catholics who want to grow. They were given hope by the words of his inaugural address. "I do not shrink from this responsibility . . . I welcome it." And by his quotation from another Irishman, "Some people see things and say 'Why'? but I dream things that never were and I say 'Why not'?" Perhaps his healthy normality, and the fullness of the life that flowed from it—the life of a man who burned with his own oil—does, in fact, give a fresh vision of the work of instructing disciples. It is far more a work of freeing the best that is in them than of getting control of them.

The healthier things are, the better. A healthy world is not a soft and empty world, but a profoundly challenging one in which men must keep their feet on the ground. The hypothesis is simple enough: If we are normal and healthy, if we are mature enough to be real with our students, then they too will be healthy and normal and grow to full maturity.

10 The Atmosphere of Growth

"The Seminary" is an abstraction that has, at times at least, as many meanings as there are clerics who refer to it. For some it brings up recollections of relatively happy, if irresponsible, years. For others, the memories are grimmer and their imagination projects a turreted silhouette against a lowering sky. Still others recall this class or that, the meals, the rules, or this escapade or that professor. The seminary is all these things, of course, as it provides the overall experience of academic training and character formation for future priests. It is difficult, if not impossible, to speak of the seminary as only a complex of buildings, although the architecture can contribute one way or another to the whole process of education. One popular style of seminary architecture, incidentally, has been described as "Early American Penal." Neither is the seminary comprehended by focusing only on the administrative procedures or the administrators. To see only the chapel or only the classes is to see again parts of a total experience that is designed to facilitate growth in the candidates for the priesthood. These various aspects of this phase of priestly preparation must be examined separately and in relationship to one another if we are to understand how they provide the atmosphere of healthy personal development for seminarians.

72

THE SEMINARY AS AN INSTITUTION
OR ORGANIZATION

The religious life is often built around the virtue of obedience, and it is the observance of the rule which is extolled as the one sure path to holiness and to the whole Christian life. A new perspective has been given to the role of rules in human living by the research which sociologists have been doing into the characteristics of organizations and hospitals. In brief, they have shown very clearly how the structure of a bureaucracy or of any complex organization differs from the structure of a family. Gradually a bureaucracy becomes more and more governed by uniform rules and formulae. Little consideration is given to individual differences and to direct personal relationships. The administration is uniform and impersonal for all individuals. While this increases efficiency, it gradually depersonalizes this portion of the life of those involved. So, for example, upon registering at a hospital one might be told, as one of the authors was, that his number was more important than his name, etc. In a family, on the other hand, there is a minimum of formulae and rules and the relationships are deeply personal. Many people spend their working day in an organization and return home to their families. They live in two worlds. Others live their whole day and year within the total institution, and this is their only world. Seminaries are such total institutions, governed by rules. We like to call our religious societies "families," but perhaps some are more like a bureaucracy or an organization.

However, it is not inevitable that with growth in size and complexity, the family spirit should be lost. Pope Pius XII, in an address in April 1956 to the alumni, students and teachers of the National Boarding School for Boys, in Rome, warns about the dangers of regimentation in a boys' boarding school:

Doubtless a life in common, away from the natural surroundings of a child and under the rule of a rigid regimentation that is unable to distinguish between individuals, presents its own dangers. However small an error of judgment is made, the students will tend to become complete strangers to a sense of personal responsibility; they will be carried along like semiconscious beings, by mechanical actions, into a state of pure formalism in studies, in discipline, and in prayer. Strict uniformity tends to stifle all personal initiative, the isolated life is likely to restrict a larger view of the world; the unyielding urgency of regimentation sometimes fosters hypocrisy or imposes intellectual levels too low for some and too high for others; excessive severity ends by turning strong characters into rebels and weak ones into spineless automatons.[1]

He gives three remedies to combat this ever present tendency toward regimentation. Every effort must be made to respond to the individuality of the student, authority must always be exercised prudentially and without rigidity according to individual needs and, finally, a spirit of love and affection between superior and student provides the atmosphere in which students inevitably respond and grow. One can afford to depart from gentleness in correction only by exception, and then only briefly. His remarks on how to preserve an intimate spirit within a big institution are particularly relevant:

They require individual attention, both in the choice of a way of life, and in being corrected and judged. One must avoid, in any case, a community that is too uniform, that makes several hundred boarders . . . differing from one another even in age . . . study, sleep, eat and play in the same building, with the same schedule of hours, under the same set of rules.

These inconveniences should be obviated by dividing the pupils into homogeneous groups, of such limited numbers that it will be

[1] Pius XII, Address to Students and Faculty of the Convito Nazionale Maschile di Roma, April, 1956.

possible for their instructor to take a fatherly interest in each member of the group.

But even though they are thus divided into groups, each of which it would be reasonable to assign a separate schedule, separate rules, and separate exercises proportioned to their needs and abilities, and even though the normal youth may be able to acquire for himself the essential elements of the complex of moral and spiritual values offered by his education and his school through good examples and good books, still it is needful that each one should feel himself to be the special object of the attention of his teacher. He should never be allowed to get the impression of being confused with the crowd and forgotten, of being neglected in his particular requirements, needs, and weaknesses, as though only his physical presence was of any account.

Only from this kind of personal attention will the pupil derive encouragement to assert and develop his personal temperament, a spirit of enterprise, and a sense of responsibility toward his superiors and his equals, in the same way as if he were living in the bosom of a numerous and well-ordered family.[2]

The rule provides training in discipline for those who have not yet developed limits for themselves. The immature person, however, is apt to get the wrong impression. He is all too eager to be dependent. He waits for directives, even begs for them. He is afraid to trust his own judgment and leans on the security which the law or rule provides. This reminds one of the dynamics of scrupulosity. A few years ago we were synthesizing the data from a number of research studies on the personality traits of Catholic religious personnel. There emerged a slowly dawning insight into the parallel between the generalized personality picture of religious personnel which was emerging from the study and the standard and familiar syndrome of the obsessive-compulsive neurosis. In the latter a

2 *Ibid.*

person is driven to adopt the repetition of certain thoughts or actions as a defense against anxiety. The person who washes his hands, the person who never gets his confession complete enough to suit him; these are obsessive-compulsives. It was in the patterning rather than in the intensity of the traits that the similarity lay.

In organized religious life, especially during the years of training, we can foster living according to the expectations of superiors and in the very same breath warn our candidate for having ideas opposite to their own. We can force him to think like us; we can try to make him into our own image. The rebel gets our attention because he gets under our skin and is told of his deficiencies. The conformist does not annoy so much, and often is not told of his weakness. The compliant candidate is often extolled and is allowed to go his own way without ever being told that he is not fully satisfactory to his society.

Living too much by rule alone has another consequence which is not beneficial for a man who will have to live with others as a priest. The rule tends to eliminate all conflicts, especially among the many shy persons attached to the seminary. As conflict areas between men arise, rules are made to cover them. The rule eliminates the need for a growing man to work out directly with others their areas of conflict. The rule forestalls conflict and protects him from it. He is cheated of the profitable experience of learning how to live with men and to transcend the multiple minor conflicts which inevitably arise. When the support which a man has is merely extrinsic, it is a fact of experience that the one who has been so supported is apt to collapse when the support is removed after ordination to the priesthood.

Gordon W. Allport, the distinguished Harvard psychologist of personality, in his writings on the psychology of religion distinguishes between the religiously immature person and the religiously mature person. The one has internalized his faith; the other has not. External or immature religion is that of childhood in which we conform to the standards and norms of our parents and our culture. Allport also makes the point that religious maturity is the least prevalent of all the forms of maturity. Many young men make a notable stride in the maturity of their religion at the time of their adolescence. For a boy, it is at about the age of sixteen that conversion experiences, either critical or gradual, are most likely to occur. This is also the age of conflict and ambivalence between dependence and independence. It is really a sign of growth when the battle is joined and the youth weighs whether he will continue to accept "doctrine" from the outside or live a genuine religious life of his own, but it is a real battle. As Allport has put it:

Commencing in later childhood or adolescence, the individual who is on the way to maturity probably will repudiate both the oversimplified products of his earlier egocentric thinking, and blind conformity to institutional or parental views. . . . Adherence to almost any Church, or to none at all, may mark those who in their maturing personalities have fought through the issues of religion.[3]

This is the age at which we receive many of our candidates for the priesthood and religious life. It is vital that our training facilitate the step from external, exteriorized values which are characteristic of immaturity to those internalized, personalized values which are the hallmark of the mature priest.

The second attribute of the mature religious sentiment is found in the autonomous character of its motivational power. The energy that sustains such a sentiment may be said to pertain to it alone.[4]

[3] Gordon W. Allport, *The Individual and His Religion* (New York: Macmillan, 1950), p. 60.
[4] *Ibid.*, p. 63.

It has often been pointed out that in the writings of St. Thomas, prudence is a more fundamental virtue than obedience, since it is one of the four cardinal moral virtues, while obedience is a part of the virtue of justice. Although the two virtues are not only compatible but are needed for mature functioning in the priesthood and religious life, in practice there are difficulties in designing and implementing a program which fosters and integrates the growth of both in our candidates. There is no doubt that the cultivation of obedience is a prominent goal of clerical education, but one frequently gets the impression that realistically the same cannot be said for prudence. It is exciting to speculate on the implications for training, if prudence were to be restored as a pre-eminent objective of clerical education.

Were prudence so restored, as a central virtue in seminary life, there would have to be more freedom, more trust, more risk, a little more disorder. We would have to tolerate mistakes. It could mean that gradually our young men would find the source of evaluation within themselves. It is in this freedom that a person learns what he himself wants and what he believes in. Such an exercise of freedom is the mark of the mature man. He does not act from compulsion or obligation but from his own personalized values. For this to happen, those responsible for training must have a respect for the individual and acknowledge his right to develop in his own way. He should be encouraged to be unique. Sometimes we are afraid of this because we confuse uniqueness with being odd or a "character"; odd people, however, are not unique, because they can be typed. It is the mature person who is unique and who cannot be fitted into any type or category.

We should be wary of overlegislating and of overinterference into the lives of our subjects. Regulations have a tendency to proliferate, and we should be on our guard against this.

Yves Simon in his Aquinas Lecture, "The Nature and Functions of Authority," analyzes with great clarity the essential problem which every social group must face, i.e., how to combine rightly the forces of authority and freedom. He concludes his philosophical inquiry with two principles which must be preserved in delicate balance in the prudential operation of authority. These complementary principles he calls the principle of authority and the principle of autonomy.

They can be formulated as follows: Principle of Authority
Wherever the welfare of a community requires a common action, the unity of that common action must be assured by the higher organs of that community.

　　　　　　　　　　　　　　　　Principle of Autonomy
Wherever a task can be satisfactorily achieved by the initiative of the individual or that of small social units, the fulfillment of that task must be left to the initiative of the individual or to that of small social units.[5]

[5] Yves Simon, *Nature and Functions of Authority* (Milwaukee: Marquette University Press, 1940), pp. 46–47.

11 The Faculty Member—
His Contribution and Development

If growth is truly to occur during the seminary years, the ordinary conditions of growth must be observed. There are no short-cuts and no adequate substitutes for the interpersonal element in this process. The seminary faculty members are of predominant importance, then, in developing the whole person of the future priests under their care. It is a simple and yet a complicated truth at the same time. Who could be surprised that solidly mature priests must be in wholesome relationships with their students to make real men of them? Who, at the same time, cannot see the problems involved in bringing this elementary conviction into reality? There is probably no educator with greater potential for good than the seminary professor. In the realm of clerical culture, however, the seminary professor is not generally perceived as having such a role to play. More often than not, he is thought of as somewhat staid and, perhaps, dull; there is little sense of wonder, much less adventure, about his well-ordered life. The seminary professor is, in fact, sometimes classified, along with wars and earthquakes, as a necessary evil. Of all men, he is surely the most often imitated, the central object of high-spirited recollections in ecclesiastical gatherings from generation to generation, the one who seems to be "fair game" for his students in season and out. Among seminarians, who are at times given to conceiving of their life as an unverbalized struggle for survival, the faculty member, curiously enough, can be thought of, if only vaguely, as "the enemy."

The Seminary professor, however, does represent the priesthood to the hopeful aspirants with whom he lives and on whom he is fated, for good or ill, to have a profound effect. It is interesting to let the seminary student express his views on the qualities which he feels to be desirable in priest faculty members. This is not to say that the seminarian is altogether right or to give him the prerogative of deciding what his teachers should be like, but presumably the interested faculty member is attentive to the needs and aspirations of those to whom his life is dedicated. It is entirely possible for any educator to be mistaken about the outlook of those whom he trains. The accuracy with which he does understand his students may be a good measure of his effectiveness with them. Few men working with the young, or with any other group, are able to help them unless they can somehow tune in on their "wave-length." There is no need for pitched battle with the "new breed," disturbing as some of their attitudes and viewpoints may seem to an older and wiser generation. But there is the danger that the needs and problems of youth will be viewed only in terms of the educator's own experience. It may be that generations become deeply estranged only because they are not trying to hear what they are really saying to each other. An example of this is seen in the research of Sister Margaret Burke, R.S.C.J.[1] In her study, students checked off the areas in which they felt that their problems lay, and the directors of guidance programs also checked the areas where they felt the students' problems

[1] *An Evaluation of the Guidance Services in Seven Catholic Liberal Arts Colleges for Women* (Chicago: Loyola University Press, 1951).

were. These lists were then correlated and were found to vary greatly. In most instances there was a noticeable discrepancy between the directors' evaluation of the general areas of student problems and the students' lists.

If the seminary professor is an all-important catalyst in the process of priestly education, he is interested as well as deeply involved in the world of the seminarian. Yet he could be in error in his judgments as much as the subjects of Sister Margaret's study were. One aspect of the seminarian's world is concerned with what he expects from seminary faculty members. What does the seminarian look for in the priests with whom he lives and from whom he hopes to learn of the priesthood?

Some of our own research gives us important clues about this.[2] We administered to 110 first- and second-year philosophy students from 14 religious groups and 23 dioceses at the Catholic University of America part of a questionnaire that had been used to sample opinions and attitudes of Belgian girls toward the Catholic priest. It is reproduced below:

Read the following 10 qualities of virtues and number them (1 to 10) beginning with those you prefer most in a seminary faculty member.

.... Will power	.... Sincerity
.... Politeness	.... Hope in God
.... Understanding	.... Respect for people
.... Zeal	.... Abnegation regarding comfort
.... Humility	.... Intelligence

The students were also asked to write a brief discursive reply on the same subject. Finally, they were asked to write a

2 Eugene C. Kennedy, M.M., "The Seminary Faculty Member: the Seminarian's View," *The American Ecclesiastical Review,* vol. cxlii, no. 6 (June 1960), pp. 390–398.

one-sentence piece of advice which they would give to a priest friend assigned to seminary work.

The results of the rankings are given below, along with the results of the rankings of the 300 Belgian high school girls (averaged).

Seminarians	*Belgian Study*
Qualities most desirable in a seminary faculty member	Qualities most desirable in a priest
1. Understanding	1. Understanding
2. Sincerity	2. Sincerity
3. Humility	3. Will power
4. Zeal	4. Intelligence
5. Intelligence	5. Hope in God
6. Politeness	6. Humility
7. Hope in God	7. Zeal
8. Will power	8. Respect for people
9. Respect for people	9. Abnegation regarding comfort
10. Abnegation regarding comfort	10. Politeness

It is striking to note the correspondence between the lists in the first two qualities of *understanding* and *sincerity*. The low importance of *abnegation regarding comfort* and *respect for people* on both lists shows another interesting parallel of judgments.

When the viewpoint of the seminarian is investigated, he seems to want priests to strive to do just that; be able or willing to see things from his viewpoint. What exactly does this concept of understanding mean to the seminarian? The discursive replies throw a good deal of light on this highly prized characteristic.

Seminarians would like priest faculty members to strive to

see and accept them as they are, to have, in a familiar phrase, "an understanding ear." This implies more than just understanding about the seminarian; it means the ability to understand *with* him. The understanding priest makes an effort to communicate his feeling for his students. He does not view them only from the outside, or in terms of his own needs. He is at ease with the students and they are at ease with him.

An indication of the views of the seminarians themselves can be found in their own statements. One writes:

My ideal seminary faculty member would be one who is understanding in the richest sense of the term. He would be able to see his seminarians, not in terms of his own experience and reactions, but as they are, as they feel, as they react. He would try to acquaint himself with the seminarians' backgrounds, not out of idle curiosity but out of a desire to know everything that might be of help in understanding them. He would manifest an interest in them—not a possessive or overpowering, rather artificial cordiality, but a genuinely manly interest. He would try to remember names and would show some concern for their progress. . . . He would speak to seminarians when he met them, and he would never leave a greeting unanswered. He would not divorce himself from seminary life. . . . He would not seek opportunities to escape. He would never give the impression that he is just waiting for someone to break a rule so that he can "crack down." He would never deal with seminarians merely as so many "vocations." Rather, he would appreciate each vocation as a unique person with his own views, strengths, and weaknesses.

A similar point of view in regard to the personal nature of each student's problems is expressed by another seminarian:

The seminary professor should also have a real concern for the individual student rather than some attitude like "Everyone goes through this period," or "This is what has helped others." Rather than tell the students these facts, he should keep them in the background as a basis for understanding how this particular person must feel now. Then he can attempt to aid the seminarian as a person with a problem which he must solve himself, rather than as a mathematical problem to which he can apply a formula worked out in the past.

A number of other students emphasized the availability of the seminary professor, a willingness to let them talk to him:

He should be, above all, approachable and understanding, never driving anybody away by his attitude or his actions. This interest means he will make himself available at almost all times and not just at his own leisure.

It is a real comfort to be able to walk up to a priest, say what's on your mind and get an honest and appreciating reaction; not to have to dress up a request with fancy phrases of obeisance, etc. If a priest has understanding, he has enough. . . .

Most priests, as soon as they're ordained it seems, forget what it was like when they were in the seminary. They don't seem to understand us—which is odd, since they were once in our shoes. . . .

I would like to see a closer relation than that generally experienced between the seminary professor and the students. The professor and the student should be able to meet freely and converse openly. We are striving towards the same goal. We should not then be considered as of a real lower group, untrained and unacquainted with their ideas and ideals. The professor then should not have to be on his guard lest he let the seminarians in on too much. . . .

Still others laid emphasis on the Christian virtue of love that they look for in their teachers:

True Christ-like love is most easily displayed in the priest's true understanding of a seminarian and his problems and a deep sincerity in desiring to help him to become a priest. . . .

I think he should really try to show that he loves the students. There is no one as effective as someone really in love. . . .

One who is in all things a man! . . .

What is needed is not merely an ascetic, for he may for all this be entirely closed to other people. True, well-established virtues can exert a very beneficial influence on students, but how will they ever come to know about them if the priest is not understanding? Only through understanding can a truly favorable atmosphere for development and advancement be achieved in the seminary. . . .

Sincerity was also a primary consideration in evaluating the qualities of a seminary teacher:

I think sincerity is an all-inclusive virtue in the sense that no matter what a teacher is, he must avoid trying to fool his students into thinking he is anything else. . . .

The only virtue I would place above the others is understanding. After all, a priest is ordained for others, and if he can't understand others. . . .

I feel the most desirable quality is that of understanding because a teacher or a director must see the viewpoint of the one he is helping and not put a personal interpretation on everything. . . .

One seminarian expressed his views by indicating the qualities he would *not* like to see in his professors:

Perhaps I can express what I mean from the negative angle. I don't like a faculty member who gives me the impression that he is around merely to impart knowledge in the classroom and you are just one of many he is subjected to dealing with. Such a faculty member would seldom, if ever, go out of his way to show an interest in me or bother to be friendly. . . . I like a faculty member who is seen often among the students and who shows an interest, an enjoyment, in dealing with them.

Several students who took part in the survey appended other qualities which they felt were highly desirable in the seminary faculty member. The two which emerged most clearly were (1) *a sense of humor,* and (2) *constancy.* Typical of the comments about the first of these are the following:

He should have a lively sense of humor. He does not have to be a guffawing back-slapper, but a priest whose geniality mirrors the deep hope and joy that his whole priestly life should be immersed in. . . .

Whether it is because they are afraid to unbend or because they have a need to preserve a certain sense of dignity, too many profs fail to see the incongruities of life, which, to me at least, are one of the saving factors that make seminary life bearable. . . .

As to the notion of constancy, a similar emphasis is placed upon stability and an even manner of life:

Another virtue necessary is consistency. The contrary situation so often pops up. "Never do that, you never know when he might be in a bad mood." . . .

Too many profs are as changeable as the weather. . . .

Nothing makes you feel so uncertain as the faculty member who is unpredictable in his reactions. One day he is friendly, the next aloof. You can hardly be yourself, when you have to put on an act to match the prevailing mood of the teacher. . . .

Perhaps these comments constitute a fairly good operational definition of the priesthood. The seminarians are not asking for anything more than what Catholics everywhere have a right to expect from their priests. Our students can learn a lot about the office of the priesthood from a veritable library of books on the subject, but they can only learn what it means for a man to be a priest from men who are priests. As one seminarian once commented, "The only time I ever see a priest personally is when he's mad at me. Then I get called to his room or office but, other than that, no contact." The correction of mistakes is a function from which faculty members will never find themselves free, but if this is their chief source of contact with the students, one might legitimately wonder whether some values were not out of balance here. A good father corrects his children but hardly limits himself to that kind of evaluative-disciplinary relationship with them. He listens to their lessons, arbitrates their fights, plays with them, and sometimes he is just with them for no particular purpose at all. Throughout this spectrum of relationships he maintains his own adult status and adult interests and occupations. So too the faculty member need not become a seminarian again but, as a mature adult, can live in a healthy and unselfconscious manner with the seminarians.

He does not have to set out to practice the pseudo-virtue of "togetherness." The healthiest associations of life are not planned. There is such a thing as just living as a priest with the seminarians with no particular purpose outside of being with them. A priest faculty member at a great Catholic university once pointed to a colleague and said, "You know, he makes me uneasy all the time. He makes me feel as though I were the object of his meditation resolution for the day." Virtue that is contrived is not virtue at all; there is a healthy spontaneity in the relationships that promote real growth in those who experience them. As Barron has put it:

. . . in health there is no awkwardness, for the moment of health is the moment of unconscious creative synthesis, when without thinking about it at all we know that we make sense to ourselves and others.[3]

[3] Frank Barron, *Creativity and Psychological Health* (Princeton, N.J.: Van Nostrand, 1963), p. 5.

What the seminarians ask is not that we be perfect but that we be real in our lives with them.

In another study, carried out in France on the subject: "What Youth Thinks of Priests and the Religious Life," with 300 girls and 300 boys of secondary school age, the same emphasis on human and understanding qualities was found. These points about the students' image of the priest clearly emerged:

The values of "incarnation" prevail in most minds over those of transcendence and separation. . . . The priest is first and foremost "the friend of man," the priest is "he who associates with their lives."

This notion of "incarnation," according to the study, implied the following values. The priest should be

(1) Receptive to all that is human;
(2) Adaptable to human interests;
(3) One with all men through love.

It is certainly significant that there is such a parallel in the attitudes uncovered by these different studies.

They have been replicated on different populations many times with the same results. It might be interesting to note parenthetically one of the results of our own experience in testing hundreds of seminarians with what is known as a sentence-completion test. In such a test the subject is asked to complete a series of partial sentences with a notion that is meaningful for him. One of the partial sentences is: *The priest I know best.* . . . In almost every case, seminarians, although they have been living intimately with faculty members for a number of years, will complete the sentence with some such phrase as "the curate at home." The priest to whom they feel closest is often someone they have not seen in years, or whom they see only intermittently at vacation times. Why, one might ask, should this be? Why is there a relaxed, wholesome, and enduring relationship of this kind elsewhere, and apparently so little of it with priest faculty members?

Many familiar attitudinal positions of faculty members may well be evaluated in the light of this study. Is, after all, "aloofness" the virtue that many have made of it? Is it really wise to say "You must not smile until Christmas," or "Who cares what the students think anyway?" It would seem, given the results of this inquiry, that the faculty member must care very deeply about what the students say in order to be effective with them.

The seminarians seem to view the process of their own preparation for the priesthood as intensely personal. Perhaps, if our ears were attuned keenly enough, that is the message that would emerge from many of the seemingly obnoxious stirrings and strivings so often reported as coming from today's seminarian. He is really asking, despite the occasional imprudence of youth, to be respected as an individual human being who wants to commit himself deeply to the salvation of the world. He cannot be dismissed for dreaming the dreams or conjuring up the visions that belong so much to youth. He cannot be forever frustrated or suppressed; that merely delays the explosion. And neither can he be ignored; that merely estranges him even further from the mature generation from whom he must learn, if ever he is to learn at all, the meaning of the priesthood.

But if the seminarians are respected and if faculty members are not afraid to be a part of their lives in a grown-up manner, it will be found that this generation is not all wild-eyed and ill-disciplined. They are profoundly good and deeply anxious to be better. They are growing and the pangs of healthy growth must not be misunderstood or mis-labelled as the hostilities of rebels out to destroy the Church. A person who has not fully grown up yet defines the word *immaturity*. Immaturity, then, connotes promise more than unrelievable lack. If the promise is to be redeemed, it is going to flow from the healthy inter-actions of faculty members and students. Nothing else can do this as long as the age-old conditions of human growth obtain.

SELECTION AND DEVELOPMENT OF FACULTY MEMBERS

It is the inescapable obligation of superiors to make it pos-sible for faculty members to grow. They too are pursuing their vocation and need the atmosphere for self-development as much as the students. First of all, who shall serve on the seminary staff? The answer is, as has been emphasized con-cerning the selection of students, those priests capable of con-tinued growth. It has been alleged that the intelligent but docile, the proper but unadventurous, priest is frequently chosen for this work:

Those who are chosen for the work are generally solid per-formers in the sacred sciences, though they may have been in-differently taught in the first instance. They are given further theological training but little encouragement to refashion the educational scheme they will be a part of. The mentality of *nihil innovetur* is likely to be assumed as that which best befits their new responsibilities.[4]

Often enough the one selected is truly shy and self-con-scious, and although he likes people, he is also threatened by them. For example, we have known faculty members to use

[4] Gerard S. Sloyan, "Seminaries in America," *The Commonweal*, vol. lxxiii, no. 2 (October 7, 1960), pp. 37–40.

very circuitous and inconvenient routes around the seminary building in order to avoid visitors. They do not dislike people, but they are uneasy with them, and the roundabout path saves them from a social situation which would put them under real pressure. It is difficult to see how such men, manipulated into social withdrawal by their own anxiety, can contribute significantly to the personal development of the students. Intellectual ability is not enough, and a seminary faculty member should be a mature, or at least a maturing, priest who is free from any obstacles to complete personal growth.

There has never been any question of the need for adequate training for a seminary faculty member. Even so, the fact remains that men who have not had the opportunity for further education after ordination have had the responsibility of running seminaries. Lack of graduate study is a heavy burden to place on the shoulders of a man chosen for the already exacting life of a seminary professor. "Any priest can teach Latin" or "Any priest can be a spiritual director"—these phrases probably have some truth in them. The question is: What is our criterion for effectiveness? To hold class is a minimal accomplishment, after all, but whether the students grow or not is the real test of the teacher. If the seminary professor is somewhat unsure of himself, then to add to his burden of self-consciousness by sending him into academic work without adequate preparation is clearly not going to help the general quality of seminary education. It is unfair to the faculty member as well as to the students.

In addition to training in his own assigned field of specialization, a faculty member should be encouraged to get added instruction in subjects which would add to his personal development. Courses in education, current biblical scholarship, preaching, and counseling are but a few examples of available developmental courses.

The faculty member deserves the conditions of life and

teaching which will contribute to his professional growth. Many newly assigned faculty members are left to shift for themselves in adjusting to life in the seminary. An intelligent program of in-service training and orientation, even if carried out informally, can contribute significantly to the maturation of the faculty member. He deserves the ordinary conveniences and facilities available as a matter of routine to teachers in secular schools of a comparable level.

The development of the faculty member is affected markedly by the conditions of his work and by the general tenor of his professional relationships. In the end, however, he must grow for himself and exercise the choices that will help him to grow steadily in his unique vocation. He can live by trying to meet the expectations of others; he can, as a matter of fact, continue to live pretty much as a dutiful seminarian. This may make him popular with superiors and acceptable to the students, but does it mean that he is really mature? Only the faculty member can answer the question, for only he can decide what values will predominate in his life. He has to effect the balance of striving for academic excellence, of creating healthy relationships with his students, and of leading a personally mature life. A healthy priest will move in this direction and cannot help bringing his students along with him. There is something engagingly simple about men of real depth, and their health is contagious. The most effective faculty members, alive and growing, fit Barron's description:

A person may be said to be . . . most healthy when his awareness includes the broadest possible aspects of human experience, and the deepest possible comprehension of them, while at the same time he is most simple and direct in his feelings, thoughts, and actions.[5]

He is also a very happy man.

[5] Barron, *op. cit.,* p. 4.

12 Defective Faculty-
Student Relationships

The subject of faculty-student relationships has been a constant source of comment in the world of seminary education. The discussion arises from the two defective extremes which bracket the wholesome and mature kind of relationship which we have advocated. Briefly stated, there are faculty members who cannot be made to relate with the students and there are faculty members who cannot be kept from relating with the students. These extremes of withdrawal and overinvolvement spring from the faculty member's own emotional needs.

WITHDRAWAL

Some professors, even when they acknowledge intellectually the value of mature relationships with the students, feel that they cannot participate in them. Sometimes this is a result of their own feelings of shyness or social inadequacy, a lack, in other words, of personal development in themselves. These are often excellent men who wish they could feel free to know the students more easily. They are frequently lonely men because their inner feelings have kept them from ever knowing anybody very well. The worst part, and this can be the source of real suffering, is that they often feel trapped because their social behavior is controlled by their emotional reactions. These professors need to grow and, indeed, are capable of it, but they have never been helped to understand their own emotional lives.

The problem is serious because it reflects a whole style of relating to others in a formal and proper ecclesiastical way that can carry over into the pastoral relationship of the priesthood. It is a confusing ideal to present to seminarians. This posture of withdrawal may generate a feeling of security for the anxious priest, but at the terrible price of robbing him of his God-given spontaneity and naturalness. He is forced by his fears not to be himself. *The Courage To Be,* the title of a book by Paul Tillich, has been paraphrased by Sydney Jourard as the courage to be known.[1] This is precisely what he means when he also says that "self-disclosure" is a symptom of the healthy personality.[2] This, however, is just what is so difficult for people who are unsure of themselves. The distant path of withdrawal is then better, as they see it. This sidestepping of human persons can contribute to a life that is quite abnormal because it is unrefreshed by any satisfying human relationships. Sometimes this professor seeks all his social relationships outside the life of the seminary and, while there is nothing intrinsically wrong with this, it represents an abandonment of one group of persons, the seminarians, for another group not so directly connected with his vocation. It is like a parish priest who would spend a lot of time getting to know people in a parish on the other side of town.

This attitude of removal from the seminary social scene is reflected in casual statements that are so familiar to anyone

---

[1] Sydney M. Jourard, *The Transparent Self* (Princeton, N.J.: Van Nostrand, 1964), p. 11.
[2] *Ibid.,* p. 15.

who has lived in a seminary. "Wait until you get out of here
and live with *real* people." "I can hardly wait to get back to
parish life so I can work with people again." Even the seminarians catch this same mood when they remark, after a visiting day, "Earth people were here today." There seems to be
little recognition in all of this of the reality of the persons who
make up the world of the seminary itself. This spirit, of course,
can generate an atmosphere from which everybody, faculty
members and students alike, would deservedly want to escape.
Human beings simply cannot live, much less grow, in such an
environment.

There is a further aspect of this fear that can move teachers
to use the defense of aloofness. This is the fear that if they do
show an interest in the students, if they do let themselves out,
then they might lose themselves. The immature faculty member, not knowing himself, finds that his own feelings are hurt
when a seminarian somehow fails him. He begins to take
refuge by establishing distance between himself and others.
"You can't get involved with others," he says, meaning "I can't
run the risk of being hurt myself." Because his own feelings
have led him into a relationship marked with emotional overinvestment of self, because, in other words, of an inadequate
personal relationship, he decides that no relationship is possible at all. It is a defense, an excuse for not growing; it is the
beginning of depersonalized relationships that are just as defective as his previous ones. Rogers makes some relevant observations in this regard:

Can I let myself experience positive attitudes toward this other
person—attitudes of warmth, caring, liking, interest, respect? It
is not easy. I find in myself, and feel that I often see in others, a
certain amount of fear of these feelings. We are afraid that if we
let ourselves freely experience these positive feelings toward an-

other we may be trapped by them. They may lead to demands on us or we may be disappointed in our trust, and these outcomes we fear. So as a reaction we tend to build up distance between ourselves and others—aloofness, a "professional" attitude, an impersonal relationship.

I feel quite strongly that one of the most important reasons for the professionalization of every field is that it helps to keep this distance. In the clinical areas we develop elaborate diagnostic formulations, seeing the person as an object. In teaching and administration we develop all kinds of evaluative procedures, so that again the person is perceived as an object. In these ways, I believe, we can keep ourselves from experiencing the caring which would exist if we recognized the relationship as one between two persons. It is a real achievement when we can learn, even in certain relationships or at certain times in these relationships, that it is safe to care, that it is safe to relate to the other as a person for whom we have positive feelings.[3]

It is frequently the fearful faculty member who will substitute theorizing about love for the much more demanding business of really loving others. Discussion groups about loving your neighbor abound among people who are not mature enough to love others in a down-to-earth and unselfconscious way. Even the liturgical renewal of the Church has been appropriated by the theorizers at times as a framework for their endless elaborations on charity. This is milk, but seminarians need the red meat of healthy relationships with strong men if they are going to learn how to love.

THE OVERINVOLVED

Few people seem to do less good than the do-gooders. Some faculty members set out to establish relationships with the students, but the good they seek is chiefly for themselves. They

[3] Carl Rogers, *On Becoming a Person* (Boston: Houghton, 1961), p. 52.

must have their followers and the know-how to cultivate the attention of the students in a hundred subtle ways. They seek emotional nourishment for themselves, and they represent a major obstacle to the growth of the seminarians. Unfortunately these teachers or guides frequently speak the language of personalism without really understanding it. The encouragement of professor-student relationships, as urged by this book, is just what they want to hear to justify what can only be described as their own selfish style of encountering others.

The inner needs that drive these men are not very apparent even to them. They may resemble the counselor, described by Patterson, "who desires strongly to be looked up to, respected, admired, to be considered clever, intelligent, and informed. . . ." Such a one may "seek satisfaction of this need in counseling."[4] One thing, however, is clear; they do not reach out to love for the sake of the other but for the sake of themselves. They do business with counterfeit money and, while it may pass as genuine for a while, it cannot really buy anything.

These professors may attract students in multiple ways. One reason for this is that there is often very little in the way of faculty-student relationships in a particular seminary, so that they merely fill a vacuum. Selectivity is a highly developed art in their initiation of relationships with students. They are never open to everybody, but only to those whose friendship will reward them in some way. A sure symptom of this kind of "friendship" with students is that it is often based on the student's weakness rather than his strength. They flatter him, grant him privileges, and quickly gain a hold on his attention and loyalty. The prime feature of this kind of relationship is the possessive attitude of the professor. They place what Horney has called "claims" on the seminarian and the hand of

---

[4] C. H. Patterson, *Counseling and Psychotherapy: Theory and Practice* (New York: Harper, 1959), p. 49.

friendship turns out to have a grip of steel. The student must follow their views not only academically but sometimes spiritually as well. The seminarian is anything but free; he is not being loved, he is being used. Clearly, the seminarian cannot grow in a healthy manner if he is in such a relationship. All he is experiencing is the lack of maturity in the faculty member, and the whole situation may prove to be embarrassing and uncomfortable for him. In this case the faculty member needs him far more than he needs the faculty member. Some immature seminarians, of course, know just how to take advantage of such a symbiotic relationship. They milk it for privileges and minor favors, but the whole relationship is empty and unworthy of real men.

Seminary professors whose inadequate personality growth makes them reach out to the students in these defective ways cannot contribute to the growth of the students. No matter what their intellectual endowments, these teachers do not belong in seminary work until they themselves have matured. These priests, mercifully few, are difficult to deal with because they are clever in protecting themselves and rationalizing their behavior. Their self-rewarding emotional relationships with the students are generally not the only manifestation of their personal inadequacy. The same lack of maturity will reveal itself in their relationship to authority and in their dealings with their colleagues. Their overall influence in a seminary is negative and divisive.

The seminarian, in these situations, finds himself forced to worship at the faculty member's shrine. He must appear when summoned, acquiesce in the wisdom offered, and subdue any impulses he may have to think for himself. These professors are jealous—there is no other word for it—of the students they have singled out for special attention. They want the students, in a manner that is basically disrespectful of them, to be dependent. The dynamics of the relationship, however, reveal that the professor is actually dependent on the students. He is easily hurt if the student does not respond to him, and with the power of criticism any faculty member enjoys, he can make reprisals on those students who try to break their ties with him. These seminarians, whose desire to be let alone is a sign of their fundamental soundness, are "ungrateful" in the eyes of the faculty member. What the latter has never learned is that in any true friendship there is a respect for the person of the other that is never violated.

One of the ever present conditions in a healthy relationship is the willingness to let the other person alone, to respect his integrity and freedom. Real friendship is not destroyed by separation, nor does it demand constant reassurance from either person. Erich Fromm has written that

to be able to concentrate means to be able to be alone with oneself ... and this ability is precisely a condition for the ability to love. If I am attached to another person because I cannot stand on my own feet, he or she may be a lifesaver, but the relationship is not one of love. Paradoxically, the ability to be alone is the condition for the ability to love.[5]

Friends, quite simply, are just friends in an unselfconscious and open manner. That is what is normal and healthy. Anything that is healthy can stand the sunshine and fresh air. It is the same for faculty-student relationships. There is never any need for secrecy or for an association that would go against the basic regulations and spirit of the seminary.

These are extremes, it is true, but they have the ring of truth to anyone who has been active in seminary training. Obviously, the development of the next generation of priests cannot be left to extremists.

[5] *The Art of Loving* (New York: Harper, 1956).

13 Counseling and Spiritual Direction

Growth is the very theme of everything anybody has ever written about the spiritual life. It is described by a handful of analogies, including mansions and stages, all implying progressive growth. The spiritual director has, then, a vocation of helping other persons grow "to the full measure of manhood in Jesus Christ." The seminarian indeed should "have life and have it more abundantly." Even the notion of perfection itself can be thought of as not merely matching an ideal criterion outside of oneself so much as the individual's fulfilling all of his own potential, of his becoming everything he can be. It is a Christian philosophical commonplace to describe evil as the "absence of a due good." What illustrates this state better than unfulfilled growth, the promise of fullness unredeemed?

The spiritual director helps somebody else to grow for himself. The director is not the source or cause of the growth. In the area of his interior development, as in so many weighty aspects of his life, man is faced with the responsibility of doing something in cooperation with God's grace for himself. The subject grows, or it is all illusion, as any experienced director would say. It is interesting that spiritual guides are often described as "directors of souls," a phrase which, however unintentionally, divides the person. It is in deeply understanding themselves as "directors of persons" that spiritual directors can see afresh the factors in their work which promote growth. Insights from psychological counseling are helpful here.

It is easy, and to an extent quite appropriate, to distinguish between spiritual direction and counseling. Among other writers, Byrne[1] has shown that direction treats spiritual problems and aims at supernatural integration while counseling treats emotional problems and aims at natural integration. These are accurate and useful statements, and they remind the spiritual director and the counselor not to intrude in each other's domain.

But what makes any helping relationship effective, whether it is the relationship in marriage, spiritual direction, friendship or counseling? Do the cautions and distinctions about spiritual direction and counseling reflect a mathematical viewpoint toward human persons? The desire to categorize may have blurred something much more fundamental and much more profound that is shared by both spiritual direction and counseling.

Recent psychological research has indicated that there are basic similarities in all good human relationships. That is to say, there is something that all good human relationships have in common. There is some quality that they must have if the relationships are to work at all. This shared characteristic may be far more important than the ways in which, on possibly accidental bases, we distinguish various kinds of human relationships. It is in this territory, in the realm of what happens between people in their most significant encounters with each other, that we need to grasp the root dynamics of interpersonal growth. We are saying, then, that what makes good spiritual

---

[1] J. T. Byrne, "Counseling and Spiritual Direction," *The Homiletic and Pastoral Review*, vol. lix, no. 6 (March 1959), p. 537.

direction effective is basically what makes good counseling effective. Spiritual direction works when there is a genuine interpersonal relationship between the people involved. There must be some real contact on a genuinely human level. This relationship implies real understanding and interest, and this arises when two people are related in the profound way that is possible only between human persons. This is far more important than techniques. In short, the conditions of healthy interpersonal exchange must be present or spiritual direction is a lifeless kind of enterprise.

It would seem that many persons view spiritual direction as an enervating and not very profitable experience.[2] This is bound to occur if the relationship is mechanical, impersonal, or ambiguous. In rereading the masters of the spiritual life, one is constantly struck by the keen sensitivity they have in common to the same truths. The writers, for example, reiterate the fact that the relationship is not one of obedience as between a subject and a superior. As Leclercq says:

Certain spiritual authors have tended to identify as much as possible the spiritual director as a true superior and to attribute to him an authority properly so called in virtue of which he decides even the minute details of a choice of a state in life; the submission to a director becomes then an obligation of obedience strictly speaking. Père de Guibert has justly remarked that this conception has no foundation in tradition and ecclesiastical teaching. That, differing from superiors properly speaking, the director is not appointed by God but chosen freely by each so that a person does not practice towards a director the same obedience that one would to a true superior.[3]

[2] Lucien-Marie de St. Joseph, O.C.D., "Spiritual Direction—Its Nature and Dimensions," *Theology Digest,* vol. vi, no. 1 (Winter 1958), pp. 39–44.
[3] Jacques Leclercq, *La Conscience du Chrétien* (Paris: Aubier, Editions Montaigne, 1946), pp. 248–249.

The spiritual director's task is far more that of the prudent guide who helps the individual develop himself in truly responsible fashion. Or, as de Guibert has it: "Such an excess in passivity would prevent the soul from reaching maturity in the spiritual life and would not result in true 'spiritual childhood.' Rather, the aim of the director should be to make the soul self-reliant, at least in ordinary spiritual matters."[4] The freedom the subject enjoys has been protected zealously by the Church. These notions give added reason for seeing the similarities between spiritual direction and counseling, likenesses they share with all wholesome human encounters. It may, after all, be a naive and unchristian approach to speak of separate treatments for the soul and the emotions. What is dealt with is the living, breathing human person who lives in a world of nature and grace and works toward the fulfillment of his supernatural destiny. Here again the whole man is treated or the man is not treated at all. The spiritual director must deal precisely with persons, not just with intellects; he must be deeply attuned to the whole complex psychosomatic unity we meet in individual men. ". . . all spiritual fathers," Lucien-Marie de St. Joseph writes, "can approach each of their sons as individuals. Each individual is different by reason of his character and his own personal history. Man in the abstract does not exist."[5]

Counselors have increasingly emphasized the quality of the human relationship as of far greater importance than any possible "techniques" or "tricks." What they have come to see with ever greater clarity is that the person seeking help will improve or grow only if the relationship with the counselor is deeply real. If the persons involved do not genuinely encounter

[4] Joseph de Guibert, S.J., *The Theology of the Spiritual Life* (New York: Sheed and Ward, 1953), pp. 173–174.
[5] *Op. cit.*, p. 42.

one another, then failure ensues. Counseling works, to borrow a well-known phrase, *ex opere operantis*. A psychologist, discussing what makes counseling successful, or not, writes:

In the first place, I hypothesize that personal growth is facilitated when the counselor is what he is, when in the relationship with his client he is genuine and without "front" or façade, openly being the feelings and attitudes which at that moment are flowing in him. We have used the term "congruence" to try to describe this condition. By this we mean that the feelings the counselor is experiencing are available to him, available to his awareness, that he is able to live these feelings, be them in the relationship, and able to communicate them if appropriate. It means that he comes into a direct personal encounter with his client, meeting him on a person-to-person basis. It means that he is being himself, not denying himself. No one fully achieves this condition, yet the more the therapist is able to listen acceptantly to what is going on within himself, and the more he is able to be the complexity of his feelings without fear, the higher the degree of his congruence.

I think that we readily sense this quality in our everyday life. We could each of us name persons whom we know who always seem to be operating from behind a front, who are playing a role, who tend to say things they do not feel. They are exhibiting incongruence. We do not reveal ourselves too deeply to such people. On the other hand each of us knows individuals whom we somehow trust, because we sense that they are being what they are, that we are dealing with the person himself, and not with a polite or professional façade. This is the quality of which we are speaking, and it is hypothesized that the more genuine and congruent the therapist in the relationship, the more probability there is that change in personality in the client will occur. . . .

I hope it is clear that I am talking about a realness in the counselor which is deep and true, not superficial. I have sometimes thought that the word transparency helps to describe this element of personal congruence. If everything going on in me which is relevant to the relationship can be seen by my client, if he can see "clear through me," and if I am *willing* for this realness to show through in the relationship, then I can be almost certain that this will be a meaningful encounter in which we both learn and develop.[6]

The counselor must have certain skills and certain qualifications, but in a great measure his effectiveness will depend on what he is like as a person. As Father Charles Curran has written:

Nor can one catch in simple description the most subtle and complex relationship that must exist between counselor and client, between therapist and patient. Here the necessity of mutual involvement in the human condition is most strikingly demonstrated. The therapist or counselor cannot stand apart in an objective, unfeeling, Cartesian way. He must be a complete person, psychosomatically committed to a deep, sensitive, and intense personal communion, a true giving of self. The counselor is first to give himself. Then, more slowly but just as surely, the person coming for help gains the confidence to make a genuine commitment of himself. Such a relationship seems to approximate what the ancients called *amor bene-volentiae*—a relationship in which one gives of himself entirely and seeks no return from the other except the other's best fulfillment of himself.[7]

It should hardly surprise us to find that this is so. After all, the purpose of spiritual direction must surely be growth in charity. Could it ever be imagined that this could be accomplished in one-sided fashion? The spiritual director must grow along with those with whom he works. Counseling research

[6] Carl Rogers, "The Interpersonal Relationship: the Core of Guidance," *The Harvard Educational Review,* vol. 32, no. 4 (Fall 1962), pp. 417–419, 429.

[7] Charles A. Curran, "Counseling, Psychotherapy, and the Unified Person," *Journal of Religion and Health,* vol. 2, no. 2 (January 1963), p. 109.

bids priests to examine the quality of the human relationship in spiritual direction.

Spiritual direction may be conceived by some as merely instructing the newcomer in the principles of prayer and the spiritual life. Others may see it as largely encouraging others with something akin to pep talks. Others, in fact, see the director as assuming a great deal of responsibility for the development of the directee. It is healthy to re-examine some of these attitudes in the light of what we are learning about real human relationships. The director, however, is not dealing just with a mind that seeks information. Neither is his encounter merely with emotions that need arousing. Nor is his the sole responsibility for the other's actions. It is an existential encounter between two persons and the outcome depends on how truly this encounter takes place. The spiritual director's main resource is not his academic degree, the title on his office door, or any other claim to wisdom; it is what he is and who he is in his work with others.

Spiritual directors, like counselors, or other faculty members previously mentioned, are capable of working with people in order to receive the rewards of gratitude, or to build their own image of themselves as wise men. They may find that they often concentrate, not on the person whom they hold theoretically to be sacred, but on the problem and, as a result, they resort to various artificial approaches and techniques. They find even that the problem they are solving in counseling is not that of the person but is of another order altogether. They solve, especially if they are given to much direct advice, the problem they are experiencing because someone has come to them for help. They tend to "handle" cases because, on some level of awareness, they feel they have to do something for this individual and send him on his way. They find that they are often very subtly trying to remake others in their own image and likeness, rather than giving persons the freedom really to be themselves. They remind one of the remark of Monsignor Ronald Knox about the possible motivations of a soliloquizing seminary professor: "Rows and rows of divines turning out just like me. . . . What could be more suitable for the Church?"[8]

The focus comes back to the person of the director or the counselor, and it may be that what they must have in common is far more important than the distinctions that can be made about their work. A further sharing is in their ability to understand another and to communicate this understanding back to the troubled person. As Father Curran says:

To understand another at the deepest level of his feelings and reactions is an immeasurably more profound, complex, and delicate kind of understanding than simply to know the meaning of the words he uses. Yet this is what the other really means when he says of the counselor after an interview, "You know, he really understood me."[9]

Reality of self and depth of understanding: these, then, are the absolute requirements for a good counselor. They are not very different from the virtues of *understanding* and *sincerity* which rank high as desirable in priests. His counseling is sterile without them. It is perhaps because these factors have been somewhat blurred in our vision of the nature of spiritual direction that it has been a disappointing and ineffective experience for many people. This is not to say that the knowledge of the spiritual director is of no account. Neither is it to say that instruction in the principles of the spiritual life is unimportant. To emphasize the personal factors of the relationship

8 Ronald Knox, *The Priestly Life* (New York: Sheed and Ward, 1958), p. 154.

9 *Op. cit.,* p. 110.

is in no sense to downgrade these other possible aspects of spiritual direction. It is translating his wisdom into human terms, it is in making it possible for the other to experience charity and understanding through him, that the spiritual director can learn from the counselor. Why, St. Thomas asks, can St. Paul say that a man could know all things, and without charity it would profit him nothing? And he answers that nobody could learn anything from him. Nobody can learn in an atmosphere that is cold and remote. Nobody can breathe in such high, thin air. What spiritual direction and counseling share arises from the wonder of the fully human person. "The glory of God," St. Irenaeus tells us, "is in a man fully alive." The glory of God is in the counselor or the director who is fully alive as well.

POSTSCRIPT

We are appending to this section the reactions of one highly talented and creative seminarian to the experience of a deep personal relationship with a priest-counselor. There were only two half-hour counseling sessions, but they seem to have been very real and helpful experiences precisely because the seminarian spoke to a priest who was both understanding and genuine. These reflections suggest the dynamic growth possibilities of director-student relationships that are fulfilled when the encounter is personal in a healthy and mature sense.

Reflections on My Experience with Counseling

I have only gone to seek counseling three or four times, but those times were like cataracts or whirlpools in a fast river. I was flowing along in a merely turbid, swollen state, ready to erupt at any moment, for several months. Seminary life, despite my expectations, had some gutty reality to it. There were periods of wild and foolish exhilaration followed by days of seemingly uncaused black melancholy. I simply could not take it any longer one day, so I made an appointment with the priest-counselor.

Let me describe my set of postulates before I spout out the conclusions. I'm an intensely introspective student (with a capital S). I'd read some books on Freudian psychology and even knew a bit about client-centered counseling. In a cold intellectual way I even knew my main problems.

Which brings me to my first big impression of the counseling experience; there are ways of knowing and ways of knowing. There's quite a big chasm between telling yourself that there's a big conflict in your life about doing so-called duty or taking the risk of initiative and telling it to another significant human being. You find that certain concepts and angles of viewpoint are just little placebo-like images that you've constructed and that others, the ones you blurt out in far less glorified and sophisticated language than that which flows through the stream of consciousness, not only come out riding on hot breath but actually pull the breath out of you and leave you feeling half-shaking and half-empty, as I imagine the wild man felt when he was sitting on the rock, after Jesus let the devils break out.

A second big impression that comes to mind is that none of this would have been possible if the counselor had not been the man he was. I had gone to our spiritual director (under the compulsion of our rule system) several times, and several times had tentatively and cautiously given a brief statement of what I conceived my conflict to be. This invariably set off ten minutes of good-old-common-sense spirituality. I used to muse over the fact that listening to the director talk was very soothing and pleasant in a way; like taking dope or watching television when you're not really a damn bit interested in the program. Since then I've concluded that I, with my occasional nods of assent, was counseling *him* and keeping his ego-structure and value system safe, strong, and secure. I say this in a joyful spirit, though; I was glad to help.

On the other hand, the priest-counselor *listened* to me. Listening is the high-priced spread of love that nobody's oleomargarine of advice will ever equal in good taste. "Please, mother, I'd rather do it myself" . . . every counselor who sees someone struggling to really know and feel and live his problems ought to engrave that on his wild and maybe perverted love of "helping others."

A third major comment involves the after-the-catharsis stage. There I was, enervated and shocked at finding out that *I* . . . *me* . . . actually had such and such a feeling that was strong enough to possess me body and soul. The next problem was, it seemed, what was I going to *do* about it? This question I seldom answered in concrete terms in the counselor's office. But, oh, it felt so good to have the problem stated! It was a return to the freedom of childhood . . . with one Olympian difference; a little healthy feeling, partly frightening, that I was the master of my destiny. The counselor couldn't tell how much time I should spend on my dull but painlessly hypnotic assigned courses of study, how much time I should spend on the outside reading and writing my whole being craved for, or how much time I should spend on the socializing that I very well knew my reserved personality needed and enjoyed, but slightly feared. *I* had to decide all these things. I was a free man, despite the first-impression chain of seminary rules that was tied and still is tied around my feet. Yes, life can be daring, risky, and exciting . . . *even in a seminary.*

It goes to show you that the Lord takes care of His children. Amen.

TWO TONGUES

If we listen carefully in even the most casual conversation, we may suddenly understand dimensions of human communication that we have never heard before. We sometimes tell or ask each other what we *think* about some person or situation. More often we are trying to tell others, just as they may be trying to tell us, what we *feel* about things. It is as if we were saying, "This is not just the logical conclusion of my intellect. This is me, all of me, and how I react totally to this person or situation." All of us share in the poet's attempt to catch in our words the feelings we are experiencing. And many times we "just can't find the right words to tell you how I feel." But the words go together with the feelings, just as the body with the soul, to form one message.

We address ourselves to the world in two languages. One is the language of intellect or cognition. The other is the language of affect or feeling. The language of cognition, the words, are like the body which is given life by the language of feeling, which is like the soul. If we hear only the words, the surface sounds, we will miss the real message and the real meaning of the person who delivers it. If we want to listen with real understanding, we might well ask ourselves, "What is this person feeling in order to speak these words to me?" The underlying emotion accurately related to the words which they motivated: this is what we must hear if we are genuinely going to understand anybody else.

Frequently we bring to our conversations preconceptions about what others are going to say. After all, haven't we heard this kind of thing a hundred times before? Our preconceptions or, as psychological research has suggested, our own needs move us to impose our own meaning on what others are trying to tell us. It was a great discovery for a young priest, who had been studying counseling, to say one day, "You know, this morning I really heard for the first time something I had been listening to for years. After Mass, a lady said to me 'Father, I want to talk to you.' I used to think people were saying, 'Father, I want you to talk to me.' And I got pretty good at doing just that, preaching them encouraging little sermons. But that's not what they want. That lady meant just what she said. She wanted to talk to me and tell me something very important, and she wanted me to listen. Why did I take so long to hear?"

The fact that we do not listen well, or even make the effort to do so, is a major barrier to the process of communication. If *understanding* is what our people, including seminarians, have a right to expect from us, then we cannot allow factors within us to obstruct our ability to listen carefully. We must, as one psychiatrist has described it, "listen with the third ear" if we are going to catch the language of emotion as it is expressed in the language of intellect.

The feeling foundation of our speech explains why intellectual or logical answers to people's questions often seem to miss the mark. Their problem is not just intellectual, and the clean, precise rational reply is not enough. We develop a certain style of handling the problems of others which betrays our overconfidence in the purely intellectual response and, incidentally, tells us something about our own feelings at the same time. Let us analyze a simple example of a seminarian's problem and and the possible reactions to it.

A young and very sincere seminarian approaches a priest for a talk with him. The priest is glad to see him and, noting that he is rather anxious, allows him to talk. The interview begins:

Seminarian: Well, Father, I just don't know what to do. I want to do the right thing, and I try to . . . but, well, it really gets me down. It's like this. I get right up with the first bell, make my morning offering, and, well, sometimes I don't even finish that before I find myself thinking of something else. Then I get to morning prayers and my mind is a million miles away. Then we sit down to meditation and I'm trying to get some ideas together and, before you know it, the bell rings and it's all over and I haven't gotten anywhere. Then Mass begins and I can't tell sometimes what has happened. I don't even remember the Consecration. I find it's time for Communion because people are getting up all around me. Then I try to make a Thanksgiving and I'm thinking of the first class of the day. . . . It's the same way all day. I come to breakfast and I don't pay any attention to the reading. I get to my room and start to prepare class and something else comes up. Then I'm behind in that. Then I plan to catch up in the afternoon and I never do. I'm behind in everything and I don't know what to do about it.

A familiar kind of story? Perhaps. And so are some of the answers that are often given in this type of situation. A skilled advisor, incidentally, could help this seminarian to grow in a very effective way. First of all, the conditions of rapport seem excellent. The seminarian has approached the priest and is willing to open himself very deeply to him. It is not, in other words, the seminarian's fault if he does not profit from this encounter. We will now listen to and analyze some actual answers given to this young man.

First Advisor (in fatherly tones): Well, you know everybody has ups and downs. The thing you don't want to do is let them keep you down. The worst thing you can do is to worry. Just try to accept things, with a little stronger Faith, and don't worry about it. We all go through these things. Why, I remember when I was in the seminary and. . . .

Comment: This could be said in very understanding fashion, and it would be hard to gainsay the principle it contains; that is, that this happens to others and that this young man should not worry. The only difficulty is that the seminarian is saying that he cannot handle the situation. He cannot "not worry about it." If he could command himself to stop worrying he would not have come to see Father about it. In trying to reassure, the advisor has completely misunderstood the seminarian. By this kind of advice he is, in fact, denying that the seminarian has a problem. He is saying, in effect, "You do not have to feel the way you say you do and you should stop feeling that way." In this response we note that the advisor slips readily into his own world of recollection. He is off the subject and is not helping the seminarian with his autobiographical touches. He probably feels better himself, but the point is to help the seminarian feel better.

Second Advisor: It sounds to me like you're poorly organized. As I see it, you need a daily schedule.

Comment: Again the advisor is looking at the situation from his own viewpoint and is suggesting what seems to him to be a reasonable solution. The seminarian would probably surprise him if he replied, "It's my daily schedule that's killing me. It's not that I don't have one. I just can't follow it at all." It is not effective, needless to say, to prescribe a solution that is already a part of the problem. No effort has been made here to understand the seminarian's feelings about the situation. The advisor has not even heard the language of intellect very well. The advisor probably feels better, however, even if the seminarian does not.

Third Advisor: Well, we can't just complain about everything that comes up. You'll have to learn that sooner or later. You ought to offer these things up.

Comment: This seems like a sensible, no-nonsense reminder to the seminarian not to feel sorry for himself. There is, however, no evidence from what he says that the seminarian is feeling sorry for himself. If anything, his statement suggests the contrary. He is ready to take a hard look at his inner self; he is willing to open up any phase of himself to try to improve. Why make him feel guilty for being so open? Why not be willing to follow along as he tries to understand himself? Again, the seminarian may already know as much as the advisor about offering things up. He knows he has to do more than that if he is going to come to grips with his problem. Again, the advisor has missed the effort of the seminarian to explore and understand himself. The advisor has remained on the outside, but he probably feels better for having delivered himself of such a straightforward piece of advice.

Fourth Advisor: You feel deeply discouraged and frustrated and you don't know how to handle it.

Comment: This advisor in very simple language has caught the message that the seminarian was trying to express and, by putting it in fresh words, has clearly expressed his deep and accurate understanding. The chances are that the seminarian will say "That's exactly how I feel," and will proceed another step in examining himself. The advisor has not evaluated, nor has he given a ready-made piece of advice. He has not condoned the statement of the seminarian, but he has not condemned him either. He has simply tried to listen and hear what this young man had to say. In other words, the advisor has tried to understand and to express his understanding. He has heard the language of emotion, filled with illustrations, and has translated it accurately into the language of intellectual understanding. The advisor has symbolized clearly what the seminarian was struggling to express. Now the latter can understand his own conflict more clearly, can understand himself more deeply. This is the first but most important step toward solving his own difficulties.

Such responses are relatively rare in advisors who stay on the outside of those who come for help. They are rarer still in advisors who have all the answers and who enjoy the sound of their own voices. But this understanding viewpoint, which catches the whole man's communication, is an absolute necessity for anyone who wishes to be truly helpful with other persons. The skilled advisor is able to see as if he were looking at the world through the eyes of the other; he can, as was mentioned in *To Kill A Mockingbird,* "wear someone else's skin for a while."

This understanding is the very essence of priestly compassion as it strives to enter into the feelings of others. To do this well, the seminary professor must put aside the satisfaction of his own feelings. As Father Curran has written of Catholic counselors: "Analogous to the manner in which the surgeon carefully 'scrubs' before an operation, the counselor should enter the counseling relationship 'scrubbed' of his own self-concern and urges."[10]

The seminary professor who would counsel the growing student must "empty himself" in real Christ-like fashion. Nowhere more than in the work of seminary training is a priest called upon to give himself totally for his "flock." If a seminarian is going to learn something about understanding and dedication, he will have to learn it from the priests with whom he lives. That kind of knowledge comes in a personal way, if it comes at all. The seminary professor who aspires with Solomon to "an understanding heart" will contribute in the most significant way to the growth of the priestly hearts in his care.

[10] *Pastoral Psychology,* vol. 10, no. 91 (February 1959), p. 22.

14 Training for Growth

"And then man is not static, but living. . . . An
urge towards synthesis impels me to seek the
common factor in them, to pass from the
lantern slide to the cinematograph film, to
comprehend man in his incessant movement."
—Paul Tournier, *The Meaning of Persons.*[1]

The healthy seminarian is one who can grow and who is interested in growing. It is not a surprise that he should reflect the behavior of someone still in the process of growing. This is quite normal and healthy in a developing young man and is ordinarily quite well understood by seminary authorities. They can appreciate the process of growth and allow for it as they share in moving the candidate toward manhood. The adolescent who has difficulties with seminary regulations need not be seen as irreligious, but more as someone who is working out, with great difficulty and pain at times, his whole idea of relationship to authority. This relationship to authority is normally worked out during the years of adolescence. Growth is not always smooth and steady, and the signs of it might easily be misinterpreted. The basically healthy candidate keeps moving forward, however, and his struggle for growth is a

[1] New York: Harper, 1957, p. 115.

good sign of his fundamental soundness. Seminarians do not arrive full grown, then, but they must be free of any major defects or obstacles that would make their own growth impossible. It is obvious that the phases of seminary formation should be appropriate to and blend with the stages of personal development.

Any elements of a training program which would inhibit growth or which tend to fixate the seminarian at a less than mature stage of development are obviously working against the whole meaning of seminary life; indeed, against the meaning of life itself. The seminary exists for the development of the students, not to provide them with secure niches in which they can remain as they are without having to grow. It is not a haven for the insecure or for those who are afraid of life. "Any dead thing," Chesterton reminds us, "can go with the stream; it takes a live thing to swim against it." An effective priest is fully alive. His life flows from deeply internalized values, both religious and moral; he is open to what he experiences, and he grows through real relationships with other men. It is clear, then, that the "raison d'être" of the seminary is the maturing of the seminarians and not the convenience of the staff.

There is a characteristic of very many candidates for the priesthood and religious life which is quite relevant in deciding on the kinds of training which will facilitate their growth. They tend, in great numbers, to be anxious and unsure of themselves. At the same time they have highly sensitive consciences and have internalized the values of their parents and their teachers. These candidates have very little to live on that is truly their own. To put it succinctly in psychological terms, these young men have weak egos and strong superegos. They need to strengthen their own self-trust and self-acceptance. They are all too alert to the expectations of others; they need to find and strengthen themselves. They must discover their own identity and, in a profound sense, become themselves. They need, in Goldbrunner's phrase, to "discover their own truth" and to begin to live it. Any system of training which places a premium on conformity to a pattern of regulations tends to reinforce in these candidates an already established personality structure which is geared to correspondence with extrinsic norms rather than to the development of their own inner sense of direction.

What, we might ask, does a young man learn in the seminary? Surely one of the early but persistent bits of learning is to do what is expected of him. This is a part of wisdom that serves him well and can certainly be a legitimate part of clerical education. The difficulty arises when this is all that he learns. His growth is clearly incomplete if his life is predicated on a self-image whose motivations and thinking are provided by others.

One form of inadequate personality growth is seen in the person who relates to others by finding out what kind of behavior they prefer and then providing that in order to get their approval. They seek constantly for the formula which will make them a success with others. What self they have is based on meeting the expectations of others. They are "all things to all men" in a strictly non-Pauline sense. This is seen in the seminary in the way in which the students become expert at "handling" the faculty. Students everywhere are good at this, but seminarians rank with the best of them. The idea is that in each course it is not the subject that is to be mastered but the professor. Subtle but deep changes take place in seminary students as one class hour yields to another. Seminarians become sensitized to producing with uncommon skill the kind of behavior, in the classroom and on tests, that is needed to survive in the various courses. Great energy, reinforced by regular reward, goes into discovering what the professor presumably wants and then accommodating him. No professor interested in teaching really wants this kind of response on the part of his students. He is annoyed by students who calibrate their responses to his teaching in this way. In this example, however, the students are not interested in being their real selves as much as they are in meeting what they presume the faculty expectations of them to be.

This occurs in many aspects of seminary life other than the classroom. Conversely, the faculty members sometimes struggle to meet the students' expectations, to behave in front of them in a way that matches the seminarians' expectations. At times faculty members view their task as doing to others what was done unto them when they were in the seminary. "Giving good example to the students" is a familiar faculty ideal, but it often means doing something in front of the students that one would not do if they were not present. "Good example" in this case means doing something that has only extrinsic value, that the faculty member does not really believe in himself. Seminaries could conceivably end up with the only encounter between masters and students at the slightly unreal level of each group's struggling to meet the other group's presumed expectations. Far simpler and far more satisfying and productive for all concerned is to meet in the real world. It is far better to be real and imperfect than to act out a behavioral form of perfection that is unreal.

Recent psychological studies have provided stimulating reading for all those who, like faculty members in a seminary, are concerned with the growth of the young. Peck and Havighurst[2] have delineated five types of character of different degrees of maturity. They have related these moral types to both family influences and personality characteristics. The two least

[2] *The Psychology of Character Development* (New York: Wiley, 1960).

mature are the *amoral* and *expedient* types. These have no internalized values, and they correspond, in stages of maturity, to the levels of infancy and early childhood respectively. Such individuals are frequently found in correctional institutions. Two somewhat more mature types, corresponding to about the same level of later childhood development, are otherwise quite different. These are the *conforming* and the *irrational-conscientious* types. Both have internalized values which they follow against the whole world, if this becomes necessary. The *conforming* follow, insofar as they can, the expectations of the group in which they live. The most mature stage of moral development is the *rational-altruistic,* which corresponds to the adolescent and adult stage of growth. Such individuals, like those who have passed "from being loved to loving," have internalized moral values which can be modified in the light of new experience.

A minority of individuals belong to the most mature type. The majority of society, as a torrent of current literature reminds us, belongs to the *conforming* group. This is true of a large proportion of those young people who present themselves as candidates for the priesthood and religious life. That is to say, when these people enter the seminary or house of religious training, they have not grown farther than the conforming stage of development. Their "life-style" is that of conforming to the values and beliefs of others.

The authors of this study go on to relate these moral types to four basic dimensions of family values and discipline. These are:

(1) Consistency—Inconsistency
(2) Severity-Leniency
(3) Democracy—Autocracy
(4) Mutual trust and approval versus distrust and disapproval.

Moral maturity in the offspring is highly related to the degree of trust and approval and to the consistency of parental control. Taken alone, democratic family practices are only slightly related to maturity of moral behavior. However, when this is combined with consistency and trust, a systematically positive influence is present. In similar manner, severity by itself has no significant relationship with moral maturity, but it does in combination with other factors.

Individuals of the *rational-altruistic* type come from very trustful, democratic families, consistent but lenient in discipline. The typical *conforming* individual comes from a family which is regular in its rules and its way of life. It is authoritarian and rather severe. The conformer does not have a strong self or personality of his own, although this is the characteristic of those capable of more mature behavior.

It is suggested by all this that if growing up in a family which is trustful, consistent, lenient, and democratic leads to moral maturity, the same should be true of seminary training. If candidates are to grow to this obviously traditional goal of self-mastery and self-decision, then the conditions that further this growth must be provided for them. What they do not need is an atmosphere which will keep them stalled at a lower level of development or which will frustrate their potential for maturity in any way. Trust, understanding, constancy, and a correctly understood leniency: these seem to be essential elements for an atmosphere of growth.

We must remember, however, that while it is frequently compared to a family, the seminary is basically a different type of structure and, as has been noted, is more comparable to an organization or a bureaucracy. Unlike most families, the seminary tends to get formalized, to become impersonal and governed largely by rules and regulations. John Gardner tells us that ". . . the last act of a dying organization is to get out a new and enlarged edition of the rule book."[3]

The rules, of themselves, do not possess sacramental power to develop persons, even though this would be a great convenience for seminary faculty members if it were true. A person, as has been reiterated many times, grows through his contacts with mature persons. The tendency, which seems to be inherent in the nature of bureaucracy, is for the rules to proliferate, and then to become rigid and petrified. The big danger in seminaries is that the rules, in reality lifeless aside from the persons affected by them, also become sanctified.

The seminary cannot be understood in impersonal structural terms. The priests who exercise authority are the dynamic catalysts of growth, and, as has been suggested, there are certain virtues which they must have in order to be effective. In any discussion of training, the question of preparation for obedience in later life is bound to arise. Candidates must be grown-up enough to be able to work effectively later on with and for their pastors or superiors. These are human relationship problems and can never be solved, or even prepared for, merely by rules and regulations. This is not to deny the necessity of rules and regulations in any institution, but they cannot be highlighted as the fundamental source of character development for future priests. It is precisely because of this that the relationships between priests on the staff and seminarians become so important. It must be emphasized again that, although the seminary is not being run for the convenience of the faculty members, neither is it to be an adolescent or young adult tyranny either.

Let us consider the concept of trust and its application in seminary training. True and mature love flowers in persons who have had others committed to them in deep faith and

[3] John W. Gardner, *Self-Renewal* (New York: Harper, 1963), p. 45.

hope. It is a universal law of growth. Faith implies a commitment to another when the outcome is by no means certain. It takes a deep act of faith for parents to raise children, a commitment to the possibilities of the helpless infant who will one day stand on his own. It is the kind of risky optimism that motivated Pope John XXIII when he said that he wrote *Pacem in Terris,* relying on "what is best in man." This means that loving others is a dangerous business because as soon as we love someone we give him the power to hurt us. We make ourselves the prey of the beloved, and this existential risk of being hurt or disappointed keeps many people from truly loving others. They find it safer to withdraw or to maintain a neutral and impersonal posture.

Father Charles Curran makes an interesting observation in this regard:

But the other kind of fear is a mistrust, and mistrust kills love. If any need is basic to our spirit, then we need to be loved. And we cannot be loved without first being trusted. St. Thomas, explaining this point that love is the form of the virtues, says that, as the soul or psyche is to the body, so is love to the psyche. In other words, as the body is dead when the psyche withdraws its integrating power, so in a certain sense one might say that the soul is dead when it is devoid of the integrating power of love. This is something we see over and over again in clinical psychological studies. If you examine parent-child, husband-wife, or any other human relationships; in industry, in the army, even in religious life itself, anywhere—you learn that people wither; they freeze; they get cornered and incrusted; they get more and more narrowly animal in their defenses; in proportion as you take away their feeling of being loved. But essential to being loved is being trusted. That is to say, it is not only in the theological order that faith and hope precede love.[4]

[4] *Proceedings of the 1959 Sisters' Institute of Spirituality,* ed. Joseph E. Haley, C.S.C. (Notre Dame: University of Notre Dame Press, 1960), p. 24.

From the psychological viewpoint it seems clear that education will never produce men capable of deeply mature relationships with others unless there is an atmosphere of real trust. And trust cannot exist without freedom. Harsh discipline, military order—these may get a certain superficial order and tone of efficiency, but they do not necessarily allow men to achieve the internal self-control that is the mark of a mature person. As Father Curran continues:

Being trusted, being believed in, is the most profound way to make a person do what he ought to do. That is to say, if you ask me under what circumstances will I do the best thing, the answer is that I probably will do the best thing if you trust me, if you believe in me, if you give me a chance, if you wait and let me try to do it.[5]

When we believe in someone we are casting a vote in his favor even when we are at the same time afraid that he might make a mistake and hurt himself and us at the same time. Overprotective parents try to save their children from every possibility of failure or injury, but they tend to cripple them psychologically at the same time because they never let them test the strength of their own two legs. Some day these parents must yield their children to the vagaries of life, and because they are unaccustomed to the risky business of living their own lives, these children frequently end up getting hurt anyway. They pay in anxiety and immaturity the price of the lack of belief and trust that characterized their fearful parents.

The essence of trusting somebody demands that we be willing to let them alone, to respect them enough to let them try this task or that sport or this trip on their own and in their own way. It means giving them their separateness and not taking it back. It rests on our own strength to handle our anxiety

[5] *Ibid.,* p. 33.

about their success without acting this out the way blundering adults all too often do in their relationships with youth. Trust, then, is something absolute; it doesn't come in small doses. It is very demanding of those who would give it. It really means loving enough to give our whole selves to others and to stay out of the way at the same time. It is hardly the attitude which says, "I will trust you, but you had better not make any mistake" or "I will trust you, but I will keep my eye on you." The pledge of unconditional trust may take a man's breath away because it means that he must be strong enough to endure the existential anxiety of the loved one's exposure to the uncertainties of his own encounter with life. Rogers has written something which catches some of the feeling of this:

Can I be strong enough as a person to be separate from the other? Can I be a sturdy respecter of my own feelings, my own needs, as well as his? . . . When I can feel freely this strength of being a separate person, then I find that I can let myself go much more deeply in understanding him, because I am not fearful of losing myself.[6]

The growing seminarian wants to try his own wings and test his own strength. As one very healthy seminarian put it:

Are seminarians allowed to undertake projects or responsibilities in which they might fail, or are such jobs given to those who undoubtedly won't fail? That is, is the element of risk removed from our development, or is there always some cover-up for a failure? I think our class project was good in this way. There was a high chance of failure, and in many little areas we did fail. But that *allowance to fail* which we had demands a good deal of trust from those in authority. I guess I have to admit that we don't want to fail in front of anybody, but still I think that such an apprehension may keep us

[6] Carl Rogers, *On Becoming a Person* (Boston: Houghton, 1961), p. 52.

from trying to do things which *may not* fail. I don't think prudence is quite as cautious as comfort would have it.

The only thing that could prevent seminarians with such a drive to meet life realistically from growing fully would be our own timidity, our own failure to respect them and to let them be free enough to fail. This is the message of the Gospels. The wicked servant is the one who was afraid to risk the talent given to him, the one who did not take any chances and who played it safe by hiding it in a secure place. The Good Shepherd is willing to risk his life when danger is near, but the hireling takes flight. Boats set out in gospel stories, not just when the sun is high and the sea is calm, but when storms are building up and the water is threatening. This willingness to take a risk is a basic dimension of Christian life. It is, in fact, by being ready to lose our lives that we end up saving them.

So it must be in seminary life as well. We must be strong enough to give our students a deep and full sense that we believe in them enough to let them make choices of their own; that we trust them enough to let them face the possible consequences of failing without trying to protect them from them. The inevitable reward of this kind of commitment to them will be that it will maximize their chances of growing to full manhood, and this, after all, is the whole purpose of seminary training.

15 The Emotional Life of the Seminarian

The chief occupational hazard for the seminarian is to live by his mind alone, to use only a portion of his personality in his encounter with life. But man is more than a mind, no matter how fine an instrument that mind is, and he can neither understand himself nor be understood by others unless his whole person is taken into account, not only his intellect but also his emotions, skills, and even his physical health. A recent tradition of spirituality inclines more to distrust emotions or to regulate them, with negative overtones, to a secondary role in personality functioning. Such a tradition, fathered and fostered by multiple philosophical cultural forces, leaves man, like the tragic city of Berlin, riven by a makeshift wall which was never meant to be there.

Man as one individual, body and soul, intellect and emotions working together in the subtle wonder of their psychosomatic unity: this is the human person. Real growth toward maturity implies an ever smoother integration of these inseparable aspects of personality. One cannot ignore or patronize the emotions if one is going to understand the meaning of man. The emphasis on the intellectual side of man, at the price of distorting the emotional side, is a feature of our culture that has been remarked on by many. A famous poet has said it this way:

To feel emotion is at least to feel. The crime against life, the worst of all crimes, is not to feel. And there was never, perhaps, a civilization in which that crime, the crime of torpor, of lethargy, of apathy, the snake-like sin of coldness-at-the-heart, was commoner than in our technological civilization in which the emotionless emotions of adolescent boys are mass-produced on television screens to do our feeling for us, and a woman's longing for life is twisted, by singing commercials, into a longing for a new detergent, family size, which will keep her hands as innocent as though she had never lived. It is the modern painless death, this commercialized atrophy of the heart. None of us is safe from it.[1]

The emotions man experiences are the reverberations, as it were, the feeling feedback that tells him what his life means. Feelings are not random and haphazard phenomena; they fit and interpret our experiences in a profound manner. Our feelings, as an integral part of our total personal response to life, give us a judgment on what we value, what importance this or that happening has for us. The single verb "to feel" bears the burden of a sweeping hierarchy of responses which is quite precise and informative when we understand it. Our feelings tell us, in a real sense, who we are by telling us what we like, what we are afraid of, whom we love and what we are willing to die for.

Although refreshing trends of personalism, which place the emotional life back in perspective, are present in the world today, the distorted image of man who is all mind and no emotion dies hard. As one observer has written:

[1] Archibald MacLeish in *The Saturday Review of Literature,* vol. 44, no. 32 (August 12, 1961), p. 24.

So in our modern culture, we are now in a reorganization period, taking a fresh look at man. We are beginning to see him as a unity again, which can help restore us to the stream of our earlier Christian, Aristotelian-Thomistic tradition. One of our operational problems, however, is that although we can verbalistically or semantically use these new terms, which are at the same time very ancient, we can be victimized by centuries of thought and feeling formed for us by Descartes, Kant, and Rousseau.[2]

In other words, while we can give intellectual assent to the beautiful truths about the unified human person, it is quite another thing to interact with him in accord with this conviction. It would be much easier if all one had to do was to *tell* others intellectually what was right for them, but the history of the world has shown that this does not work. Knowledge, we learn painfully, is not virtue. The problem, in seminary training, is to make education a full-bodied experience which will help the learners to grow as well-integrated persons.

Where feelings have not been tried and found guilty they have at least been under indictment, and a rather rigid intellectual framework has been offered as the basic structure of seminary training. The emphasis on the intellectual approach, that is to train man through telling him, makes it easy to misunderstand man, to listen to the words and to fail to hear the music.

It is quite clear that we are never in a completely non-feeling or neutral state. As long as man lives, he feels. This is perfectly natural, and man can look on his feelings as his friends. An unnecessary burden of guilt is generated sometimes by socio-cultural forces that make men feel anxious about having any feelings at all. This is further complicated when certain

[2] Charles A. Curran, *Some Concepts of Psychological and Spiritual Maturity* (privately printed at St. Meinrad Archabbey, St. Meinrad, Indiana, by the Conference of Major Superiors of Men, July 1963), p. 3.

feelings are labeled, even vaguely, as dirty or disgusting or un-fitting. Frequently the forces generating these negative self-attitudes are pseudo-religious. Man's confusion about his feel-ings flows less from the spontaneous emotions themselves than from the extrinsic interpretations and values that are forced on him from the outside. Man must be able to view his emotional reactions clearly, be unafraid of them, and call them by their right names. If he does not understand his emotional reactions in this mature way, they will master him.

Man does not live rationally by being at war with his own feelings, by being a stranger to himself. He can be fully a man only when he can face everything in his experience and still exert rational self-control. We are not implying that man's emotions are always pulling him away from rational goals. This is far from the truth. In the truly mature person there exists a harmony between feeling and thought, a genuine inte-gration of these aspects of the person. The individual who is growing toward this state of maturity must obviously learn to understand his emotional promptings well. It is only then, when his understanding is deep and sure, that he can bring real order and integration to his feelings. This is not achieved, how-ever, through ignoring emotional reactions or by mislabeling or suppressing them.

Emotions, like murder, will out. They literally make them-selves felt in a disguised way if we cannot face them as they are. The revelations of psychosomatic medicine, which gives unintended testimony to the unitary nature of man, have made us all aware that the body can artfully symbolize inner anguish in physical symptoms. Man speaks to himself through his feel-ings, and the language is quite clear if he will but listen. If he does not listen, the message is translated into another language. Sometimes, of course, it is much easier to listen to the second language of physical illness rather than to the first language of psychological unrest. It is far more tolerable, and perhaps even more socially acceptable, to have an ulcer, which confers the secondary gains of an executive illness on the person, than to face an inner conflict of emotions. Denial or suppression of emotions is not only basically unhealthy; it is also ineffective.

Frequently the seminarian is confused because others seem always to be telling him how he should feel rather than helping him to understand what he does feel. This compounds the basic problem of self-understanding by making him feel chagrined, uncomfortable, or even guilty because what he finds himself feeling is not what others suggest that he is or should be feeling.

Very few persons experience the feelings that preachers and directors describe as ideal or desirable. Often this is true because the ideal that is presented is quite inhuman and quite unattainable; it just does not fit man as he is. The best of men can still be distracted or feel discouraged or depressed at times. As long as they share the human condition, men will be subject to an almost infinite variety of emotional reactions. All of these testify to their humanity, to the healthy normality of imperfect human beings who are not yet gods. Man is changeable when he is normal; it is a sign of sickness when our patterns of reaction become rigid and inflexible. Dead things never move, but all living things squirm and look around and inch toward the light. If it is bad to insist that everyone should think the same, it is just as bad to insist that everyone should feel the same.

The insistence on certain feeling reactions when dealing with normal healthy people only tends to confuse them. When they do not, for example, experience "first fervor" upon entering the seminary, they frequently feel that something is wrong with them. Seminarians can be made to feel somewhat guilty because they have only the feelings that are theirs at the moment and not those that some well-meaning spiritual authority says they should have. Normal seminarians may, at the time of entering the seminary, experience some anxiety and very little of what could possibly be described as fervor. More illusions of religious initiation have been spun out on the theme of "first fervor" than can be imagined. This example could be extended to include many other aspects of seminary life. ("Our hearts should be full of joy this morning," someone intones from a much used book of meditations at 6 A.M. on a dark and cold winter morning. "The seminarian," a veteran professor tells a new and not as yet adjusted batch of candidates, "must love suffering and seek it out." The list is endless.)

If we are going to help seminarians to grow, we begin, not where some stained-glass ideal might place them, but where they are. We accept them as they are, even though their emotional reactions may reflect only their adolescent, and hence incomplete, stage of growth. To insist that the seminarian should feel differently than he does may imply real disrespect for him. A refusal to accept him as he is, is tantamount to telling him that he *should not* be what he really is. The real possibility of helping someone else to take a further step on the path of growth lies in perceiving and accepting this other person just as he is. Buber describes this as confirming the other person. He says: "Confirming means . . . accepting the whole personality of the other. . . . I can recognize in him, know in him, the person he has been . . . *created* to become. . . . I confirm him in myself, and then in him, in relation to this potentiality that . . . can now be developed, can evolve."[3]

FEELINGS IN THE MATURE PERSON

The mature person is open to himself, is in a good relationship with himself. He knows how to love himself correctly. Our Lord commanded us to love our neighbors as we love our-

[3] Quoted by Carl Rogers from an unpublished manuscript in *On Becoming a Person* (Boston: Houghton, 1961), p. 55.

selves. There is, then, a right way to love oneself, and this becomes the model for loving others. St. Thomas Aquinas says that

the love with which a man loves himself is the form and root of friendship. For if we have friendship with others it is because we do unto them as we do unto ourselves, hence we read in *Ethic.* ix. 4, 8, that the origin of friendly relations with others lies in our relations to ourselves.[4]

A recent comment by a well-known psychologist not only re-echoes St. Thomas but also suggests the source of our self-knowledge. Rogers writes:

. . . if I can form a helping relationship to myself—if I can be sensitively aware of and acceptant toward my own feelings—then the likelihood is great that I can form a helping relationship toward another.[5]

Charity, as we have long aphorized, begins at home. The fully grown man loves himself in the right way, and this flows from his clear knowledge and understanding of himself. He is, therefore, capable of loving other persons in a profoundly Christian manner. Because he is in harmony within himself he is also in harmony with the rest of men.

This understanding relationship with oneself is conspicuous in many people by its absence. The man who does not know himself, who is not a friend to himself, is full of anxiety and self-accusation. He harms himself, like the alcoholic or the dope addict, but often far more subtly. He destroys himself and destroys others, not just by his actions but, more fundamentally, through his attitudes, his basic inability really to

---

[4] *Summa Theologica*, trans. by the Fathers of the English Dominican Province (New York: Benziger, 1947), II–II, q. 25, art. 4, p. 1288.

[5] Rogers, *op. cit.*, p. 51.

love. It remains true that if by real love man can bring others to life, so too by a failure to love, he can kill others. One is reminded of Péguy's grim remark about people who "because they love no one, imagine that they love God." But it is all one piece and in the healthy, growing Christian, a real love for self reflects itself in his real love for his neighbors. This love of neighbor, in turn, is the "acid test," as Pope Paul VI has said, of a man's love of God.

The man who truly loves himself is open to himself and is not afraid to look at any of his experiences. He does not have to defend himself by exaggeration or denial, because he can look at himself without fear. This quality stands out in the mature person. He does not apologize for his own existence and does not constantly have to prove himself. He trusts himself and lives an integrated life. This openness, this willingness to expose his real self to others, makes him approachable and trustworthy. The tragedy of the man who does not know or love himself is precisely that he cannot be himself, cannot trust himself, and, therefore, can neither love nor be loved. He is unloved because he has made himself so. To form a relationship with these persons is like trying to build a bridge across a river where there is no opposite bank to receive it. The man who does not love himself estranges himself from others, but this is only the fruit of his own self-estrangement.

The pain the self-alienated person experiences is the anguish of an emotional life that is literally *dis*integrated. The suffering is intense, and the process of helping such people to become integrated centers on helping them to understand their twisted emotions and to face their feeling selves in the hard light of day. If they are going to know and love themselves, they must be open to their own feelings. This is where their defenses must come down. The process of therapy is designed to help a person move deeply and non-defensively within himself. Rogers writes of it in this way:

. . . The individual is becoming more able to listen to himself, to experience what is going on within himself. He is more open to his feelings of fear and discouragement and pain. He is also more open to his feelings of courage, and tenderness, and awe. He is free to live his feelings subjectively, as they exist in him, and also free to be aware of these feelings. He is more able fully to live the experiences of his organism rather than shutting them out of awareness.[6]

This has consequences not only in the individual's attitude toward himself but also in his attitude toward the world of reality around him:

. . . The individual becomes more openly aware of his own feelings and attitudes as they exist in him at an organic level. . . . He also becomes more aware of reality as it exists outside of himself, instead of perceiving it in pre-conceived categories. . . . As you might expect, this increasing ability to be open to experience makes him far more realistic in dealing with new people, new situations, new problems.[7]

The mature person does not have to experience therapy to be at ease with his own feelings. Because he is sensitive to them and can "own" them, he is integrated and in control of himself. He is unified in thought and feeling and can be the person he really is. He hides nothing from himself and does not then hide anything from others. Neither is he, like the neurotic, a stranger to himself ("I don't know myself") or to others ("I don't have any really close friends"). Obviously this kind of person enjoys a healthy sense of well-being and self-

6 *Ibid.*, p. 189.
7 *Ibid.*, p. 115.

control and is also capable of deep and enriching personal relationships. Not enslaved or confused by his feelings, this man is psychologically free and, because of this, can lead a truly responsible life. As Rogers has said, ". . . the person who is psychologically free moves in the direction of becoming a more fully functioning person."[8]

The free man who is in control of himself is, in the terms of St. Thomas, the individual in whom the virtue of prudence is truly operational. He sees things as they are, is open to his experience and makes free choices about himself and his behavior. His whole being is in tune with what is right, and the coordination of feeling and thought is governed by the total prudential process. In the concrete, the mature person's feelings contribute to his ability to live a virtuous life. In a sense, the prudent man can feel his way through life because he can trust his feelings as reliable guides to action. He reacts in unitary personal fashion to what he encounters in life, and his emotional reaction is appropriate and instructive to him. The prudent man can validly say, "I won't do this because I don't feel it would be the right thing," or "I will do this because I feel that it is correct." His total organism, intellect and emotions in harmony, senses and evaluates the situation and renders the real prudential decision.

This picture of an integrated human person, whose total personal reaction concretizes the meaning of prudence, is far different from the individual who is constantly divided by convictions and feelings which oppose one another. The mature state of harmony between thought and feeling is not achieved in a day but is the result of real growth. This kind of growth can take place only when the individual is able to look deeply at the roots of his own feelings and to see himself without distortion.

[8] *Ibid.,* p. 191.

Quite the opposite, and often quite unnecessarily miserable, is the person who depends solely on "will power" to govern himself. Much advice and many spiritual books place strong emphasis on the need to "strengthen the will." Exercises are sometimes even prescribed to help in this, as though the will were some independent executive power which governed the individual without reference to the other aspects of personality. The will is, of course, important in the person but, as Curran has pointed out, it "must be trained as a part of a team, as it were. Kantianism and our present culture . . . tend to make the will the only member of the team."[9] On this point, another contemporary Christian observer has urged:

. . . In a personalistic theory of freedom the act of decision and voluntary choice belongs, properly speaking, to the person and not to the volitive function. It follows then that that training whose essential task is to develop in an individual the control of his conduct will have to aim at the integral formation of his personality, and not at training the will alone. The formation of a habit in man's conduct does not depend on the repeated training of his will, but on an attitude which is a function of the entire personality. It excludes, therefore, the training of the will for its own sake. . . .

Progress in training will, therefore, consist in progress toward the integration of personality. This is obviously based on the presupposition that a well-integrated personality, which is physiologically and psychologically balanced, can act in conformity to the laws of its rational nature and therefore can respect the moral laws of social life. . . . In order to reach the goals of training, then, it is of the greatest importance to develop in youth that psychic harmony which is an evident sign of personality integration.[10]

[9] Charles A. Curran, "Some Basic Factors in the Formation of Feminine Character and Spirituality," *Proceedings of the 1959 Sisters' Institute of Spirituality,* ed. Joseph E. Haley, C.S.C. (Notre Dame, Ind.: University of Notre Dame Press, 1960), p. 20.

[10] Roberto Zavalloni, O.F.M., *Self-Determination: the Psychology of Personal Freedom* (Chicago: Forum Books, 1962), pp. 299, 300.

Aggressive assertion of the will can, in fact, put a person under great and unnecessary strain. He is using brute force against his feelings. Being blind and depending on the information of the intellect, the will can be no more than this when it is the only faculty employed by the individual. The exercise of rational control, the outcome of the total prudential process which includes the function of the will, is more easily attained when the person first understands his feelings and their source within himself. This is a more human process because it involves all the resources of the person.

This also means that man is not sentenced to a life of "putting up" with himself or his feelings. He is not the victim of emotions that can be handled only by rigid control mechanisms. There is enough suffering in life without adding any more, especially when it is unnecessary. The person who is growing totally can go very deeply into his feelings, uncover their source, and experience a remarkable development and change in them. If man is made to grow, then we can hardly believe that there is a part of him destined to be forever stunted.

The wife of a famous English novelist said once, "For me, Heaven is a place where I won't have to be shy any more." This is very much like the feeling of many seminarians and religious who have never been helped to understand their emotions and how they fit into their personal lives. Feelings are not important, seminarians are told, as they are urged either to ignore them or overcome them by sheer will power. This is to see man as a psychological dwarf, someone not fully grown but incapable of doing anything about it.

Despite its popularity, there is something grimly unchristian about settling for a statement like this: "You don't have to like everybody, but you have to love them." Perhaps that cliché is helpful at certain stages of development, but it sells the possibilities of real Christian love very short. There is, in fact, a great deal that the individual can uncover about his feeling reactions of "liking" or "disliking," and these can change as the whole person grows. The healthy Christian finds no opposition between *liking* and *loving*. He is not afraid to like people and to communicate this to them. The love of Christians cannot be a cold and sternly disciplined attitude toward others if it is the very heart and meaning of life in the Mystical Body. Pope John seemed capable of liking and loving and did not distinguish between the two. His love, the love of a mature Christian, reached men everywhere and is excellent testimony to the creative power of genuine love when it is truly experienced.

The worst of all illness is marked by disturbed emotion. A better-informed public realizes that the mentally ill person is not a howling beast or a benign eccentric passing himself off as Napoleon. It is not yet clear, however, that the public is sensitive to what a person caught in the frightening confusion of mental illness really experiences. He is something less as a person. There is a disintegration of the aspects of personality and the "split" of the schizophrenic is precisely between his thought and his feeling. In the consulting rooms, the wards, the endless corridors of hospitals, one senses deeply the suffering of these faulted human beings who can no longer live in relationship with other men.

Here we find the terrible flattening of emotional reaction that is sickness, not self-control; here the surging psychopathic assaults where there is no control at all. Nothing reflects sickness or health more clearly than the emotions of man; deep psychological pain for the ill person and deep satisfaction in living for the well person. There must, then, be a keen sensitivity to the affective dimension of the seminarian's life and a constant effort to maintain the atmosphere of health.

16 Creativity in the Seminarian

"Listen to one of them talking to Socrates,
just waked up in the early dawn by a persistent
hammering at his door: 'What's here?' he
cries out, still half asleep. 'O Socrates,' and
the voice is that of a lad he knows well,
'Good news, good news!' 'It ought to be at this
unearthly hour. Well, out with it.'

"The young fellow is in the house now.
'O Socrates, Protagoras has come. I heard it
yesterday evening. And I was going to you
at once but it was so late. . . .' 'What's it all
about . . . Protagoras? Has he stolen something
of yours?' The boy bursts out laughing.
'Yes, yes, that's just it. He's robbing me of
wisdom. He has it . . . wisdom, and he
can give it to me. Oh, come and go with me to
him. Start now.' "
—Edith Hamilton, *The Greek Way*.[1]

The world owes more to the creators than to the copiers, but
it has not always made life easy for them. Anybody who has
an unslaked thirst for truth or the vision of a new way to do
something can be very disturbing to his companions or to his

[1] New York: Norton, 1964, p. 30.

142

elders. But the true growth of a people depends on the intuitions of the truly creative, and any society that wants to progress is obliged to get the best out of its gifted citizens. A seminary has the unique obligation, in preparing men through the Holy Spirit, to "re-create" the face of the earth, to foster the creative potential of its seminarians.

Recent psychological research has told us a good deal about people who are creative. They are, refreshingly enough, not stereotyped Bohemian rebels. They are simply separate, independent persons who are strong enough to follow their own paths. The staggering richness of human growth potential is revealed in them. Here is what the human person can become, bursting with the spirit of inquiry and restless with visions not yet seen by other men. The challenge comes to this: can the seminary make room for creative people and also maximize the chances of developing their individual personalities?

The person whose creativity goes unrecognized by masters less gifted than he can be made to suffer great pain. This is a possibility in any school, but at times it is intensified in a seminary where spiritual values can seem to be in contrast with the creative person's drive for growth. No conflict can possibly exist here: God cannot will that the gifts He has given should not be used, that growth should be frustrated. Human beings can make mistakes, however, even though they be titled teacher, director, or counselor. They err most seriously when they are insensitive to the inherent possibilities of the people among whom they work. St. Thomas reminds us that humility is "the reasonable pursuit of our own excellence," and no rationalization, no matter how buttressed by spiritual-sounding phrases, can justify deadening the creative potential of another human person.

Oliver Wendell Holmes once wrote:

A few can touch the magic string,
And noisy Fame is proud to win them:—
Alas for those that never sing,
But die with all their music in them.

Any educator who wants to foster creativity commits himself to viewing his students as individuals, and this is always demanding. Certain slogans have worn themselves into our minds, and the need to live by them can obscure their limited application. "Treat everyone the same" echoes a fond hope of democracy, but "Treat everyone individually" catches the idea better.

IDENTIFYING THE CREATIVE

Some significant characteristics of the creative person, as revealed in recent research, are the following: he is fairly intelligent but, beyond a certain point, being more or less intelligent does not crucially determine the level of the individual's creativity. "Creatives," as they are called, show early in life special aptitudes necessary for their ultimate careers. Many of them have a number of skills, and they find it difficult to choose among them.

Something that is true of all creatives is their ability to integrate apparently contradictory aspects of personality successfully. For example, in a well-known test of values, they score highly on both the *aesthetic* (an emotional concern for beauty and form) and the *theoretical* (a rational concern for knowledge and truth). Usually it is found that individuals who score high on one of these will score low on the other because the values are polar opposites. Creative persons can tolerate the inner tensions that must arise when one holds conflicting values. They can, in other words, express opposite sides of their nature at the same time. They can balance reason and passion, science and art, the rational and the irrational. Creatives are not one-dimensional characters, and, in a way that heralds individuality rather than describes rebelliousness, they cannot be called "well-rounded." They have their own rough edges, and, as one researcher described them, "they are real people; they are not protoplasm."

All highly creative male groups score high on the psychological variable known as "femininity." This is not the same as the state of "effeminacy." It indicates rather that the creative person is more open to his feelings and emotions, that he is more sensitively aware of himself and others, and that he possesses wide-ranging interests. They are not effeminate in appearance or behavior but are, on the contrary, assertive, dominant, and self-confident. A further indication that creative people are attuned to their inner experiences is that they seem to have a positive preference for complexity. Less creative people have to impose order immediately, but the more creative sees the possibility of a higher level of order since he has been able to tolerate previous disorder. Highly creative people are overwhelmingly intuitive. That is to say, they are not alert only to *what is* but to *what could be*. The creative person looks for the link between what is present and something not yet thought of. His is the vision of possibilities. The expert, it is said, bores you because he talks about what he knows, but the creative person will excite you because he talks about what he does not know. For them the path of learning leads up a cloud-wrapped mountain, and they ache to climb it because it is there.

The truly creative person is a hard worker, and he gives himself to it with a self-discipline that would give good example to any monk. This is a point frequently unappreciated by a world that often wants the creative person to live and work exactly like the rest of men and which would judge him unruly because it cannot understand his deeper and more demanding self-discipline. He is given over to the creative task with all his bone and spirit, and he is not made for eight-hour days and forty-hour weeks. There is, nonetheless, a striking sense of purpose and order in his life, and, unlike so many other people, he gets something done.

Probably the most arresting aspect of the creative personality is the spiritual economy of the creative process itself. Above all, and like any true lover, the creative person risks himself in his effort. He constantly imperils his own security in order to achieve something new and better. He is unafraid of the leap in the dark or the plunge into waters that are icy and, perhaps, bottomless. The person who is afraid never moves out into life for fear of losing himself. He is fearful, and his terror rules him. He holds the sure position and settles for it. He wraps his talents in a napkin, he buries them in the ground, for is not the master a hard man?

But the creative person knows that to live fully he must be ready to die, and for him there is no other way. He is willing to give up his security, to take the risk, to die the death in order to achieve a newer and richer form of life. In a parallel with the deepest ascetical demands of Christianity, the creative person sees that the seed must fall into the earth and die, or it is fated to remain barren and alone. Commenting on a creative person's description of his work as "throwing himself away," a leading researcher on the creative process says this:

What this man meant by "throwing himself away" is what in this context we mean by permitting diffusion to occur in the service of a need for an enrichment of conscious experience—a need which is felt with such intensity that the individual is willing to "die unto himself," i.e., to permit an achieved adaptation or state of relative equilibrium to perish. And there are no guarantees that something better will thereby be arrived at. Looking backward from the endpoint of the creative process, we are inclined to say, "Ah, yes, it had to be so; the chance had to be taken; the chalice could not be passed; the agony was necessary for the redemption and the resurrection." But facing forward in time we see only risk and difficulty, and if we have not the courage to endure diffusion ("suffer death") we cannot achieve the new and more inclusive integration ("gain the light").[2]

The spiritual destiny of the potentially creative is identified with his seeking and striving. There is a singleness of purpose about him, a oneness about his convictions and vocation that fairly shouts for recognition. No split in this person, one might say somewhat in awe. In his life *"laborare est orare"* takes on a luminous meaning. There is a clear need to assist the creative person to walk on his own path, to be, in the deepest and richest sense, himself. His spirituality must flow from his essential work, but this is sometimes a difficult truth for those who think that nothing done outside a chapel can be supernatural. It is a monumental misunderstanding of the meaning of creativity to force those gifted with it into some kind of group behavior that can never develop or satisfy them. The creative person needs some "give" in his environment if he is going to fulfill himself. If there are, as some suggest, creative possibilities of different kinds in many people, then the educator's task is to sense it and free it wherever it may be found. On this point, Rogers writes this:

. . . Watching my clients, I have come to a much better understanding of creative people. El Greco, for example, must have

[2] Frank Barron, "Diffusion, Integration and Enduring Attention," *The Study of Lives,* ed. Robert W. White (New York: Prentice-Hall, 1963), p. 247.

realized as he looked at some of his early work, that "good artists do not paint like that." But somehow he trusted his own experiencing of life, the process of himself, sufficiently that he could go on expressing his own unique perceptions. It was as though he could say, "Good artists do not paint like this, but *I* paint like this." Or to move to another field, Ernest Hemingway was surely aware that "good writers do not write like this." But fortunately he moved toward being Hemingway, being himself, rather than toward someone else's conception of a good writer. . . . This is not a phenomenon which occurs only in the artist or the genius. Time and again in my clients, I have seen simple people become significant and creative in their own spheres, as they have developed more trust of the processes going on within themselves, and have dared to feel their own feelings, live by values which they discover within, and express themselves in their own unique ways.[3]

Researchers have suggested that the condition of education which will maximize the flowering of creativity is the presence of creative teachers. The creative seminarian, the one who wants to make the best of himself . . . perhaps becoming a saint is the greatest of creative acts . . . deserves the best attention a seminary faculty can offer. He will be helped greatly by a mature and understanding relationship with a faculty member who can see not only *what the seminarian is* but also *what he can be*. The faculty member should be wise enough and strong enough to trust and believe in the vibrant potential of the seminarian. He will not force him to be anything that denies or distorts his true personal potential. A basic but most effective attitude is that of respect for the sacredness of the person and his gifts. The flowering of the Church may depend on the measure of deep respect we have for the creative individuals put for a time in our care by God.

[3] Carl R. Rogers, *On Becoming a Person* (Boston: Houghton, 1963), p. 175.

Freya Stark says that "the deepest love of young people goes, I think, to those like my father . . . who feel tenderly about the 'living space of other human souls.' "[4] The root realization of the human dignity and promise of a creative student makes us sensitive to the "different drummer" his talents enable him to hear. The big job, as Thoreau reminds us, is to "let him step to the music which he hears, however measured or far away."

[4] *Traveller's Prelude* (New York: Penguin, 1962), p. 321.

17 The Problems of Seminarians

The following section deals with the problems of seminarians in terms of their own perceptions and reactions. The problem areas have been chosen, on the basis of research and counseling experience, as representative of the seminarian's world. Too often problems of seminarians and religious candidates are discussed or written about from the viewpoint of the superior, the spiritual director or somebody else who is on the outside looking in. Nothing is of less value, in any walk of life, than sermons which miss the audience to which they are directed. Nothing is more keenly resented by any congregation than a preacher incapable of entering into the world of those to whom he addresses himself. We hope that a presentation of the seminarian's problems from his own viewpoint will make it easier for all religious formation workers to be more understanding and more effective.

This cannot be done by an intellectual process alone, any more than these problems can be solved by intellectual answers alone. The curious overinvestment of directors in simply "telling" their subjects how they should behave is one of the chief obstacles to the process of effecting deep personal growth in candidates. The whole person of the director must be involved in a meeting that is genuine and mature. The real key to this is the ability to understand the world of their subjects, the world we enter now.

ONE HUNDRED THOUSAND WAYS TO BE PERFECT

Man would be better, it is generally agreed, if he could learn the lessons of the past. When he does not, according to Santayana, he is condemned to repeat the mistakes of his elders. History has seen the older generation constantly trying to hand on its hard-bought wisdom to the younger. Never has there been a lack of advice-giving; the problem always arises in following it. Nowhere is this more true than in the formation of priests and religious.

Everybody who is ever in contact with seminarians, novices, postulants or other aspirants to a life of perfection is tempted to hand on his own formula for success. Each spiritual director, retreat master, lecturer, and even teacher sometimes, has his particular view of how other people should lead their spiritual life. So too, every spiritual writer emphasizes certain means to holiness, and these are also found in the traditions of every seminary and religious house. There is no question about the validity of the advice or the good will of the advisors, but this abundance of counsel is the source of the prime problem for seminarians. How does one make use of the wisdom of one's elders? The seminarian, being generous and good-hearted as a rule, tries to do everything he is told that it would be good for him to do. Extrinsic urgings attain a disproportionate value in the life of the developing religious; this is the core of the fundamental problem of perfection.

The task for the seminarian is to integrate in his own life the multiple external values proposed to him as he goes through his years of training. He can suffer a great deal of anxiety when he finds that he is not able to do everything that he is told he should be doing. This "tyranny of shoulds" hardly gives him time to make deeply his own the principles by which he will have to live. Not only does the seminarian get too much advice, but it is also often quite contradictory. He is told in one breath that he is worthless and in the next that he is called to perfection and that he should realize his dignity as a Christian. Humility is the path, but next week it is zeal, and the week after that, contemplation, and then someone says that charity sums it all up anyway. There is the rule and the often tortuous regulations which go into minute detail about how the young man should spend all his time. It can easily become a life by formula, and while the advice-givers never intend it to be this way, it preserves the seminarian at an immature level of growth where he is constantly striving to meet the expectations of other people. It is a frustrating and bewildering time for him because he senses himself a failure in so many of the things he undertakes in the name of perfection. He can hardly feel the warmth and wholesomeness of the Gospels when he is trained to strain out gnats.

We once heard a lecture on the spiritual life entitled "A Recipe for Perfection." This captures the nature of this problem very well. Some good-intentioned spiritual father offers his ingredients, to be mixed and served in a certain way, as the food for all. Perhaps it nourished him well, but it may not suit every taste. It seems very difficult for some spiritual directors to see that, in the long run, people have to decide what they are going to eat for themselves. As one seminarian has put it, "Before all else a seminarian must realize that his life is his, his actions are his responsibility, and that he will be whatever he wants to be."

Surely the spiritual life should not appear to the seminarian like a maze which he must learn to run in order to find the reward at the end. His gigantic challenge is to become responsible for his life, to become himself as fully as possible. Perfection, which implies full growth from within, can never be found in things outside of a man. It is not measured by external criteria no matter how finely they are graded. The ultimate test of whether the seminarian is perfect or not will be whether he has become the person God intended him to be. Growth goes from the inside out, and, while the seminarian must learn the lessons of the past and keep himself open to the wisdom of his directors, he must ultimately shape himself. That is the only way he can become whole. And holiness, as Goldbrunner reminds us, "is wholeness."

Seminarians experience great frustration and discouragement, however, when all they can see or hear are the solutions of other people to the problems of life. Genuine suffering, all the more poignant because it is unnecessary, fills the life of generous young men and women who are always led and never allowed to find for themselves their path to perfection. Seminary educators do well if they grasp the fundamental Christian truth that each man must be responsible for himself and that nothing else will do in the sight of God. No one will get into heaven by explaining to St. Peter that he performed this or that action because his spiritual director thought it was a good idea. The truth of Christianity must be presented clearly, but it must not be forgotten that it promises to make men free. Eloquent advisors might examine themselves on who gets more out of their product, their listeners or themselves. It is a difficult task to herald perfection and at the same time to be sensitive to the need young men have to find their own way toward it.

This insistence on the individual's responsibility for his deepest beliefs should not be confused with the pursuit of personal sanctification without reference to others. Real Christian love does not develop under a bell jar where the world and its possible contamination is kept out. The genius of the apostolate is in loving our fellow men. On the point of the social implications of the priest's sanctity, Fichter writes:

The point is that the apostolic orientation in spiritual development is toward the service (salvation) of others, just as the professional orientation in technical development is toward the service of others. Exclusive concentration on self-perfection is almost necessarily a block to successful external apostolic performance. In this limited concept of sanctity, personal perfection is supposed to spill over into charity toward others. . . . The central problem here lies in the supposition that the apostolic function will somehow *automatically* occur when individual sanctity has been taken care of, and will occur *only* as long as one focuses his efforts on his own spiritual perfection. This is similar to the bald self-interest theory among economists . . . who claim that what is good for their business is good for their country.[1]

The individual seminarian must work out his own answer to the problem of perfection, but he will not find it except in the world of the men he is called to serve.

The mature priest cannot live long on slogans, superficial pieties, on the introjected ideals of others; this is building a fragile edifice on sand. The hothouse flower may please its cultivator, but it pays a price for its fragile beauty. It is not tough enough to stand the storms because its life depends on the artificial environment of the greenhouse. The wildflower, with an inner hardiness, survives the worst of wind and weather.

The seminarian's spirituality cannot have the deceptive but fragile beauty that can exist only in the artificial environment

[1] Joseph H. Fichter, S.J., *Religion as an Occupation* (Notre Dame: University of Notre Dame Press, 1961), pp. 110, 111.

of the seminary. His strength of character must be the outcome of his own growth if he is to survive the storms of life. Nothing exposes both weakness and strength as clearly as a crisis. The seminarian must be given the opportunity to confront himself during his years of training and to internalize the values and convictions that must last for a lifetime. Nobody can cry for him, or suffer for him, and nobody can grow for him either; he must find his own way. In this spirit, surely, St. John of the Cross inscribed on the summit of the mount of perfection "There is no road here, for there is no law for the righteous man."[2]

THE PROBLEM OF DEPENDENCY

The problem of dependency is closely related to the problem of perfection and, indeed, is often an aspect of it. Dependency arises in a life where everything is planned and where few occasions for individual choice are permitted. This is very unlike any real life situation. The mature man does not need a careful framework or schedule to hold him together. He puts order into his life, but he does so on his own. Order flows out of him; it is not imposed on him. Often newly ordained priests find that they do not know how to do very much for themselves when they are on their own. Excessive directiveness and insistence on authority's knowing all the answers can obviously foster dependence. This difficulty in subtler form is not readily recognized. For example, seminary students tend to live in a predictable world where someone else provides Mass, meals and the other necessaries of life. They never have to think about these things. The classroom often reproduces this atmosphere, especially where rote learning is emphasized and where

[2] St. John of the Cross, *Ascent of Mount Carmel* (Westminster: Newman, 1953), XXXII.

professors spell out assignments in great detail. In this situation the students are forever trying to find out what kind of tests the professor likes to give and just how much matter they will be responsible for in order to get a good grade.

This search for the correct formula of academic success becomes the central quest of their lives. Young priests are frequently dismayed when they are assigned to graduate studies after ordination. No one is looking over their shoulders or holding their hand; they discover that they must keep themselves afloat or they will sink. Their favorite excuses, "We didn't cover this in class," "You didn't say we would have this on the test," have a childish sound to them in the unforgiving adult world of learning. The adjustment to autonomy in the pursuit of knowledge is a new and bracing experience for these students. The game is no longer played according to little-boy rules.

Study is not the only aspect of a seminarian's life where he can be led too long by his elders. The normal, healthy young man must learn to impose order in his own life, to balance his time and his tasks, to respond maturely and on his own to any challenge of life. Carefully planned and supervised schedules give the young man little chance to grow toward mature independence. Frequently the healthy seminarian will feel a certain irritation at schedules, bells, at being one of the obedient herd. Neither he nor his mentors may understand that his restlessness is a sign of the conflict between his healthy drive toward being separate from others and the constant frustration of this by the conditions of his life. A recent study of highly talented graduate students, for example, revealed that fifteen years after leaving the campus, their primary goals in life were in achieving freedom, autonomy, and self-expression.[3] A sensitive

[3] Eli Ginzberg *et al., Talent and Performance* (New York: Columbia University Press, 1964).

teacher will understand that this sign of the student's struggle to grow up is a good one; it does not represent rebellion that needs immediate suppression. The latter response is often given when the faculty members are threatened by this normal stage in the student's growth toward manhood. Docility suddenly becomes the indispensable virtue for the seminarian. The insistence on it is often not so much to develop the seminarian as it is to control or suppress him. This is the fatal but common defense mechanism of the faculty member: add the spiritual dimension, and the faculty member can preserve his self-esteem by feeling righteously indignant. At the same time this generates undeserved guilt feelings in the students for a crime no greater than being normal. Typical of this "We are right, you are wrong" school of training is the writing of Dubay, who presents the ready-made argument for docility in these words:

The docile seminarian takes cognizance of the fact that he is young and inexperienced, that there is much for him to learn. He recognizes that the rule is accepted by his bishop and the faculty, and that, since they are much more experienced than he, his would-be complaint is, more likely than not, ill-founded.[4]

The pile-up of authority on the side of the faculty and the demeaning tone applied to the seminarians' attitude are worth noting. In another place, to underscore the guilt feelings, the same author says:

. . . a seminarian who sins against respect due the faculty member commits objectively . . . a sin of several specifically different malices, which actually are equivalent to several numerically distinct sins.[5]

[4] Thomas Dubay, S.M., *The Seminary Rule* (Westminster: Newman, 1954), p. 132.
[5] *Ibid.*, p. 125.

This approach is, in the long run, self-defeating. It can only cause real resentment on the part of the students and further defensiveness on the part of the faculty. These tactics put the generations on a needless collision course. A striking description of the estrangement of the students and the faculty is given by Nevitt Sanford. The dynamics described underlie many a pastor-curate, superior-subject hornlocking after ordination:

Much of the life of a college community involves interaction of the faculty and administration on the one hand and the students on the other. The conception of students responding to an environment that has been largely made by the educators is, of course, central. But faculties and administrations react to what the students do and thus create new and often peculiarly important stimuli to student behavior, thus starting a fresh circle of interaction.

Let us consider an example. In a traditional college of high quality a majority of the faculty believe they note a serious decline in the general level of the students' effort and performance. As the phenomenon is discussed in formal and informal faculty meetings a sense of outrage builds up, and the general feeling is that there must be a tightening up all along the line. There are heavier work assignments, more frequent examinations, longer papers, more required reading, and classes are conducted in an atmosphere of increased grimness. Now, since for the individual student this discipline comes not from a particular teacher who knows him but from an impersonal "they," and since it is plain that for some of the faculty members narcissistic needs rather than devotion to intellectual aims are involved, the tightening up is generally perceived by the students as arbitrary punitiveness. The students generally, with a nice appreciation of the realities of their situation, but not necessarily with any conscious deliberation, do not rebel openly but respond rather with a kind of passive resistance. They do precisely what is required but no more; they invent and share among themselves numerous devices for judging the exact nature of the requirements and for carrying them out with a minimum of effort; they establish a kind of "norm" for amount of work and make life difficult for the individual who threatens to exceed it. Particularly do they look askance at any student who "gets too close" to any of the faculty, for this tends to break up the general strategy of doing what is required by the faculty without being influenced by them in any positive way. (On the other hand, a certain pretense of going along with faculty values may be allowed —may indeed become fairly general—if it appears that this will help make life more comfortable.) Since this general pattern of response is very similar to that which upset the faculty in the first place, it is likely to be met with even stricter requirements. The vicious circle becomes increasingly taut. Now the students seek ways to hold the faculty strictly to their obligations and, if possible, to embarrass them by requesting more office appointments, expecting papers to be corrected on time, asking about books they suspect the instructor has not read, remaining silent and unresponsive in class. Some teachers do not go along with the majority; they seek to break what has become the common pattern, to "reach" the students. The students will have none of this. They have developed an effective system for handling their situation and they do not intend to be put off by any new or different methods of teaching or any appeals to their curiosity or creative impulses. They hold the deviating or innovating teacher to the pattern that has become common. They have the power to do this, for there are channels through which their complaints can reach the department chairman or the administration, and by now faculty morale has so deteriorated that the enterprising teacher has no assurance that his colleagues will back him up. Happily, the term now ends; the student leaders graduate, the faculty leaders take vacations, and there is a chance for a fresh start.[6]

THE PROBLEM OF CHASTITY

Chastity emerges as a problem for the seminarian, but not in the way that many people expect. It is a problem in itself, of course, but far more real is the problem that is caused when

[6] *The World of Wiley,* vol. i (Spring 1963), p. 8.

this subject is not sufficiently well treated in class or in other conferences. It is frequently not treated at all. One can only speculate at the reasons for this conspiracy of silence about the facts of life. There is a great deal of anxiety on the part of the professors, and, as one seminarian once put it, "In our place, it is obedience, poverty and ah-hem." This not unlike the uneasiness of parents who avoid helping their children understand sex. This same kind of discomfort probably lies behind the sudden switch from English to Latin in certain textbooks when the subject of sex comes up. A kindred anxiety motivates some retreat masters to give a distorted emphasis to sex and its dangers in anti-climactic conferences which usually abound in pieties and euphemisms. There is very little straightforward, honest, and wholesome discussion of sex as an aspect of normal personality development.

If the professors and retreat masters are unsure of themselves, this is what they communicate to their hearers. There is a culturally derived aura of guilt about sexual feelings and experiences that is merely reinforced by an unwillingness to face the facts in a wholesome and mature manner. Sex can readily be discussed as a problem; that is easy. It is far more difficult to present it as an aspect of human personality which must be faced, accepted, and understood without unnecessary fear and anxiety. Sex, after all, will be a part of every man's life as long as he lives. Unless he can face it without guilt and anxiety, he will never be able to obtain mature self-control. Nothing helps the seminarian more than a frank and non-mystical confrontation with the facts of life. Because of so much unnecessary mystery and lack of clarity, many seminarians never clear up basic confusions. It gets more difficult as the years go by. The worst result of this, of course, is that they are often made to feel guilty because they are human and capable of sexual feelings. An impossible ideal of sexual morality sometimes emerges from spiritual conferences which, whether they are correctly understood or not, make young men feel that they have done something wrong merely because they have reacted in a normal and healthy manner in the face of life. Sexual neutrality would seem the ideal proposed, but there is nothing wonderful about the discovery that they are human; it is only when they understand this deeply that they can truly make a choice of celibacy and live as unfrightened grown-up people.

Sometimes books and conferences on marriage idealize the married state beyond anything that any human being could ever expect of it. It is made to seem to the struggling seminarian an unending Valhalla of delights. They then tend to feel that because they have given up marriage they have offered the ultimate human sacrifice. Because they have failed to see marriage as it truly is they often lead lives that slowly fill with regrets. But married couples know the deep struggle to understand and love each other as persons that is the heart of wedded life. The meaning of their love is not unending honeymoon bliss but the day-to-day, unchanging love of one person for another that is stronger than the thousand strains it can feel every day. Books on marriage, often written by anatomically inclined Catholic physicians, tend to stress its physical aspects, and this is a distortion in another way. It presents a partial picture, but only the immature can think that this is the meaning of marriage. Its real heart is in the working out of a relationship between a mature man and a mature woman. Obviously, the husband and wife must grow as persons if their marriage is to be a success. There is no choice for the serious couple. If they do not work out their relationship with each other, then their marriage collapses. It is unfortunate that the seminarian is not helped to get a more realistic view of the deep challenge to the person that married life represents. Nothing could be better for him and nothing would help him

to feel less sorry for himself than a vision of the mature demands of wedded life.

The easily aroused guilt feelings about sex sometimes force
seminarians to abnormal maneuvers in the effort to preserve
their purity. They are so cautious that they omit reading the
Bible because they find sexual things described in it. For
others the resolve is to stay at a distance from other persons
because they are all perceived as potential dangers. These
seminarians are being controlled by fear; it forces them to
deny themselves normal and healthy activities. This is a neurotic effort to handle the anxiety that arises in their life because
of an uninformed attitude about sex.

The priest is not called to be a bachelor but to be a friend.
He must be a grown-up person to do this, not an adolescent
uneasily fascinated by the mysteries of sex. He must learn to
face the presence of sexual feelings in his life in a calm and
mature way. It is only then that he can choose celibacy maturely and enter into a life, not weakened with wistful longings
for things he never had, but ordered to the deep love of the
persons who constitute his flock. Let him take a good look at
things; let him understand himself and what he is really like
and let him see the celibate priesthood as it really is. The truth,
presented by men who are sure of themselves and unafraid, is
a simple way of eliminating much of the unnecessary anxiety
that surrounds this subject.

Women are perceived very negatively by some seminary
professors. Many priests cannot recall women ever being
discussed in the seminary except as sources of conflict ("Be
careful in dealing with Sister Superiors") or as temptresses
("Be careful of all women"). This jaundiced presentation is
frequently motivated by the fears of men who have never
learned to relate with women in healthy and mature ways.
Half the human race is made up of women; that elementary

fact cannot be ignored by priests ordained to help them save their souls.

Women can hardly be perceived as persons in an atmosphere which constantly casts them in the role of Eve. There is hardly any wonder that many priests feel uneasy and awkward in dealing with women after ordination when they have learned only to fear and keep their distance from them during their seminary years. The command to love our neighbor includes women, and this is impossible unless we can know them in a wholesome manner. We cannot know them abstractly or vicariously; opportunities for relating in healthy and normal ways with the opposite sex should be built in to all training houses. Men and women must learn to understand their feelings toward each other in normal fashion. This can only be accomplished if they are enabled to meet in a number of ordinary but healthy ways. The influence of a female faculty member, for example, would bring both priests and students into constructive relationship with a woman's personality. Freedom to be a part of the normal healthy social life of their age-mates would be productive of mature growth. This is not an encouragement to date or dance, but it suggests that a seminarian's presence at mixed parties can be virtuous rather than sinful. If they cannot maturely associate with girls, then it would be better to find this out before ordination rather than afterwards in any case.

The contribution of the feminine principle in the development of priests has long been neglected. Seminaries are over-masculinized institutions and are out of balance because of it. As Priestley has written about the supposed matriarchal character of American Society:

Where is the feminine principle, where is Woman in this madness? Where is the feminine emphasis here upon love, on the happiness of persons? . . . Here is a society shaped and colored by male values. It is almost as much like a matriarchy as the Marine Corps. . . . Society itself must be as thoroughly permeated by womanliness as it is by masculinity, that *as a community,* not simply as separate persons, we must accept feminine values with their emphasis upon love, people, relatedness, synthesis as opposed to analysis, intuitiveness as distinct from purely intellectual discourse.[7]

Creativity and maturity in an individual or a society demand a balancing of the masculine and feminine aspects of personality. The fullness of a human person's growth depends on his healthy integration and appreciation of both of these forces. This is no less time for the full growth of the Church. Father Charles Curran, in writing of devotion to Mary, captures some of the profound implications of this needed synthesis of masculine and feminine gifts. His words should be meditated on by all of those responsible for the training of seminarians and religious. He writes:

It is not surprising then, that the devotion to Mary in the Church—seen Biblically as the Woman—also meets with some psychological reactions in both men and women. In the light of these psychological awarenesses we can see how such a devotional encounter with Woman, in a religious way, also poses similar difficulties and challenges. As the psychological process of understanding and integrating the feminine element makes high demands on individuals and relationships, so the theological process must make equal if not even more exacting demands. There is here, therefore, much more than simple sentiment or emotion. A purely sentimental devotion to Mary would only barely suggest the complicated psychological process we are treating here. It would, at best, probably be an early stage. This helps explain why the concept

[7] J. B. Priestley, "Women *Don't* Run the Country," *The Saturday Evening Post,* December 12, 1964.

of devotion to Mary in the Church is often not easy for people to accept and practice. Such devotion, as we see it psychologically, calls into play, at its deepest level, a person's whole relationship with himself and others because it would seem to imply not only the highest regard for femininity but as well a profound sense of persons. This, one would have to have both towards himself and others for an adequate theological encounter with Woman in Mary and the Church.[8]

THE PROBLEM OF POVERTY

The poor in spirit are blessed, and today's seminarian is attracted by this ideal no less than his predecessors. The difficulty here is not in questioning the ideal of apostolic poverty but in learning how to practice it in a land of plenty. It is an age-old question: how does one render to Caesar what belongs to him and render to God at the same time all that belongs to him?

The demands of the vow of poverty are carefully spelled out in the constitutions of religious orders, but the question is not so simple for secular priests. They must make their way in this world, pay their taxes, buy their clothes, finance their cars, and manage some reasonable leisure, or they will not be able to operate in the apostolate at all. They cannot deny the world of things that they are meant to transform; they must come to terms with it as a priest who is a man of his age. Most seminarians do not have much understanding of the economics of priestly life. They have not yet been admitted to the reality of supporting themselves on salary and stipends. These notions seem somewhat base and unfitting to them from their viewpoint before ordination, and they tend to view poverty in very idealistic fashion.

[8] Charles A. Curran, "Psychological Factors in Marian Devotion," *Proceedings of The Mariological Society of America, 1964*, p. 18.

Quite often seminarians are sharply critical of the way priests spend money, but at times this is because they do not understand the economics of clerical life from the inside. There is no doubt that some priests live too well, but for many priests there is no choice about being poor in spirit and in fact as well. We are not here concerned with the intricate problem of the virtue of poverty as much as we are with the seminarian's perception of the meaning of poverty. He cannot be educated to apostolic poverty as an ideal isolated from the other aspects of his personal development. His values must be so proportioned that his attitude toward this virtue falls into place organically. He will not be made virtuous by being made poor, as the world too well knows. He cannot think that poverty endured stoically will convince the world of the truth of Christianity. The seminarian's poverty of spirit will flow from his having sought first things first, from having valued persons and his growth in loving them more than things and his growth in loving them. It is all one piece, as are so many other things in the mature priest's life; it cannot stand alone as the sole virtue and the only pillar of Christianity.

Seminarians frequently parallel their unrealistic criticism of priests and their possessions with the pursuit of an ideal of poverty that has a highly adolescent flavor. They criticize any improvement in the seminary grounds or building, any acquisition of furnishing beyond what is absolutely necessary. They condemn anyone who would try to make the surroundings a little more human and livable. They tend rigorously to simplify their lives and, while this is a highly commendable effort at detachment, they may be straining to live as though the things of this world did not exist at all. But food must be bought and clothes must be paid for, and the car does not go without gasoline in it. A business manager who must buy furniture that will last for several years cannot surrender to students' values which would insist that he buy the cheapest brand in the name of poverty. Too little attention is paid to helping seminarians understand the undramatic but realistic prudence that must be used in wisely spending money in the work of the Church. It is not unusual to find that those seminarians who herald poverty in an histrionic way are those with the least sense of responsibility for community property. It is as though they would enjoy being poor in an exhibitionistic manner. Neither scrip nor shoe would they claim as they kneel in the spotlight of sympathetic attention from the rest of the world. Not for them the simple but much more basic sense of values that uses things wisely and well and does not put on a show about it. This desire for the rags of the beggar is not unusual in a developing seminarian, but he must not be allowed to confuse this with the meaning of apostolic poverty. For most seminarians the development of a deep sense of responsibility for the care of their own and the community's possessions would constitute a good basic education in being poor in spirit. The only flaw in it as far as they are concerned is that it does not seem very heroic. This is a part of their growing up that should be expected during their years in the seminary, and they should not be ridiculed for being attracted by the luminous vision of the poverello. We can help them understand the much less dramatic forms of practicing poverty without destroying their eager generosity at the same time. This is a task which may have to be done in the highly individual way and will not, of course, be accomplished outside of their overall personal maturation.

A related question is whether, in this century, there can be a private practice of the virtue of poverty. Can a seminarian exercise poverty of spirit without reference to the world of living men who are poor in fact? In the age of *Pacem in Terris* a deep social awareness is a necessity for every seminarian.

Perhaps part of poverty of spirit for the seminarian is a thorough understanding of Catholic social principles and a practical grasp of their application in a world of want. As Peter Riga has written:

The situation is very serious. The mute and individual worshipper who does not realize this Christian and human solidarity and therefore responsibility, who busily promotes his private bartering with God, is a contradiction in terms. . . . The vital unity of doctrine and social justice as the concrete application of doctrine in practical life, cannot be over-emphasized in the training of future priests. . . . The students' and seminarians' minds must be as totally imbued with it as they are with their scholastic theology, because on this will depend whether we shall have anything meaningful to tell the world; or whether we shall continue spouting our irrelevant "natural law theories" to a world which neither understands us nor is in any way attracted to us by what we have to say.[9]

The seminarian must learn to "empty himself" of the selfish pursuit of personal virtue. The world of hungry men bids him to learn that if he is to be poor in spirit, he cannot do it alone. He must "make himself poor," as did Christ, in order to make men rich.

THE PROBLEM OF AUTHORITY AND OBEDIENCE

It is a fair question whether more heat or light is being generated by the current arguments over authority and obedience in the Church. Quickly ignited feelings give evidence of psychological defensiveness and may indicate the discussants'

---

[9] Peter Riga, "Liturgy and Action," *The Commonweal*, vol. lxxxi, no. 14 (December 1964), p. 446.

uncertainty and uneasiness about their own positions. Indeed, the language of combat has become common in these exchanges. The mind's eye sees two embattled camps but, as is the question in so many wars, what is the fighting all about? War has never proved an adequate solution to man's problems; there is no hope that it can resolve the current difficulties about authority and obedience. Today's seminarian finds himself in the middle of the battlefield, unsure of whether he is a contestant, a hostage, or part of the prize each side seems to be seeking.

It is clear that authority is not going to win the war merely by asserting itself; that reminds one of the question "Have you got the answer or are you part of the problem?" Solution by *fiat* may be, like patriotism, the last refuge of the scoundrel; it clearly shows that the person in authority has failed, because he can exercise his authority only by insisting on it. Equally unrealistic are the subjects who think that the war will be won by blind rebellion. They inch toward placing themselves outside anybody's authority; nothing shows more clearly their failure to understand the basic facts of human existence.

Throughout history the Church has not had as much trouble with heresy as it has with heretics. The reason is simple. Heretics have feelings, and these complex reactions interfere with their communication with other men. When the heretics and the churchmen finally can get together they find, in a surprising number of cases, that their differences are not as great as they had at first supposed. How else can one explain the recent proposal about the possibility of canonizing Martin Luther? It is the human dimension that is vital if authority and obedience are ever to be interrelated in a healthy way. It is not enough to discuss the concepts of authority and obedience abstractly, but this is what has been done, despite lively examples, in many recent articles. In truth, authority and obedience are found only in human situations as exercised by human persons. In an operational way, then, authority and obedience are profound questions of human relationships. The growth of the Church rests, not just in the theoretical realm of defining obedience and authority, but in the existential working through of the relationship between those in authority with their subjects. "Man can neither rule nor be ruled," Pope Pius XII has told us "by fear and force."[10] This is a problem of the persons, not just the concepts, involved, and it will be resolved only through their real communication with each other in love.

It is easy to dramatize the excesses of incompetent authority. We know both Captain Bligh and Captain Queeg and the celebrated literary mutinies they engendered. Their mutinies were reactions to their defects as persons, not challenges to the existence of naval authority. Someone else stepped into authority as soon as they were turned out of it. Their crews' rebellion was not against the necessary structures of authority in life but against the destructiveness of those unfit to administer it. Authority within the Church can easily serve the ends of the person who exercises it. It is no challenge to the concept of ecclesiastical authority to face the fact that some superiors are inadequate persons who derive their self-esteem from the authority that has been given to them. These persons must defend their authority because they have nothing else as a source of satisfaction. As Cervantes, commenting on the problems of religious administrators, remarks: "One of the chief reasons for employee discontent is that a supervisor or employer really is not sure of himself, what or how he wants done, so of course he is satisfied or dissatisfied according to the mood and whim of the day."[11] The worst tragedy of the incompetent superior is

10 Pius XII, "Address to the Women of Italian Catholic Action," July 24, 1949; trans. in *The Catholic Mind,* vol. xlvii, no. 1043 (November 1949), p. 689.

11 Lucius Cervantes, S.J., in *Hospital Progress* (November 1961), p. 58.

the suffering he causes, suffering which he often does not see because he does not let himself see it. Nothing can interfere with the growth of Christ's Church in the world but the weakness and failures of human beings; when these human beings are superiors their crippling effect is increased unbelievably.

But there is another side of the coin in the lack of sympathy for the complex responsibilities of those in authority. There are many competent people in authority who are helping their subjects and, through them, the Church to grow. Seminarians and religious subjects evince a strange adolescent need at times for their superiors to be absolutely perfect. They excuse no human weakness; no superior may get fatigued, have a headache, or make a mistake without being criticized roundly. Only the superior can know the burden of petty complaints that come to him from subjects who are unable to handle their difficulties with others in a mature fashion. These subjects, actually quite dependent, live like parasites, drawing all their strength from the way they can manipulate authority to strengthen, soothe, or comfort them. No religious house is without its prima donnas; these are a source of great strain on even the healthiest superior. Some flocks demand an amazing amount of care and feeding from their shepherds. Many superiors spend most of their time with subjects who have never learned to care for themselves in a grown-up way. This is a part of the terrible complication, in human terms, of the authority-obedience question. While there are persons in authority who are incapable of exercising it maturely, there are also many subjects who, although they are critical of authority, cannot live without it because of their dependent character structure and their incapacity to govern themselves.

Several other human factors also affect the authority-obedience question which can be so dangerously oversimplified when thought of only in abstract religious terms. The superior faces

the fact that his authority will not solve his difficulties of relationship with his subjects. It is an aspect of what James Reston
describes as "this modern dilemma of the powerlessness of
power."[12] Just as the least effective thing that the United States
can do in international relations is to use its incredible military
power, so the least effective thing the superior can do to further
the work of his organization is to use his authority. The goals
of seminaries and organized religious life would be minimally
achieved if everything were done under the constraint of the
superior's orders; the subjects must want to cooperate actively
or the work collapses.

This generation does not respond wholesomely to authority
when it is exercised in an absolute commanding way. We may
not like this, but it seems to be one of the facts of life. So
Likert observes that the "trend in America, generally, in our
schools, in our homes, and in our communities, is toward giving the individual greater freedom and initiative. There are
fewer direct, unexplained orders in schools and homes, and
youngsters are participating increasingly in decisions which
affect them."[13] Another author, commenting on a new generation of students, puts it this way. "This underlies and creates a
new and different attitude on the part of college students to
the authority of their parents. It also creates a different attitude on their part to the authority of their college. Such a shift
in attitude has been foreshadowed by the change in the social
structure of the high school and preparatory school. In place
of the disciplinary methods of twenty-five years ago has come
a philosophy of student responsibility, worked out in the early
progressive schools and spreading from there to the rest of the
school system. There is a great deal more structure than before

---

12 *The New York Times,* August 31, 1964, p. 2.
13 Rensis Likert, *New Patterns of Management* (New York: McGraw-
Hill, 1961), p. 1.

in the social organization of the American high school and . . . at the same time, students are given more responsibility for sharing in educational and social policy making.[14] This is the generation that we have urged, for good or ill, to think for itself. We are confronted, then, with young men and women unaccustomed psychologically to the exercise of authority in an autocratic manner. Whether this is good or bad is an academic question now. These are the candidates and the subjects of today, and it will do little good in dealing with them to insist on forms of obedience that were appropriate and effective with an older and possibly more passive generation. We must learn to relate to this "new breed" in an effective way so that they will be helped to grow and will serve the Church well. This is an extraordinary challenge for today's superior because he will often find it inconvenient and irksome to deal with such persons when it would be much easier to give commands which are obeyed quickly and without question. But this is unmistakably the task, and today's conflicts will be resolved only when superiors have the vision to reach their subjects as they are, not as they would like them to be.

The seminary model more often than not finds the Rector as the keeper of all the keys. Life revolves around him because he dispenses permissions and patronage to faculty and students alike. Most superiors, of course, discharge their responsibilities conscientiously. At times, however, some fail to sense the father-figure role that they can so easily assume when they are clearly all-powerful. This tends to link the growth of the future priests closely to the person of the Rector. In paternally operated seminaries, the lines are quickly drawn, so that the students are generally passive to the influence of the Rector. He is the head of the house, the giver or withholder of every good

---

[14] Harold Taylor, "Freedom and Authority on the Campus," *The American College,* ed. R. Nevitt Sanford (New York: Wiley, 1962), p. 783.

thing, and he may like it that way. The possible combination of students who want to be dependent and the superior who wants to be depended upon does not result in growth for either party.

A recent research project on the passive attitude of the Mexican peasant in questions of authority and obedience is stimulating in the light of the possibilities of paternalism in seminary life. Raised in a culture where life centered on the hacienda and its master as the source of all good things, the majority of the peons are incapable of generous love or much productivity. Theirs are listless lives where the shame is "not that they die, but that they die like sheep."[15] The researcher found that only those villagers with a loving orientation towards life are productive. The others "react with passivity or resignation to the hardships which eroded confidence in their own powers. Instead of creating love, they want to be loved, and they receive little from the land or from others who also feel their inability to give. A concept of love most often stated by villagers reflects the feeling that all good things of life lie outside oneself, beyond reach; one must await passively the experience of happiness or love, being grateful if it arrives but without power to keep it."[16]

This passive dependence is all too similar to that which is revealed in counseling interviews with seminarians and religious. Monsignor Knox writes of encountering a young postulant and saying cheerfully, "It's a fine day, isn't it?" Her reply was, "I'll have to ask Mother Superior."[17] This only half jesting story catches the real pain of the passive religious who

[15] Vachel Lindsay, "The Leaden-Eyed" in *Collected Poems* (New York: Macmillan, 1946), p. 70.

[16] Michael Maccoby, "Love and Authority," *The Atlantic Monthly* (March 1964), p. 121.

[17] Ronald Knox, *The Priestly Life* (New York: Sheed and Ward, 1958), p. 105.

cannot trust himself. The author of the Mexican study finds the roots of the peons' dependence at least partially in their cultural and psychological relationship to the hacienda. He writes:

Peasants lacking faith in themselves still seek patrons with whom they act the part of humble supplicant. In fact, when land was partitioned, some villagers refused to accept *ejidos* because they feared that the old hacienda would return to punish them. . . . These social attitudes mirror family relationships in which bonds between brothers are weakened by the tie to parents. The parents, like the hacienda owners, demand strict obedience from children. . . . Their strictness is rooted in the idea . . . that willfulness and independence are signs of *lo malo* ("badness") that must be eradicated. With this attitude parents probably save their children from getting into trouble with the hacienda masters, but now it cripples the growth of self-reliance. After the age of six . . . the child is expected to obey without question. He is taught what is right is what his parents consider right. He constantly feels guilt and seldom learns to distinguish between his own rational conscience and the fear that he will transgress a parental command. Since parents often punish but hardly ever reward, the child lacks a sense of doing anything worthwhile; it is enough to avoid trouble.[18]

Unable to form a truly cooperative and productive agricultural club with the village youth, the author met with them in what were equivalent to group therapy sessions. They discussed the ever present guilt which crippled their own initiative. The author continues:

He had been taught that to anger authority for whatever reason meant punishment. Therefore, with parents, with employers, or with us, it was better to remain silent, to do only what one was

[18] Maccoby, *op. cit.*, p. 121.

told to do, to avoid any initiative. I pointed out to them how this attitude was rooted in centuries of hacienda life and how as long as they kept it, they would remain peons in their souls and never be free men. By accepting the idea that the right thing to do depends on another's judgment, they never could develop their own sense of right, they could never be the masters of their own activity, and they would always be more interested in escaping punishment than in their work . . . the other side of guilt about disobeying authority was the conviction that nothing they did could be praiseworthy, for no one had ever stimulated their sense of satisfaction in a job well done. Their only rewards resulted from obedience.[19]

Too many seminarians sell out and become "peons in their souls" when they are not helped maturely to interrelate with the person who exercises authority in their regard. The task of the superior is not that of creating an hacienda-like life, where the dynamics of obedience rest on rewarding men for acting like boys. Far different is the view of an administrator mature enough to write:

A good president regards it as his prime duty to stock the university with experts all of whom constantly have new ideas and are constantly pressing for more money, more accommodations, more staff. If any of them are *not* enterprising, the institution tilts out of balance; the more enterprising they are, the greater is the centrifugal toll on the administration. In any healthy institution, innovation and enthusiasm outrun resources and so there arises a succession of conflicts. The purpose of the institution is cooperation, but its vitality depends on conflicts; he has to encourage them, and when they arise he has to take steps to insure that they are resolved —an equilibrium continually disturbed by forces and enthusiasms generated within the faculty. . . .[20]

[19] *Ibid.*, pp. 125–126.
[20] Eric Ashby, "A University Presidency: What It Takes," *The Saturday Review of Literature*, vol. xlvii, no. 47 (November 21, 1964), pp. 59, 77.

Ashby's remarks are those of a man with a vision of what real leadership can mean; he cannot speak of it except in dynamic terms, of vital sparks that must fly whenever men of purpose struggle toward a goal together. The pseudo-rewards of passive obedience crush the breath out of the man with a hunger for life; they are the sacred seals of approval only for the unloving and the inadequate. In too many seminaries, the concept of obedience has been presented in terms of the closed-off seminary world alone. The good priest is the one who does what he is told. He stays home and keeps his own counsel, and the seminary regulations, with about equal circumspection. But there is yet a larger world, and the priest of today must be obedient, first of all, to its profound needs. It is required of him, as Holmes said it was required of every man, "that he should share the passion and action of his time at peril of being judged not to have lived."[21]

Lost too in the deadening dialogue about abstract authority is the sense of the way a real leader can electrify his followers and bring out the best that is in them. Men follow the real leader not just because he has authority but because he inspires them, because he resurrects them when they are dead and breathes into them life and hope. Such leaders have shaped the course of history; theirs is a special magic, and the terrible question of today is whether we can make room for these men in the Church. Perhaps our glorification of the virtue of day-to-day fidelity to the common tasks has made us incapable of utilizing the uncommon man in the evangelization of the world. Perhaps the question of obedience and authority is edged with unnecessary strain, precisely because our seminarians have been in relationship with so few real leaders. It is a sad dawn for the Church when it settles for safe and

---

[21] Oliver Wendell Holmes Jr., Address "Memorial Day," Keene, N.H., May 30, 1884.

uninspiring leaders, and when it seems afraid of its strongest and most able sons. It means real leaders can suffer intensely when the Church does not make the best use of them. To them could be addressed the melancholy and reluctant tribute, "You will burn up the world at last, you are too healthy for the world."[22]

Many superiors are constantly conscious of their power and responsibility for ultimate decision. There is more to authority than making decisions, however, and it is a larger view of their challenge to move men and to help them grow that they must have to merit their insignia of office. A recent commentator on the American presidency put it in this fashion:

It is only in recent years that power has been represented as "decision-making" or a president as a "decider." . . . The language is, one sometimes feels, reductive, demeaning, and misleading. Power is more than "ultimate decision," and decision is perhaps the least of its mysteries. A president is not first of all a man thinking over what (or what not) to do next and then doing (or not doing) it. This may describe the central role of a purchasing agent or a speculator, but it does not describe that of a president. . . . Had Kennedy lived to serve a few years more, he might have staked a claim to greatness by the rightness of his decisions, which is unmistakably the claim that Truman makes upon our consideration. As things have worked out, Kennedy will not be judged by this but by his presence—always surprising, bracing, promising much in the way of new departures. . . . Mere presence, of course, cannot promote the general welfare. . . . Power is given in order that it may be used, and it is true that, with a few exceptions that should not be overlooked, great men have been those who used it boldly, imaginatively, humanely. But not every exercise of power is an act of "decision"—preceded by rigorous deliberation, fol-

[22] Gilbert Keith Chesterton quoted in Maisie Ward, *Return to Chesterton* (New York: Sheed and Ward, 1954), p. 84.

lowed by vigorous execution. One of the mysteries is that there can be palpable power in mere presence.[23]

The able Church leader can move his subjects toward a common goal without insisting that there is only one path to its attainment. Men and movements die quickly when their focus on means blinds them to the horizon that should beckon them onward. There are newer and better ways to do things; that is what the new generation, with its surging energy, has to teach us. This is the way of progress in all of history. There is no stopping the clock in this age of the Church; the establishment of the Christian community in the world is the goal shared by all. Authority must see part of its task as that of bringing out of the rising generation of priests and religious all the richness of their creative gifts. This is the way to fulfill the Church and to fulfill its clergy as well.

The Church, if its true authority is to be understood and its spiritual goals achieved, must be seen as a community of love, one whose real strength arises from the mature relationships between the persons who are its members. Seminary directors need not fear the loss of their authority, nor the loss of their students' respect for ecclesiastical authority, if they try to bring this vision to life in their communities. As McKenzie has said:

When I read a letter in a clerical journal in which the writer reaffirms as traditional his conviction that obedience is THE WAY (sic), I can only reflect that the Father has not been reading the New Testament lately. I know the sources of his conviction, I think, and I know that he, like many others, has mistaken the part for the whole. Unless authority commands in love and the subject obeys in love, we are not dealing with Christian obedience. And at

23 Richard Rovere, "The Loneliest Place in the World," *American Heritage,* vol. xv (August 1964), p. 30.

this point one must risk being banal by recalling that love is directed toward persons, not ideas or objects. Christian obedience is intelligible only as a work of love, not as a substitute for love.[24]

The seminarian must learn to give himself generously to his life of work in the Church, not just to submit himself reluctantly to abstract authority. It is curious that we have not presented obedience in a more positive psychological fashion. More often than not, speakers and writers depict obedience as a dramatic virtue that involves carrying out something we do not want to do. The seminarian, they say, must be ready to surrender to the situation where he will have to embrace a decision that contradicts his own interests and judgment. Is this, in fact, the truth about life in the priesthood? How many times, we might ask ourselves, does this critical occasion arise? Many priests and religious will answer that the Church demands this kind of acquiescence rarely, if at all. Obedience would be a strange virtue if it were designed to be exercised only two or three times in a year, or in a lifetime.

Obedience is more realistically understood in quite a different way. We are challenged by our vocations of service not to do the things in which we don't believe, but to do the things in which we do believe. We are asked, not to do the things that contradict us, but the things that fulfill us. Obedience to the needs of suffering mankind asks us to give ourselves wholeheartedly to the values we prize most highly. We are charged to do the things we want to do—to empty ourselves in our effort to bring the Gospel to men, to give our inner selves up, to die every day to bring life to others. The apostle is invited by any serious commitment to the apostolate to be "poured out like water." It is as if Christ took us seriously when we decided on the priesthood; He seems to say "All right, if you believe it is better to love than be loved, to understand rather than be understood, I will fill your lives with the opportunities to do this until there is no time left over for yourself." This is the heart of his vocation for the priest who says that his "heart is ready," who believes that "now is the acceptable time." Christ invites men "to follow" Him, and this is along a road of self-giving that is without respite; this is the profound existential challenge of "obedience unto death." Only men who have learned how to love are fit for this kind of life. A genuine, loving and Christ-like obedience does not stunt us; it demands that we grow up fully and give ourselves away generously. Obedience is not, then, just a negatively-toned aspect of a priest's vocation. Neither is it designed as a support for the half-grown, dependent man. Virtue is never so mean as this. Obedience is a strong and positive aspect of the total response of a mature man to the deepest convictions of his faith. Only a healthy man, a real lover of the Church and the men it is meant to save, can practice it. How refreshing it would be to present obedience in this light for a change.

The debate about authority and obedience rages in an airless and empty hall when it is not referred to men in relationship to each other in the community of Christ. We are, in this age, experiencing the painful demands of working out realistic and effective ways for men to cooperate with each other for the development of the Church. The situation is tragically misperceived if we can only see it in terms of the rebellion of youth and the counterattack of old age. We are witnessing the Church moving in time; it is a state of growth toward the *pleroma*. The theme of this book is the growth of vocations through healthy human relationships. The growth of the Church depends upon the same factor—do Christians love one another? The question is too hard for many; others are afraid of its implications because it means that issues like those of authority and obedience, indeed the success of the mission of the Church to mankind, depend, not on abstract reasoning, but on our own individual answers.

PROBLEMS OF COMMUNITY LIVING

Modern man is preoccupied with his alienation from his fellows, and our culture has been described as a "lonely crowd." Despite the superficial cheerfulness, this is exactly what many seminaries and religious houses are, places where strangers live closely with one another. It is a curious historical development when we consider that one of the motives for establishing monasteries was to bring men together, in an age of great distances and limited communication, in order to have them enjoy a common life. Now, with instant communications and people living more closely than ever before, candidates come together in religious houses and end up living quite separated lives. There is little sharing of even the simplest of their internal experiences, and even after many years together seminarians and religious find that they do not know each other at all.

Life in a seminary can be something like a ride in an elevator. Everybody recognizes the mild tension that develops as an elevator, crowded with a random community of strangers, descends to the lobby of a building. No one speaks, and a person hardly knows where to look. People are embarrassed if they are caught sneaking a glance at their neighbor; they are soon bored with reading the certificate which tells the last time the elevator was inspected and found safe. Never are people closer together physically and farther apart psychologically. The tension mounts until the doors finally open and there is a sudden sense of relief as the passengers plunge into the anonymity of the outer world. What is strange about this is that everyone has had exactly the same experience, the same feelings of tension and embarrassment and awkwardness, and yet they have experienced these things separately. Everyone nods in appreciation at a description of this experience. "Yes," they will say, "that's just the way it is." It is a touching spectacle, this elevator full of strangers who are so much alike in their own private and insulated worlds. Unfortunately, many seminarians and religious experience this same tension and lack of real sharing in life as they take the elevator ride of seminary existence together. They are experiencing the same things, and their reactions, although they may seem unique to each one, are strikingly similar. But the burden is not shared; the journey is a lonely one. How else explain the sense of relief in seminarians or religious when they are allowed to plunge into the anonymity of the world outside their religious houses? The tragedy is that it need not be this way. Several aspects of community life constitute problems for seminarians and religious.

Loneliness

Many seminarians see the path of the priesthood as a long dusty road that a man must walk alone. Here again we are dealing not necessarily with the truth of priestly life but with the students' perceptions, and these represent the psychological reality with which they interact. The seminarian can and does feel lonely here and now during his seminary years; he is afraid of the future into which he projects these same feelings.

It is frequently argued that the seminarian should not feel lonely; after all, the priest is in the midst of people all the time. "Keep busy and avoid idleness": there is no room for loneliness or self-pity in a life lived according to these maxims. These injunctions to industry reassure the seminarian about his future happiness. Quite rightly they suggest that it is in his power to do something actively to control this dimension of his life but, as with so many reassurances, these tend to ignore the reality of the individual's own reactions. They substitute the encouraging pat on the back for what could be mature insight into the individual's experience of loneliness and his fears about it in the years ahead. In other words, the significant thing is the seminarian's reaction to the loneliness which he rightly or wrongly sees in the life of the priest.

In science the simplest explanation is the preferred one. The priesthood looks lonely because many priests are lonely. They have carried their isolation from others into their ministry. This can easily seem true of seminary professors who, scholarly by nature, can seem out of contact with each other and with the human community. This is not always the case, but it is true often enough to justify the seminarian's fears about what his life as a priest will be like. What matter all the reassurances about the priest's life being deeply involved with others if the priests he sees are not like this? The growing seminarian does not want to be a bachelor at heart, frustrated and alienated from the community. The seminary staff has a major obligation of reflecting the deep contentment of well-rounded priests who are capable of enjoying their priesthood and the people they serve through it.

Other questions may be asked as well. Is there shyness in the seminarian that can be overcome and social development that can be achieved during the seminary training itself? Is the loneliness a genuine sensing that he is ultimately on his own in the face of life, a sign that he senses that wrenching of the spirit that comes as a man realizes that he really "can't go home again"? Or is the loneliness a self-inflicted and self-defeating result of a spiritual regime which casts other men in the role of the enemies of his spiritual welfare? Is he alienated from men in the name of a pseudo-perfectionism that denies him the healthy and necessary supports of good relationships with other people? Is holiness presented as only "Jesus and me"?

These questions are difficult, and a man must answer them for himself. A seminarian can be helped to face his own feelings in this area of life just as in any other. He can and will experience loneliness; it is the lot of every living man. How he is able to deal with it depends on how deeply he understands himself and his own needs. There are many superficial attempts at covering up loneliness through shallow and restless recreations. A man's footsteps sound all the more hollow when, through this din of unsatisfying activity, he lets himself hear them. If the priest is not capable of facing the facts about the experience of loneliness, he will be driven by its pangs towards solutions that are not only frustrating but sometimes disastrous as well.

The worst of these solutions flows from the regret a man can experience when, after ordination, he says, "I never knew it would be like this." It is very easy for a priest, gripped by these feelings and seeded with self-pity, to justify antidotes for loneliness through unhealthy and self-indulgent relationships with other people. It is quite remarkable to see how easily priests, presumably imbued with the highest Christian ideals, can literally "use" other people to heal their own wounds. These inadequate adjustments to life are the fruit of superficial self-knowledge. Too often unhappy priests begin the tale of their recriminations with the phrase, "If I had only known I would feel this way. . . ." The tragedy of this is that they could have known and been better prepared to understand both loneliness and their own reaction to it.

Loneliness is a fact of life, and the best way to prepare a man for it is to insure his overall personal growth. To experience loneliness is not necessarily an evil to be avoided at all costs; it can and should be a tempering and maturing influence. The seminarian who is helped to understand thoroughly the wide range of his own reactions will handle his moments alone in manly fashion. Just as he has had to grow personally to weather solitude maturely, so too he will grow through the experience itself to be a stronger man.

The man who has not learned to relate to his fellow men condemns himself to loneliness that is tragically unnecessary. The seminarian who has not learned to love has failed himself and his fellow men as well. Love is not an abstract notion, and the seminary years are the "acceptable time" for the student to develop deep and healthy relationships with his fellows. The priest was not made to live in splendid isolation pursuing a self-centered spirituality. A man who is able to love will never really be alone.

Frictions in the Community

The other side of the coin from living alone is the problem of living with others. The problems are, of course, not unrelated, and they have supplied the theme not only for spiritual writers but for dramatists and novelists as well. Broken communication between individuals who receive Communion together mocks Christianity as well as the pursuit of perfection in religious life. In a recent study of a religious community the results showed a decline in all the "human variables."[25] The longer the subjects of this study were in religious life, the less highly did they score on measures of objectivity, sociabil-

[25] Sister M. Odelia Urschalitz, I.H.M., Selected areas of personal adjustment as related to length of community membership and vocation values among religious women educators. Unpublished doctoral dissertation, Fordham University, 1959.

ity, and personal relationships. This curious possibility of becoming dehumanized in the pursuit of perfection seems to be part of a vicious circle. When people are unable to communicate with real confidence in one another, then friction is an inevitable result; this friction leads to misunderstandings and stresses which further cripple the communication process. Many of these difficulties flow from the great ignorance of the place of feeling in the life of the seminarian or religious. This is practically a constant theme in this book. When the whole person is not understood, then healthy growth is impossible. While friction is inevitable wherever human beings gather, it does not have to be the totally defeating phenomenon that it sometimes seems to be in religious life. When people do not understand their hostile or aggressive feelings, they are not able to exercise mature control over them. The burden is increased by the guilt that they feel for having experienced these feelings in the first place. An application of very basic principles of mental hygiene would eliminate many of the difficulties that arise in this area of religious life.

A case history of friction in the community begins when one individual does feel strongly about the behavior or personality of someone living with him. It is not, however, proper for a seminarian or religious to have hard feelings toward another person. These do not fit into the self-concept of a "good" religious. They consider themselves bad if they experience these feelings. Instead of being able to face what is a very normal occurrence in most people's lives, these seminarians, convinced that the very experience of hostile feelings is wrong, are made anxious by them. They feel guilty even before there is any question of whether they are or are not responsible for their emotional reactions. They attempt an unsure control by means of "will power" alone. The feelings fester when they cannot be faced and admitted, and this kind of infection spreads rapidly.

It is no wonder that such people are irritable, tend to flare up and then grieve in deep remorse. They have not learned to love themselves enough to accept their own feelings without fear.

A second attempt at solving the problem of aggressive feeling is to deny them or distort them. This, of course, is another example of the individual's failure to face feelings and their roots; this leaves the person still smoldering with resentments which must find more subtle ways of expression. When the person cannot openly express the anger he feels, he will make it known in ways that are not so dramatic but that are more destructive. Passive aggression, a lack of cooperation, and the failure to voice opinions when they are asked for, are merely some of the ways in which real hostility is expressed in religious life. It is a commonplace to measure the health of a seminary atmosphere by the amount of griping that occurs in it. This bitter complaining, which is always done about authority but never to authority, is a sign of strong feelings being handled in an immature way. The great gripers seldom have the courage to present a complaint in adult fashion to someone who could do something about it. But the hostility will out because there is no real way to hide it. When the person cannot handle his negative feelings in grownup fashion, they emerge in adolescent and corrosive forms.

The two most common efforts at handling strong feelings which cannot be faced directly are either through withdrawal or attack. The person who pulls away from others whenever heated emotions arise is being controlled by fear and his own inability to face conflict. There is an incredible amount of running to the mother or father figure in religious life to settle problems which healthy people handle in much more direct fashion. The pettiness of these complaints can be known only to the superior who has had to listen to them. This withdrawal can be masked in righteousness and a seeming spirituality of detachment. It is easier at times to pray for our enemies than to confront them and try to reach them in a human and loving way. But it is not a better thing. The attack, when it comes, is often an animal-like response made all the more furious because of the long suppression of the feelings beneath it. These are regrettable events that amount, at times, to psychological murder. The wounds heal slowly at best when the feelings tumble out under stress. The violence of the explosion may alienate the parties concerned forever.

What is needed is an atmosphere of education in which people are not afraid of their feelings, no matter what they are. The possible range of human experience is wide, and there is nothing in the experience of feelings themselves that is either good or bad. They are signals of what we are like, signposts that tell us we must go deeper in this direction if we are to understand ourselves. The advocacy of suppression is unhealthy because it is never a completely successful mechanism. Healthy people are able to take a look at their feelings and go deeply beneath them and discover something about their cause. It is when they can admit them that they can control them, but a certain inhuman school of spirituality brands feelings as evil from the start.

Unfortunately, seminaries sometimes try to eliminate all sources of conflict in a vain effort to control strong feelings. This is something like the philosophy of a mental hospital, which tries to simplify life for the confused patients and make all the tasks minimally challenging. This is not the kind of life for healthy people. The "Rule" frequently dictates so many of the minutiae of life that any opportunity for people to work out an intelligent compromise even in the simplest aspects of their shared life is denied them. It would be much better to allow seminarians and religious to face conflicts and to give them the freedom and understanding that will help them to work these difficulties out. This is the best preparation they can have to handle later conflicts in mature fashion.

There is no denying the fact that immature and complicated emotional involvements can arise in seminaries. It is against these that the authorities write their rules and preach their sermons. While they grow righteously indignant about emotional friendships, they frequently offer no help at all to the people who get involved in them, to aid them to understand what is happening to them. The individuals are told that they can be friends no longer, but this is confusing in a situation that is already tense and difficult. The seminarians are left with something that can be a very painful experience; they feel guilty and hurt, and often develop a mistrust of others and the feeling that friendship is something they can never have.

Friendship

The forbidding and abnormal conditions of life in some seminaries are the things that need criticism, not the seminarians who are driven by these circumstances into relationships which may be immature. What would we expect to find in institutions where healthy and unselfconscious friendships are difficult to cultivate because of the very structure itself? What else can grow in an abnormal atmosphere but abnormal relationships? The ultimate solution to this difficulty is not just in breaking up any "particular" friendship with stern reproofs but to examine the whole atmosphere of the seminary and see if this is not the very reason that such friendships tend to flourish. The more wholesome and open the atmosphere, the fewer will be the difficulties with the emotional relationships that are not friendships at all. Seminary educators are trying to correct a symptom when they break up two people who are in a bad relationship; let them look to the possible roots of these unfortunate human relationships and the unhealthy conditions of their institutional life.

Nothing is more bewildering for a healthy person than to enter an abnormal atmosphere where the only thing he hears about friendships is a litany of their potential dangers. This is in no way to deny the dangers that may exist, but it is a misdirected solution that holds aloofness and being impersonal as heroic Christian virtues. There is no wonder that healthy people become frustrated in such situations. Let in the sunlight and fresh air because anything that is healthy will thrive on it, and anything that is abnormal or unusual will wither up. This is the best rule in regard to human relationships in the seminary. A control through prohibition and threat merely makes people who are in emotional relationships furtive. There are then meetings in the library alcove, discussions late into the night, secret signs and a proliferation of presents. All these are truly indications of unhealthy relationships, but it is an underground life, this life of the so-called particular friendship. Those seminarians involved merely become more defensive when they are attacked. They deserve something better than this, and what they deserve is the mature understanding of educators who are able to help them understand their own emotional development and the nature of the experience that they have gone through. The typical course, however, of those in a particular friendship is to defend against it through rationalization. They soon call it a "spiritual" friendship, a name as erroneous as the "particular" friendship classification. These friendships are preoccupying and emotionally exhausting. Those in it protest too much about its sacredness; what they need is understanding help from good priests who are able to do more than scold them for having experienced this difficulty.

Friendship is an important subject for any seminarian. Real friendship is not a self-conscious thing, however. Seminarians will learn most about it through healthy friendships with priests and through witnessing the wholesome relationships that priests have with each other and with all the people with whom they work.

"There is little in life," Belloc tells us, "worth the wear of winning save laughter and the love of friends." Friendship is not paid the same tribute by the seminary, and this is precisely why it becomes an area of difficulty for the seminarian. Man was made to have healthy relationships, friendships, and the priest was called by Christ not to be a servant but a friend. This subject is not often treated in a positive manner in the seminary world. This is not to say that seminary educators do not value friendship and its importance in a priest's life; they presume an appreciation of these values and tend to concern themselves with the dangers which they know can be present in ill-starred emotional relationships between seminarians or other candidates in religious life. This is fine from the faculty member's point of view, but it is not what the seminarian sees or hears, and this is the source of much confusion for him. "All I ever hear about friendships," one seminarian has said, "is that you have to be careful of them." This unintended negative emphasis is a source of concern for the seminarians whose health is attested to by their wholesome friendships with others.

Here again this subject is a difficulty which is complicated by the way it is presented. If friendship is always discussed as something potentially evil, if human beings living together are only reminded of the dangers of perversion, then we hardly have an atmosphere of healthy normality. Robert Frost said that before he built a wall he would like to know what he was "walling in or walling out." This question is not asked by those who write into the seminary rule careful prescriptions about the nature of the friendships that seminarians are allowed. Particular friendships are to be avoided at all costs. People must walk in groups of three or more. These common rules attest to the anxiety that seminary educators feel, or think they must feel, about the seminarians' relationships with one another. They are so preoccupied with what can go wrong that they hardly try to provide a vision of what is so wholesomely right about strong friendships.

18 Apostolic Work: The Expression of Vocation and the Test of Growth

In his book *Religion as an Occupation* Fichter writes: "The point is that the apostolic orientation in spiritual development is toward the service (salvation) of others, just as the professional orientation in technical development is toward the service of others. . . . If the novice or seminarian is not given an apostolic perspective in his early years, we can expect that he will become a spiritual jack-of-all-trades."[1]

If the seminary is a period of true development, we should expect not only the pains but the proof of growth during these years. The young men headed for a life in the apostolate must do more than dream dreams and see visions. While there are many areas of activity in which the seminarian can show his increasing maturity, he must be able to manifest it in his participation in the works of the apostolate. This area should not be just an outlet for restless energy; it is an opportunity for personal growth and a test of whether it is really taking place. To work even as an apprentice in the vineyard is not a substitute for the academic preparation of the seminarian, but it may be far more realistic than many of his other experiences in allowing him to encounter himself as he encounters others.

[1] Pp. 110–111.

It is interesting to note that in the training of priests there is close supervision of the seminarian's private life but practically no supervision of his professional life. In other professional training (medicine and psychology, for example) there is close supervision of the student's professional life and practically no supervision of his personal life. It would be difficult to say that seminaries have been more effective than professional schools in developing mature men. The seminary may make too much of a distinction between the individual's so-called personal life and his work, whether it is concerned with study or the active works of the apostolate. These latter kinds of works, in seminaries where they do exist, are ordinarily extra-curricular activities. The moderators function in widely different ways, but often they are figureheads who supervise the activity only in a very broad sense. This is very different from the supervision that a physician or psychologist gives to an intern in their professions. These professionals tend to look on the students as their future colleagues and successors and take very seriously the reponsibilities for the physical or mental health of the patients with whom their trainees work. The supervisors' demands are usually very great; they do not tolerate slipshod professional performances, and they probe very deeply into the intern's knowledge, skills, and motivation. The intern gets immediate feedback on his performance; his internship quickly becomes a time of real growth as he experiences, often with great pain, the challenge of matching his textbook knowledge of sickness to the encounter with human persons suffering these sicknesses. The truth of his grasp of the meaning of his life's work is not found in the medical student's quiet room. It is in meeting and becoming responsible, as a member of the healing profession, with sick human beings. Too often the truth of the seminarian's grasp of the meaning of his life's work is restricted to his quiet room; he can find truth, as one seminarian has observed, "if it is on property." When he does act as a professional religious person, when he does assume responsibility for preaching the Gospel in some way or other, he is hardly supervised at all. He gets no immediate feedback about his mistakes and little opportunity to profit from them. What could be a healthy growth situation is instead a frustrating and disappointing experience.

Apostolic activities range from teaching catechism to ecumenical dialogues, and perhaps growth can come from these experiences alone. Experience is undoubtedly a good teacher, but it is even a better one when a skilled and mature priest can help the individual seminarian to understand himself and what he finds in the apostolate.

As it is, the seminarian, even one just a few months from the priesthood, generally lacks supervision in this area of his life. In fact, where apostolic activities are permitted, they are more often considered desirable but extraordinary. That is to say, they are not perceived as the powerfully educative and maturing experiences that they can be with increased faculty cooperation and participation. All too often, the activities are isolated from the seminary curriculum. They are nice but generally "harmless" chances for the seminarian to "practice" virtue by visiting the sick, "being good" to orphans, or "being tolerant" of non-Catholics. The truly sacramental aspect of this participation in the human condition is often ignored. It is even possible that these activities can be grist for the "do-gooder's" mill.

If the seminary at the theology level is comparable to the professional school for "professionals in religion," as one seminary dean has put it, then it has lessons to learn from the other professions. Many seminaries have had the goal of presenting to the world a man with the answers. Indeed, some priests recall that this was precisely their feeling at ordination time; experience quickly corrects this view of the freshly minted apostle. The first years of the priesthood have made many men unsure of themselves, and unsure of their faith, because their answers did not work, or they did not fit the questions of modern man. Alone with his doubts, many a young priest has prayed for a sharper faith and a subtler wisdom as he wept over the world. The seminary could prepare a man for his apostolate much more realistically if it capitalized on the opportunities for apostolic supervision during the seminary years.

A recent study of the training of doctors suggests some instructive parallels. In the third year of medical school the neophyte healer brings his textbook knowledge into the existential world of the sick and dying. Uncertainty shadows his days as he begins to perform the elementary tasks of being a man of medicine. "First, there is the uncertainty that comes with realizing that, despite all the medicine a student has mastered and all he will learn, he can never hope to 'shovel out more than a corner of what there is to know.' "[2]

This uncertainty arises, according to this study, at "major transition point in the student's training—it is the beginning of his total immersion in clinical medicine" (p. 223). There is a time when the medical student begins to look at himself in a new way, a period when he begins to identify himself not just as a student but as a member of the medical profession. This is obviously an important phase of his growth as a physician. It is during this time, the authors note, that

a third-year student looks back somewhat wistfully on what he regards as the relative "organization and continuity of the academic classroom." How do you "approach learning," he wonders, now that these things are no longer grouped by courses—and the

[2] Renée C. Fox, "Training for Uncertainty" in R. K. Merton, G. C. Reader, and P. L. Kendall, eds., *The Student-Physician* (Cambridge: Harvard University Press, 1957), p. 221.

choice of study is so completely your own? . . . Part of the student's difficulty in evolving a plan of study lies in the fact that what he is really seeking is nothing less than an organized way of learning to think like a doctor. . . . As a student quickly discovers, however, the way of thought of the doctor is something other than a sum total of the ideas he has already mastered. (P. 223.)

Is there a comparable period in the training of a seminarian when he begins to look at himself in a new way, when he begins to identify himself not just as a student but as an apostle? The answer to this question is given by the countless numbers of priests who have remarked about the abrupt transition they experienced on ordination day. They awoke as seminarians and went to bed as priests. The adjustment, the learning to think like a priest, has been very trying for many a young man. Yet, in most cases, he is left to make the adjustment as best he can with little really constructive supervision from older priests.

In recent years a number of fifth-year theology programs have been developed to ease this period of transition into the priesthood. There is a wide variety of practice and effectiveness in the way these programs are carried out. The first question that comes to mind, however, concerns the addition of a year to the already lengthy seminary training. Is this an implicit admission that the previous years of the seminary have failed to do something that they should have in the formation of priests? Frequently these pastoral years are largely made up of more of what went before, that is, theory divorced from supervised practice. Such a solution may be something like treating a man with a broken leg by breaking it again. Even when this year offers the young priests the opportunity for parish work there is hardly any close supervision built into it.

This is also true of the dioceses in which bishops have assigned their deacons, in the summer before ordination, to various parishes to exercise their orders. This has been profitable for many men, and yet the general picture is one of inconsistency. The pastors may have little time to supervise the deacons' work in any but a general way; they generally do not have the training or skills that would make such supervision profitable even if there were time for it.

It is possible to consider a carefully planned "apostolic internship" as a part of the seminary training itself. This would obviously require mature thought, but its advantages would be very great in helping the seminarians not only to think like priests but also to feel with the Church. Right now, without adding anything to already crammed class schedules, such supervision could be applied to the whole range of apostolic activities. Instead of random experiences they could become genuine sources of personal growth. The seminarian would, in a realistic way, begin to sense the imminence of his priesthood just as the medical student senses "the imminence of his doctorhood" (p. 224).

The third-year medical student begins to handle his uncertainty more maturely; he begins to be able to live with questions unanswered, more secure even though his knowledge is imperfect. Part of this reassurance comes from his "close relationship to the clinical faculty" (p. 226). The words of one medical student catch this notion clearly:

During the first two years it was possible to remain completely removed from the faculty and yet still do O.K. by reading and going to lectures. While some departments made an effort to develop a close student-faculty relationship, you never had to depend on this to get the things you were supposed to. But now only 50% of what we need can come from books. The other 50% has to come from the teachers we work with. And so, there is a 180-degree shift in the class' reaction to the faculty. (P. 226.)

It is not difficult to apply these concepts to seminary training where this kind of faculty-student relationship would be so healthy and so appropriate. It is also rare. The word "seminarian" could easily be made the subject of the following observations from the same study:

Because he finds that listening to experienced doctors reason out loud is the only way he can get "a sense of how to approach clinical problems," the third-year student welcomes the opportunity to learn through direct contact with his instructors. Meeting with members of the faculty or house staff in small intimate groups and discussing patients with them is "the heart of clinical medical education," so far as the student is concerned. Sessions like these, he says, "give (him) insight into how a doctor organizes and uses his information," and a "real sense of colleagueship." ("You catch the feeling you must have in a craft: the father passing the secrets of the craft on to his son.") The closeness of his relationship to the faculty in the third year helps a student to think and feel more like a doctor, and consequently fosters his sense of certainty. (P. 227.)

A great deal of thought has been given to the nature of practicum and internship training by the professions. The Division of Counseling Psychology of The American Psychological Association, for example, has set forth the purposes and conditions of this training in detail.[3] These statements could be applied to seminary training with stimulating results:

[3] Albert S. Thompson and Donald E. Super, eds., *The Professional Preparation of Counseling Psychologists* (New York: Teachers College of Columbia University, 1964).

The internship is the terminal phase in the practicum training of the counseling psychologist and ... should occur at that time in the student's experience when he has developed a sufficient mastery of both theoretical-didactic materials and practical skills to be able to assume the role of a fully-functioning although junior member of the staff of the internship agency. (P. 141.) ... Since the exact nature of the internship will necessarily vary . . . careful collaborative planning between the internship agency and the university, together with the prospective intern, is required before a suitable plan can be arranged. (P. 142.) . . . The climate of internship is probably best set by accepting the student as a professional colleague even though he is neither expected nor required to carry the same responsibilities as fully qualified staff members. It should be expected that he assume his place in staff meetings commensurate with his point of view whether the meeting be concerned with staffing cases, deciding policy, or preparing a budget. The intern treated as a professional person will more likely and quickly learn to be one. (P. 143.)

It is clear that many of the trying questions of the day could be worked out maturely if such programs were built into the seminary years. Perhaps the seemingly inevitable clash of the generations could be minimized if not eliminated by this gradual incorporation of the student into the work of the priesthood. Internship is a disciplined and demanding experience for those who participate in it. If anything, it would make far more adult demands on the student than any possible seminary rule could. Its dimensions are those of reality itself, and this would be as refreshing as it would be maturing.

The notion of a professional internship includes the necessity of evaluating the candidates, a traditional task for seminary faculty members. The difference here, as has been mentioned, is that this evaluation centers on his performance in a professional capacity, the rough-edged world of his life's work.

This is far different from trying to judge a man on his keeping of the seminary regulations or on some other parameter of behavior that may not fully reflect his state of development. This is not to say, of course, that these aspects of his behavior should be ignored; it is, however, to say that a richer estimate of his potential could be obtained from observing his actual function in the works of the priesthood. The model of evaluation offered by the professions could augment, if not replace, the methods already used in seminaries. Is the candidate growing? This is the question that must be answered; it is the same question proposed, for example, by the psychologists. Several principles of evaluating the growth of the intern are suggested:

1. The underlying philosophy and approach of evaluation should be directed constructively toward strengthening the intern both personally and professionally.
2. Evaluation should be *with* an intern rather than merely *of* an intern.
3. Evaluation is properly regarded as a continuing process, not as a single event in time.
4. In its most helpful form the evaluation will also provide an opportunity for interns to evaluate objectively the internship supervision and setting.[4]

It may seem obvious that a focus on the apostolic performance of the seminarian would have the advantages of providing a real opportunity for his mature development as well as a clear evaluation of his capabilities, but these possibilities have remained largely unexplored up to this time. It may require a new "set" on the part of faculty members to see themselves participating in such a program, but it would, at one time, make their work of formation more satisfying and more effective. These notions illumine the possibilities of faculty-student

[4] *Ibid.*, p. 149.

relationships that transcend the recreation room and the hand-ball court. Supervisor-intern relationships concerned with the essential practice of the priesthood among men would be healthy, mature, and productive of growth for student and faculty member as well. The relevance of their studies, something so often decried by today's seminarians, would emerge far more clearly, and their motivation for further study would be deepened.

The chief advantage of whatever program of supervised apostolic experience that prudent planning could offer would be that its roots would be in a deep respect for the seminarian and the vocation to the priesthood. Respect for his individual potential is too little experienced by the seminarian during his years of training. He would have to be taken seriously, and he would have to take the seminary and the priesthood seriously as well. This would create the conditions for mature growth; indeed, without this respectful base, there could be little true growth at all.

This new dimension of seminary training needs careful thought and planning. It may require added staff members or additional training for those already present on the faculty. It would require cooperation and negotiation with dioceses, parishes, and schools, and, clearly, it will fail without careful preparation. Its great hope, however, is in the dynamic impetus it would give to the growth of tomorrow's priests. This program would help seminarians to do more than learn their lessons; it would let them "become priests" in the deepest meaning of that phrase.

III *The Priest*

19 The Source of Growth

"Every high priest is taken from among men
and appointed to act on behalf of men in their
relations with God. . . ." (Hebrews 5.1)

Ordination day is long awaited but suddenly upon the seminarian. He kneels before his bishop, the hands are imposed, and he stands up as a priest. Neither the story of his life nor the story of his vocation is over; a new phase of growth for the priest and the man has begun. The dynamic base of his vocation is not suddenly frozen securely by the rite of ordination. The young priest has run the course and attained the goal, but the race is far from over. He must still pursue his vocation just as he must continue to grow as an individual person. These are inseparable processes; the choice is between growth or decline.

How does a priest grow? The question demands a careful and mature answer. St. Vincent de Paul reportedly advised a group of deacons that if they wanted to be good priests, they should go to bed early. The new priest has a lot of similar advice about desirable habits of life, the faithful carrying out of his spiritual exercises, and the protection of his virtue. He has the seminary's seal of approval on his technical competence in theology and canon law. He has the example of good and indifferent priests to follow and to avoid. He knows what he should do and what he can do. But this is not the same as understanding how to grow fully as a human being who is also a priest. The advice and the good example can certainly help him. He may even gain a lot of worldly wisdom on how to get along in the priesthood in the same way that a businessman or politician may learn the secrets of affluence and influence in his career. But this is also quite different from understanding real growth. The freshly-minted priest, full of feeling about preaching the Gospel and administering the sacraments, is in a new relationship to mankind. It is in working through that complex and challenging relationship that he will grow.

Growth does not come for the human person, even when he is a priest, just through thinking or even praying about it. These are necessary aspects of his development, but the heart of it must be, as it is for every man, in his relationship with the people he serves. If he grows, it is because he loves other men, maturely and unreservedly, and is loved but not possessed in return. This truly is the genius of the apostolate, this knowing how to love. No other road leads to growth either for himself or for others.

The core of healthy growth for the priest must be the pastoral relationship. All the hymns to the priesthood have been sung to its commitment to the Christian community, the human family, the people of God. This is not an abstract ideal or merely grist for the dreamer's mill. The pastoral relationship means the existential sharing of life, its burdens and its boons, by the real man who is a priest and the real men who are his people. This is not preaching from a lofty pulpit to a faceless congregation; it is a deep entering into the tumultuous and tortured human condition, not as an onlooker but as a participant, not as a moderator but as a mediator who can bring meaning to the lives of men. It is precisely in his work as a priest that he relates to men. The priest is called to be a friend, who embodies God's love for man in his real love for real men. No man can understand God's love and forgiveness unless he experiences these from His priest in a deeply human way. The pastor's life is filled with people, and it is in ministering to their needs generously that he pursues his growth and his vocation.

Human relationships are the warp and woof of priestly existence. The priest is challenged through them in a way that no other group of professionals can understand. Recent surveys, for example, show that almost fifty percent of Americans bring their emotional problems, in the first instance, to their clergyman. The priest, along with the minister and the rabbi, is a man exposed to an incredible spectrum of human suffering. Unlike the psychiatrist or psychologist, the priest cannot be selective about the kinds of people he will see. Unlike many other helping professions, the priesthood does not allow for neatly scheduled appointments. The priest must answer every knock on his door, every ring of his telephone; he is committed to a loving response to all these confused or confounded people. He may not be able to solve all their problems, or heal all their spiritual and psychological wounds, but he must be a priest to them in some way. He must try to understand despite his own confusion, to forgive despite his own fatigue and possible irritation, to share, even for a brief few moments, the world of the casual passerby. His vocation does not permit him to turn away anybody. The person staring at him in his doorway has a right to the priest's time and person. This seeker of his help can never be perceived as just another drunk, or just another marriage case; there is never "just another" of anything for the priest. He empties himself, when he has a pastoral vision of his work, in a genuine effort to understand everyone as an individual human person. There is no challenge like it in any other life. It is in this urgent invitation to comprehend the scarred and suffering procession of human beings that come into his life that the priest finds the meaning of his own life. It is in this incarnation in relationship to men that the priest is himself redeemed. When there is no healthy pastoral relationship there is no growth for either priest or people.

It is surprising to note how often this central notion about the priesthood is ignored in practice. The members of the parish, the daily round of human encounters, can be drudgery for some priests. These priests may find their satisfactions in activities that are other than pastoral; old friends, holidays, hobbies. This arises when the priest has either never learned to relate well with others or where he finds it too fearful a prospect or too great an effort. Often enough priests look on their pastoral relationships as necessarily professional and therefore impersonal. This happens as a withdrawal reaction sometimes after a priest has become overinvolved emotionally in a parishioner's problem and has vowed to himself, "Never again will I get my fingers burned!" The impersonal relationship, as has been discussed earlier in this book, is used, then, as a defense against emotional reactions that the priest does not understand and which he feels he can control only through withdrawal from close personal ties. He is stalled in his growth, and his solution is understandable, but unhealthy and self-defeating in the long run. It is precisely in working out his myriad relationships and his own reactions to them that he can continue to grow. He must be able to look into himself and understand his reactions if he is going to carry out his fundamental task of loving his neighbor. This is the heart of his work and the only possible source of genuine growth for him.

The priest must be a strong person, then, to function at all well in this demanding routine. His must be a hardy self, one not marred by any major impediments to personal growth.

When these are present in the forms of neurotic character structure, he cannot develop healthy patterns of relationship as a pastor. In other words, the priest cannot move into the world of persons with exaggerated or distorted needs of his own at work. If he does, these emotional lacks will master him and the people with whom he works will subtly become sources of unhealthy gratification rather than growth. The priest who is half grown will find himself plagued by conflicts and tensions that will make his life a torture. These undeveloped priests find their greatest difficulty, rather than their healthiest satisfaction, in meeting and dealing with people in mature ways. They are uneasy with them and tend to avoid contacts that are deep and productive of growth. This fear can follow them all day, and their efforts are directed to controlling this, literally toward holding themselves together rather than opening themselves up. This suffering is as unnecessary as it is tragic; it crucifies the priest while it contradicts his priesthood.

Celibacy is not a freeing condition of growth in personal relationships for the immature priest; it is a sterile bachelorhood that insulates him from a deep, loving relationship with the human race. St. Thomas presents celibacy as a virtue, not as a penance. In the context of the pastoral relationship to men, celibacy is not a state chosen out of fear or inability to love. It is the circumstance of life that enables the priest to enter into the lives of many people instead of just one family circle. It is not a denial of human love; it is a celebration of its necessity in a priest's life. His sacrifice of sex and fatherhood makes sense only if he can love in the healthiest and fullest sense. Celibacy, according to St. Thomas, gives greater freedom and "leisure for contemplating divine things *for the beauty* and *welfare* of the whole human race" in contrast with the more limited purpose and love of marriage. It is not, St. Thomas continues, a type of leisure that allows a man to be "as insensible as a country lout." The celibate priest is not to be deadened to humanity but dedicated to it in a total loving commitment.

The core of Christianity and of the priesthood lies in lives full of love. This love cannot be selfish or sentimental, but neither can it be totally abstract and cold. The priest who is alive and growing is so because he loves, and is loved by, the people he serves.

20 Obstacles to Growth

Since his relationship to his flock is the source of the priest's personal growth, then anything that interferes with this will keep him from growing. Professionalization, for example, may affect the healthy Christian character of his relationship to people. This professionalization, however, is a fact of life in American Catholic culture. A priest is not only an individual related to others in terms of his own personality; his role as a religious functionary, independent of his own characterstics, automatically refers him to others in a specialized way. He is not just a private person but a public figure as well. He stands for the Church and functions within its framework, and this necessarily affects the conditions of his relationship to his fellow men. Certain duties are prescribed, and these are to be carried out largely within the accepted pattern of parish life. The enormous pressures of carrying out the basic service obligations to his parishioners tend to minimize the opportunities he has to meet them in a more personal way. Even though he is aware of the dangers both to his effectiveness with others and to his own development that are inherent in this official religious position he may find it difficult, if not impossible, to strike the healthy balance that a more personalized apostolate demands. The sociological aspects of the problems of the professional religious person have been treated by Fichter.[1] Here we are primarily concerned with the psychological results of the conflicts that arise because of the various roles of the priest in our culture.

This sociological dilemma makes it increasingly difficult for the priest to maintain deep and life-giving relationships in his priestly work. Many individuals are able to adapt to this because of the strength of their own personalities, but many others are forced to make a bitter peace with themselves and the world that tends to divide their lives and frustrate their growth. They perform their priestly tasks in an impersonal but efficient way. They tend to withdraw from making healthy and deep contacts in their work and relate in a more standardized and impersonal fashion. They have a private life which they do not share necessarily with their people, and it is in this private world of friends and interests that they derive the greatest personal satisfactions. They have been forced by the enormous burden of their professional tasks or by the frustrations of their structural setting to divide themselves in order to stay alive. Maintaining life is not the same as growing, however, and that is precisely why the situation is so unsatisfying for so many priests.

This already difficult situation is complicated by the fact that many priests feel that they are not well prepared to work in a close and effective way with human persons. They must necessarily assume a professional stance in order to shore up their own weaknesses and, in a real sense, to protect themselves from the highly personal demands to which they do not feel they can give an adequate response. They are often trapped by their first experiences in dealing with human suffering and find, because they have had little effective preparation

[1] Joseph H. Fichter, S.J., *Religion as an Occupation* (Notre Dame: University of Notre Dame Press, 1961), p. 126.

for this kind of work, that they become emotionally involved, easily discouraged, and psychologically drained in the process. The professional relationship becomes a necessity, a defense for themselves. While these opportunities to share in the human condition are the occasions for real Christ-like relationships which would be highly productive of growth, many priests cannot enter into them fully because of the handicap of never having learned how to do so in a healthy manner. Any human relationship looks inevitably engulfing to them, and they are genuinely afraid of losing themselves in it. This is a major problem that affects the very core of their activities with human persons and chokes off the possibilities of their true growth. They can neither give life nor gain it; they become fixed in a deadened and immature state of development. They feel "in a rut" because psychologically that is exactly where they are.

This is an unnecessary form of suffering for any priest; uneasiness and fear are swift cripplers of wholesome pastoral relationships. If contacts with people cause him anxiety, they can hardly be the source of his growth. Instead, and often unconsciously, the priest puts all his energy into controlling his own fears, and fear, as always, kills the possibility of love. He finds that he is self-conscious and superficial even when he longs to reach people in a genuine way. There is a barrier between himself and others through which he can make no opening. His pattern of adjustment to people is ordered more to controlling his own anxiety than to meeting others in a mature personal way. He defends himself, in other words, in an effort to solve his own problem, and these defenses, spurred by hidden dynamics of interpersonal inadequacy, are what show on the surface of his pastoral encounters.

The seemingly charming shyness of some priests may often be the manifestation of a man who can only use the reactions of a boy in the face of the world. It has a certain appeal at times, but it is a clear sign of a lack of growth. Another priest may assume an authoritarian, omniscient pose; this barely covers his own unsureness about himself. Still others fashion what could be termed a "just relationship." They treat everyone exactly the same, to every man a penny, but without warmth and without giving anything of themselves away. There is a real strain in this for the priest and a terrible emptiness because his relationships are flat and unrewarding. We are familiar enough with priests who play favorites because their own needs must be satisfied. They become quite exclusive about their friends and their parishioners; they even show signs of jealousy at times if another priest seems to be getting to know "his people" too well. These are all signs of unsureness, all signals of immaturity in relationships. They are as dangerous for the priest as are the excesses of uncontrolled emotional involvement.

The question comes down to this: the priest must be able to relate like a man called to be a "friend" of other men in a mature and healthy way, or his life will be truly empty and lonely. The defective forms of relationship that spring from the half-grown person do not endure, do not bear fruit, and frequently lead the priest down the road towards self-centered bachelorhood. A bachelor is a man incapable of genuine loving relationships. He fails because he cannot form Christian relationships, and this, for the priest, is total failure.

We have previously discussed the importance of helping the seminarian to learn how to relate in grown-up fashion to other men. The seminary must make this kind of growth possible. Superficial relationships during the years of training do not produce the kind of growth that the priest will need when he emerges after ordination into the world of men. It may be that the only deep relationship that some priests have experienced is that which they have with their parents. Devotion to their mothers and fathers is a praiseworthy characteristic of many good priests, but in a certain kind of priest it is not quite the sign of health that it may seem to be. His only deep personal investment in other persons may be in his parents; he may never learn through the years to relate to them in any but a "little boy" fashion. McAllister and VanderVeldt have suggested that priests who have suffered psychological difficulties may have been more deeply affected by parents with psychological problems precisely because they never experienced any other deep personal relationship in their lives. In interpreting the fact that 11 of 32 clergy with alcohol problems had alcoholic fathers they say that the findings

suggest that the psychological importance and the psychic impact of parental figures is greater among the clergy than among a comparable non-clergy patient group. Moore and Sullivan might say that the parataxic distortion created by parental figures remains more effective in the clergy group. This seems a reasonable conclusion, because these early meaningful relationships are not as easily displaced or modified as in the non-clergy group. Laymen have new, deep and close interpersonal relationships with associates in love affairs and courtship, in marriage, and with their own children. These interpersonal experiences tend to modify and frequently to mollify their earlier experiences with parents so that the effect of parental influence is diminished.[2]

In other words, while their brothers and sisters are growing through the new relationships that come into their lives, the priest, because he does not experience these, may not be growing in his ability to make close relationships, and in a mature fashion, with people his own age. It is only at the death of a

[2] Robert J. McAllister and Albert VanderVeldt, "Factors in Mental Illness among Hospitalized Clergy," *The Journal of Nervous and Mental Disease,* vol. 132, no. 1 (January 1961), p. 84.

parent, for example, that some priests suddenly find that they are quite alone in the world. This is a very critical time for some of them, a period of great distress and conflict. It may be the occasion for their breakthrough into learning how to relate to others in a healthier and more satisfactory way. For some, however, it is a time of withdrawal and confusion. This is hardly a criticism of the affection that priests have for their parents. Obviously, growth and relationships with peers in no way threaten or destroy the wholesome relationship of a son for his mother and father. His relationship with his parents, in fact, should change as he matures. He is no longer a dependent boy who has to check in and spend all his free time with them. He is no longer the child coming home on his day off to be comforted and caressed. He cannot expect to grow to full manhood if he is unwilling to drop his dependence on his parents for his total supply of affection and understanding. He must be able to relate as a grown man with a wide variety of other people. If he cannot do this, then his attachment to his family circle is indeed an obstacle to his growth in the priesthood.

In this connection it is interesting to speculate on the connection between the candidate's perception of his vocation to the priesthood or religious life and the nature of his relationship to his parents. It is still possible for mothers to be powerful persuaders and subtly to manipulate their children into some form of religious life. Anyone who has worked intimately with seminarians, brothers, sisters or priests, has encountered more than one person whose chief motivation was to meet parental expectations. These are basically unhealthy callings, and they occur only in people who have not outgrown a relationship of dependence on their mother and father. It is their inability to go beyond this that keeps them in the seminary or other house of training. They maintain, often enough, the same kind of relationship toward their rector or spiritual director.

He merely takes the place of the parent in urging them to persevere and in manifesting disappointment when they try to discuss their feelings about some other form of life. They must do what they are told, these candidates feel, and even in their relationship to God they maintain the same immature passivity. This can be reinforced by spiritual reading and conferences that emphasize submission, a willingness "to be formed," and, in general, childish responses to life. After the parent dies, or the influential superior passes out of their life, these priests and religious find that there is little that attracts them to the lives they have chosen. Many crises that mark the middle years of religious life are directly related to the severance of the fundamental and dominating personal relationships that the priest or religious has experienced in his own family constellation. It is a difficult time for him to begin to grow, and while many in this dilemma make an adjustment that is almost heroic their problem is actually an expression of the unfortunate relationships that have controlled their lives and prevented their true maturity. On the other hand we find that religious superiors who can relate only in authoritarian and impersonal fashion merely reinforce these difficulties. Even if the number of these situations is relatively small in comparison with the total number of priests and religious, it is a tragic and unnecessarily large number. It is the unhealthy growth from abnormal situations that have never been studied very carefully; it is a bitter harvest of unnecessary human suffering, where the burden of the Lord's service is heavy and the yoke is not sweet.

As has been discussed often enough in these pages, the measure of an effective man in the priesthood or religious life is surely the health and range of his personal relationships. In the renewed liturgy, the priest is presented as the president of the Christian community. His task is defined in terms of his mature relationship to the people of God; his priesthood has meaning only in the relationship to the individuals who constitute the community of his parish. Neither the priesthood nor the Church can be understood without a clear view of people in relationship to each other in the Mystical Body. Life with each other in Christ is not sentimental, but it obviously cannot be impersonal.

We have noted before that marriage is essentially a test of the love of two persons for one another. They do not have the choice of learning to love one another or not; they must have a healthy relationship, one strong enough to survive all the struggles of long years together. This relationship is the source of growth for the married couple. When they cannot relate in a truly personal fashion, the couple drifts apart, communication ceases and growth stops. Often enough death for the marriage itself follows through divorce. The vocation clearly fails when the relationship fails. Unfortunately, nothing so dramatically signalizes the failure of a priest to relate in a strong and wholesome way to his people. He can be inadequate, half-grown, or even impersonal in the extreme, but he can still survive as a religious functionary. He will not be growing and, in fact, neither possesses nor is capable of handing on life to others. Ordination does not automatically confer on him the ability, not just to get along with people, but to love them truly and unselfishly. His relationships with others will be the expression of his love for God. But this can only flow out of a man who is alive and growing in the service of his brothers. There is no way to do this except by learning how to love in a profoundly Christian way.

Some current writers on the liturgical reform make the dangerous error of reassuring us that the liturgy will "create the Christian community." The liturgy can only provide the occasion and symbolization for the existent Christian community, one that has been achieved by people who have grown up enough to love each other in a deeply respectful and freeing way. This does not come easily, nor will it ever come through the performance of new rites. Men are not friends because they sit down and eat together; they sit down and eat together because they are friends. How does modern man worship God? Guardini has asked the question for us:

Is not the liturgical act and, with it, all that goes under the name of "liturgy" so bound up with the historical background—antique or medieval or baroque—that it would be more honest to give it up altogether? Would it not be better to admit that man in this industrial and scientific age, with its new sociological structure, is no longer capable of the liturgical act? And instead of talking of renewal ought we not to consider how best to celebrate the sacred mysteries so that modern man can grasp their meaning through his own approach to truth?[3]

Man worships God profoundly when he is in a healthy, loving relationship to other men. This is the meaning of Christianity, the meaning even of the Last Supper, which was not so much a meal as Christ gathering his close friends together. The important thing was their relationship to each other, not the meal that they ate or the utensils that they used. These constituted only the setting for their sharing together. Recently we have become preoccupied with the menu, the position of the headwaiter, and the texture of the bread we are going to serve; these preoccupations with the setting of the meal that is the Mass may give current testimony to our lack of understanding that the real meaning lies in our relationship to one another, our genuine sharing of life in Christ. If this revitalized liturgy fails to celebrate our union with one another, it will

[3] "A Letter from Romano Guardini," *Herder Correspondence*, vol. i, no. 0 (Special Issue—undated), p. 26.

only be because we have failed to grow to the real maturity that is needed for Christians to love one another. Training for a life in the priesthood will flow in a healthy way from the liturgy when it is perceived in its true meaning as a celebration of Christians in loving relationship to one another.

21 When Growth Stops

As his relationships with others sensitively reflect the priest's healthy growth, so too they reflect his inability to grow. The symptoms of his frustrated personal development are seen clearly in his distorted and tangled relationships with his fellow men. These faulted relationships are the signs of his immaturity or illness. The interpersonal area is where his stunted growth shows itself.

MAJOR PSYCHIATRIC ILLNESS

The previously mentioned study of McAllister and Vander-Veldt[1] reveals some of the pathology that is encountered in priests who have been hospitalized for mental illness. Their analysis of the characteristics of these deeply suffering men indicates how their personal relationships both shaped and mirrored their psychiatric illnesses.

Seventy-seven percent of the clergy who responded to the author's questionnaire on background factors admitted to having experienced serious emotional problems in the semi-

[1] "Factors in Mental Illness among Hospitalized Clergy," *The Journal of Nervous and Mental Disease,* vol. 132, no. 1 (January 1961).

nary. These included "severe and continued doubts about their vocation, advice from authorities to leave, sexual maladjustments, gross problems with authority, morbid scruples, severe anxiety attacks, and acute emotional illnesses." The authors suggest the need for "more careful attention to the emotional growth and health of seminarians on the part of seminary faculties."

Forty-eight percent of the hospitalized clergy were "A" students, and sixteen percent more were "B" students. This preponderance of mental illness among the more highly gifted intellectually led the authors to recommend that seminary officials "look for more than intellectual endowment in their candidates," because "emotional maturity and intellectual acumen are not necessarily correlated." The intellectual superiority of these priests enabled them to win the approval of their professors. The "halo effect" of their good grades won the respect of faculty members who either did not understand or were willing to overlook their other personal defects. In many cases, individuals who are not really capable of mature growth, because of psychological weaknesses, form relationships on the basis of their intellectual strength alone. They do not relate as full persons because they do not have to, in order to be successful and approved. This partial relationship, through intellectual achievement, is a defense against full growth. It is only in the years after ordination, in many cases, when this inadequate type of relationship is no longer effective, that the real weaknesses of these individuals show up.

The importance of the priest's relationships with his family is illustrated in these additional findings:

Ninety-one percent of the hospitalized clergy came from homes where the mother was described as the dominant figure. The authors suggest that this maternal dominance "may create some distortion in the priestly role or in the relationship to authority figures. . . ."

A significantly greater number of clergy patients had parents with psychiatric symptoms than did the lay group. For example, the clergy more frequently had alcoholic fathers than did the lay group. Eleven of the thirty-two clergy with alcohol problems had alcoholic fathers.

The authors of this book have had extensive experience in doing psychotherapy with psychologically ill priests and religious. In almost every instance of deep disturbance, the roots were to be found in the relationship of the patients with their families.

It is worth repeating here a previously quoted section of the study because of its relevance to the question of the priest's personal relationships. There was "a greater number of sociopathic personality disturbances" among the clergy group. The authors note that

seminary training and the clerical life lend themselves easily to lack of duration and depth in interpersonal relationships. For many "the spirit of detachment" becomes synonymous with "fugitive, fleeting, involvement with other people," words which Sullivan used so aptly to describe the sociopath. Sociopaths are perhaps attracted to the challenge of the clerical life, since they need to prove themselves. They are perhaps more comfortable in the impersonal relationships of seminary life, in their need to keep a distance between themselves and others.

The difficulties of seriously ill priests often have a long history. Forty-six percent of the clergy were diagnosed as having personality disorders, suggesting the presence of lifelong patterns of maladjustment.

Treatment problems with the clergy are complex, and the authors summarize them in this way:

Whatever factors may be involved in the difference between the clergy and lay groups, it is clear that clergy patients have more difficulty with psychiatric hospitalization than do lay patients. The clergy have more negative attitudes about their hospitalization; they require longer periods of confinement; they show less improvement at time of discharge; and they are less able to return to their previous duties.

In other words, serious psychiatric illness, often the outcome of defective familial relationships, removes the priest from his pastoral relationship and makes it difficult for him to resume it.

DEFECTIONS

Defections from the priesthood are frequently associated with the patterns of illness just described. Very frequently the priest who attempts marriage is seeking, through this action, to solve one or the other deep personality difficulty. He is frequently dependent, undeveloped emotionally, and it is a relief of the misery these conditions engender that he seeks in marriage.

Frequently it is difficult to see that the person involved in the situation is actually suffering deep personal conflicts. This is because the illness is often subtle and because a life of withdrawal tends to protect someone with deep personal shortcomings.

There is great difficulty ordinarily in getting these men back into priestly work. This is often because the inadequate solution of attempted marriage provides at least for their neurotic needs. In other words it is easier to handle regret, guilt, and shame than it is to give up a relationship with someone who meets their needs for affection, attention, and warm interpersonal support. Sexual satisfactions are only a small part of this pitfall into which the stunted person can fall and from which he hardly ever wants to emerge. This relationship in attempted marriage is an expression of their psychological impoverishment and a sign of how poorly they were related to themselves during their seminary years. They related superficially in turn with others in the controlled atmosphere of the seminary. Only after ordination did things fall apart, only after the controlled atmosphere was gone. Then their profound personal needs broke through in a painful and tragic fashion. These unfortunate individuals are often more sick than sinning. Their action, in attempting marriage, places them outside of relationship to the Church. They are willing to bear this in order to preserve their relationship with their "wives" and families. Some men actually do grow up more in this situation than they did when they were priests, but this is a sad footnote in most of their life stories. The plight of men who may want to find a way back to the Church from which they have exiled themselves has been studied by the Vatican Council II. The willingness of healthy friends in the priesthood to keep in touch with these men, to keep in a loving and understanding relationship with them, has been the most effective way of helping them. Love does more than ecclesiastical warnings and excommunications because it preserves the possibility of reaching them in a life-giving and human way.

PROBLEMS OF IMMATURITY AND LACK OF PERSONAL GROWTH

These problems can only be described today as all too common among priests. The priests who suffer from these difficulties are usually on the job, but they are anxious and unsure of themselves. They frequently find adjustment to priestly life a trying and unhappy time. Their solutions are often as immature as their problems. The pursuit of entertainment in multiple forms becomes a big part of their lives. This is illustrated in television, stereo, cars, boats, the theater, and, a prime example, self-identification in a surrogate-life of sporting interests. These activities are obviously good in themselves, but they are, in the normal man's life, recreations or avocations. For the immature these activities become a way of life.

Briefly, this type of priest is adolescent, half grown to maturity. It is as if the machinery of growth ceased to function during the period of seminary training. This psychological hibernation is rudely interrupted shortly after ordination, when the inevitable effects of working closely with people register on him. A whole aspect of his personality stirs to life again, and his problems are almost exactly the problems that the normal man went through during his adolescent years. These are: (a) working out his relationship to authority and (b) working out his relationship to women. When a young priest encounters these problems he suffers all the confusion of the adolescent, but the role he is expected to fill in life is that of a man. He is bound to disappoint superiors and to give his parishioners the impression of immaturity. He cannot change simply because someone tells him to. It is not a question of intellectual lack but a question of inadequate personal growth, and the help he needs to achieve this is often unavailable when he needs it most. He needs a relationship that will make fuller growth possible. He must, literally, grow up in the priesthood, but he cannot do this if there is nobody around to help him effectively. He needs the understanding of a mature priest who is able to help him understand himself. He needs the interest and consideration of authorities capable of seeing that he is not yet a fully-grown man. It is a difficult time for an underdeveloped priest, and he cannot pass through it alone. Too many priests, however, cannot even locate a good confessor very easily, much less the kind of person who can help them in basic problems of personal growth. This should have been done in the seminary; the confusion and ineffectiveness of these boys on men's errands is the price paid for training houses that do not promote genuine manly growth. Thought must be given to providing help for these priests at the time when they need it and can still profit from it. The availability of mature older priests who are capable of relating in a grown-up way to these younger men is a basic need in most dioceses and religious orders today.

22 Priests in Crisis: the Pains of Growth for Subjects and Superiors

In this age God seems, to many priests, to speak to them out of the whirlwind. The times are difficult for superior and subject alike: the world is rumbling beneath their feet and the fixtures of the Church are rattling on the walls and crashing about them. Are these merely tremors that will soon pass and leave things more or less intact? Or is the earth about to open an abyss into which everything that is familiar will fall?

We believe that priests and religious of today, uncomforted by the long view of history, are suffering with the Church in a period of growth. It is evolution rather than revolution, growth not decline, but it is a time when mere mortals are hard-pressed to be sure which is which. This chapter tries to capture and reflect on some of the common feelings and experiences of God's servants in this age.

PARISH PRIESTS IN TRANSITION

The aggiornamento has brought to priests not peace but a sword. Within the last year, as trumpets of new hope have been heard throughout the world, many priests have experienced deep and searing conflicts. Paradoxically, as unparalleled opportunities seem about to open for the Church, her priests have tasted a bitter harvest of self-doubt and frustration. This suffering is complex, and the finest priests, because of their sensitivity, have felt it most keenly. These problems are not symptoms of sickness as much as they are signs of health. These are the problems of men born to be free and called to be lovers: the worst question, hanging motionless over their lives like an atomic cloud, is whether they can fulfill these basic human needs in the framework of the priesthood. Can they grow as Christian persons in lives which, as they view them, are operationally truncated, bureaucratically frustrated, and, as far as the great thrust of the world movement goes, sadly irrelevant? In this changing world, where they feel suddenly alone and confused, the old reassurances do not work even when they seriously wish that they would. It is not enough to argue that they are wrong or that they have failed to take the long view of eternity. It is not lukewarmness or worldliness that motivates them; they love the priesthood, the Church, and the Christian community. Their conflicts arise from their deep desire to bring the Church to men and men to the Church. Their frustrations spring not from wanting to escape work but from trying to do it. They are mediators caught in the middle, servants suffering because they cannot serve as fully or freely as the needs of men demand.

The recurrent question among many serious priests concerns their own future. In a world of changed liturgy and emerged laymen, the function of the priest in relation to the Christian community is being examined. If it is true that many of the activities he now supervises, such as clubs, teaching, and other tasks of administration, will gradually be assumed by an eager and better-prepared laity, what new dimensions will his own work assume? If he is to be less of an administrator, how will he be more of a pastor?

Beyond this is the question of whether the present parish structure, with decades of delegation as assistants in the larger cities, can provide the conditions for the full and healthy functioning of priests. The parish model is being re-examined because many of the frustrations of good priests center on it. It is not simply a question of restive men who are trying to escape their pastor's authority in order to have undisciplined freedom of life and action. At the heart of this matter, zealous men feel that the present structures are suffocating them in the mature exercise of their priesthood. There is a general feeling that something must change in the traditional conditions of the priestly apostolate if it is to keep up with the modern world. The problem reflects the view of an American philosopher who wrote:

The rate of change in our time is such that an individual human being, of ordinary length of life, will be called on to face novel situations which find no parallel in the past. The fixed person for the fixed duties, who in older societies was such a godsend, in the future will be a public danger.[1]

Various experiments in American dioceses reflect the concern of bishops for this question but also feed into the general yearning of priests for new answers in a new age. Their own consciences trouble them because their faith in the older structures of the Church's mission to men has been shaken; what does burgeoning ecumenism mean, what does a renewed ceremonial which celebrates the Christian community imply, what does freedom of conscience demand of them? Where are the arguments for the truths they teach when their seminary notes and textbooks have fallen hopelessly out of date? What does the Bible tell them when they have not been able to absorb,

[1] Alfred North Whitehead quoted in Arthur E. Jenson, "Why Executives Study the Liberal Arts," *Country Beautiful,* vol. 2 (1962), p. 56.

much less keep up with, the tide of scriptural scholarship? What answers can they give to other men when they find it difficult to answer these questions themselves? The priest affected by these problems does not want to withdraw from their challenges; he does not want to sell out for respect and security. That is precisely why it is the priest who is concerned about the mystery of the Church who suffers so acutely. He rubs the well-burnished lamp of his training, but the genie with all the answers no longer appears.

The luminous vision of a resurgent Church beckons these priests, but they find it difficult to respond because of the administrative structure which seems to shackle them. The priest is incarnated in the world of men; he must pursue his redemption through his relationship to mankind. The profound core of his problem is his painful awareness that mankind needs him but is generally indifferent to him. Men have rejected what they perceived as the unbearable authoritarianism of the Church, and priests have lost faith in the explanations that have reassured them that this was not really so. The bride of Christ is too beautiful in their eyes to be further scarred with the mean faults of unloving men. It is no challenge to authority that they suddenly find themselves unable and unwilling to bear the cross of authoritarianism any longer. They cannot function freely under it, and neither can they, in conscience, adopt it as their mode of relating to men. Paul VI has said of the apostolate that it "is not a conquest but a service." No banners flying over marching armies, no militant crusade. These priests cannot reconcile coercion with the scriptural emphasis on coming to minister, not to be ministered to. They meditate deeply on the words of Christ to the effect that authority in the Church is to be exercised by men who make themselves "lackeys" and "slaves." How do they fulfill these functions in a structure that lends itself, as they see it, so readily to the abuses of authoritarianism?

These are not men bent on disobedience. They feel a deep sense of responsibility to their mission to the needs of men. Respond they must—obedient unto death—to the deep convictions of their own consciences. They want to serve the Church as the community of love it is revealed to be in the New Testament; they feel hampered by the accidental forms of political power and medieval city-state trappings that churchmen have used to harness the energy of the Spirit.

These are the kinds of problems shared by all healthy men; they want to grow and to help others grow. They move towards the values of freedom, self-expression, and self-control that are the marks of maturity. Can the Church make room for men who cannot and will not settle for anything less than full growth? This inner striving for fulfillment is the sign of a healthy and normal person. Authority, at its root meaning, means to make able to grow; the person in authority must be an "increaser" not a controller. The challenge, then, to the authorities of the Church is very great, for their charge is not to constrain their sons but to make it possible for them to grow. That is the normal, healthy relationship of a father to his child; it is a dynamic relationship worked out in love. The healthy father fulfills his vocation by helping his child, through love and a consistent use of intelligent discipline, to become a man. It is an unhealthy paternalism to keep him a dependent child. If grace builds on nature, then the laws of healthy personal growth cannot be ignored in the life of the Church.

The priesthood cannot flourish unless it provides the atmosphere in which strong men can grow to the "full measure of manhood in Jesus Christ." Normal men want to move in this direction; it is only the abnormal individual who would settle for being a dwarf if full development were possible. This means they want to become mature, and part of this growth would produce a greater ability to obey maturely. They are not trying to escape or destroy the meaning of authority. They do not, however, want to live as children who get all their rewards for being passively obedient. The world will obviously not be saved by men who are afraid of loving it. But Paul VI has said, in words that bring healthy priests to life, "The fundamental attitude of those who want to convert the world is loving it. This is the genius of the apostolate: knowing how to love." Too many priests, faced with frustrations of their burning and healthy urge to grow, become bachelors in their souls. A bachelor is frequently an abnormal person, dried up and selfish, incapable of generous love. They retreat, within the structure of the priesthood, to self-centered lives filled with hobbies and distractions. This is not healthy for them, their people, or the Church.

There is a curious and far-reaching possibility here: the healthy men will ignore the possibility of becoming priests because they will perceive the structure as one that does not permit full, normal, adult growth, while the inadequate and passive, those without initiative and without love, will be attracted by a structure which they will perceive as protective. These candidates, in other words, will do considerably less for the priesthood than it will do for them. Many seminary educators have already become concerned at the large numbers of relatively inadequate applicants they have encountered in recent years. This, in some cases, is precisely why we find the priesthood used by some men to bolster themselves and to feed their own unhealthy needs. They have not come to minister but to be ministered to; they have sought a secure and respected status. This has not gone unnoticed by contemporary observers. For example, in the *New York Times Magazine* for August 2nd, 1964, one of them writes:

The diminishing power of the clergy over the people may be reaching its nadir in Western history in our times, but this decline is no new thing. The privileges which clergymen still retain in our modern society—exemption from military service, commercial discounts, tax leniencies—demonstrate rather than dispute the clergy's declining prestige. These are merely residual courtesies, inherited but now meaningless and unnecessary customs, or they are political differences society invests in the clergy for equivalent returns.[2]

The forces that contribute to this trend, a problem far more dangerous for the Church than is Communism, are complex, but the conditions of the priest's apostolate are surely a factor in them. Unfortunately, many of the solutions proposed aim only at symptomatic relief. Longer vacations and higher salaries may alleviate some of the pain of modern-day priests, but they will not cure it. Basically healthy men will not be satisfied with these ideas; they want something more substantial, more challenging to their zeal, more fulfilling for them as human persons. They do not want things made easier in a material way. They want a life where they can grow; they want freedom in order to be more responsible. As mentioned earlier, all too often the normal person has been made to feel guilty because he cannot lead an abnormal life perfectly, while the abnormal person has not only been tolerated but rewarded. No solution that does not examine and renew the basic structure of priestly functioning can possibly work.

The priest feels tension in his life from a variety of sources. For example, he senses his removal from the main currents of world forces that are, in fact, shaping and controlling man. He feels isolated from, and incapable of communicating with, the men who need him most. Cardinal Doepfner has even commented on the apparent "irrelevancy" of the priest in the

[2] Kyle Haselden, "11 A.M.: America's Most Segregated Hour."

modern world. His renewed liturgy celebrates the community of Christianity, but the priest senses the emptiness these ceremonials may have if they do not represent a deepened love and trust between the members of the human family.

Ceremonial changes fail if the priest is not speaking a language that means something to modern man. The priest's dilemma may only be increased if he cannot participate more fully in the lives of his fellow men. To be called the "president" of the Christian community may only intensify his awareness of his lack of real relationship to the people of God. Either that, or he will be nourished by the delusion that because he talks about the Christian community he has actually done something about it.

The priest is fair game for criticism, and it has become quite open and frank in this age. He is getting progressively less sympathy from the faithful, who look on him as a distant figure. A good deal of the criticism is unfair, but at least some of it flows from the fact that priests are caught in a structure that tends to isolate them from, rather than incorporate them into, modern life.

The main source of this psychological suffering, as we have said, is in the traditional parish structure, in the pastor-curate, religious superior-subject relationship. This structure, as it has developed in large metropolitan areas, leaves most priests in a lingering and stultifying apprenticeship throughout the prime of their lives. They have no authority until they are in their sixth decade of life. Even though they may dutifully offer all this up, they deserve, as normal healthy persons, something better. There is no easy solution to this problem of the organization of parish life, but it must be faced if the priests of the world are going to minister more effectively to it. Deferred hopes, paternalistic insistence on passive acceptance of an untenable situation: all these serve to increase the pressure on the basically healthy man. He wants to suffer with the world but cannot suffer much longer from the structural frustration that dispirits him.

He feels also an inadequacy to respond to the world that arises from his ineffective seminary preparation. The roots of his problems are entwined in a structure of seminary training which seems often to be aimed at soothing the abnormal rather than helping the normal to grow. A dead preparation for a live apostolate; a life of rules for men who must live maturely without them; a cold, impersonal life, safe from the evils of the world, for men called to transform it through the depth of their human love: these are the impressions many priests have of what happened to them during their seminary days. It was a good life, free of many cares and responsibilities, but it was not life as they suddenly encountered it on ordination day. One must sympathize with the struggles of seminary faculties who are trying their best to improve their programs in a time of transition. They sense the unrest of the age and are seeking solutions that will enable their institutions to be genuine sources of growth. But they are caught in a structural crisis of no small proportions. How can they open up their seminaries unless they can freely investigate the possible need to renew their structures radically? How can they improve when the risk of destroying time-honored values haunts them? Can the Church stand the maturation of its seminaries when it may seem far safer to stay put?

Can the seminaries, in fact, grow when many seminary faculty members have been chosen precisely because they are safe and conservative by nature? Can withdrawn men, chilled by the winds of change, respond to the human needs of normal youths who want to fill their lungs with fresh air? On the other hand, pellmell solutions (for example, the prospect of the wholesale transfer of seminaries to college campuses) are typical of Americans who, when in crisis, feel they must do something, anything, and almost immediately. These solutions may not have much thought in them either; they may be the panic button moves that are more confusing than constructive. The solutions to the problems of seminary training will not come easily, but come they must if priests are to "have life and have it more abundantly."

These are merely a few aspects of a deep and distressing problem. Difficulties abound, and the way will not be easy as we seek solutions fit for healthy men. This must be the goal, however: to create conditions in the priesthood where the Church's most vital sons can achieve their full growth as men. The problem is only further complicated by answers that contradict the basic needs of normal men. The solutions must be consonant with the nature of men and the nature of the Church as a community of love. Men's hearts will be restless until they find their rest in this. There are great risks involved, and something will have to die if new and fuller life is to follow for priests; this is the age-old economy, and only hope, of Christianity.

THE ANXIOUS SUPERIOR AND THE MEANING OF FREEDOM

James Reston described President Kennedy, in the year before he died, as having reached that midpoint of maturity between the rising and the retiring generations. President Kennedy, like any man in his prime, was obligated to his stricken and elderly father as much as to his growing infant son. Every man reaches this point, usually at the height of his own powers, when he must care for his parents as well as his children. Real stress arises with the pull that comes from these opposite directions; this is exactly where many rectors and religious superiors find themselves in 1965. They belong to the generation that is responsible for the Church and its many works. At the same time, they are obligated to those priests and religious who have a right to a graceful old age as much as they are to the generation that will succeed them, whose growth they must encourage. Never has the stress been so great, because the age of renewal has underscored dramatically the apparent difference in outlook and methods of the older and newer sons of the Church. The superiors are the men in the middle, the mediators who must maintain themselves, the Church, and peace between the generations all at the same time.

The Victorian age of seminary and religious training has ended. The present problem will not be solved by a retreat into it. Out of fashion now are many of the repressive aspects of religious formation programs. The space age finds a new breed questioning the unquestionable and thinking about the unthinkable. This is a heady wine for a generation bred in prosperity and inflamed by the banners that demand "Freedom now!" Veteran religious and priests, as well as laymen, whose faith has been tried by prejudice, depression, and wars, are genuinely upset at the pace of, and passion for, change in the Church in which they grew up. Young liturgical geniuses have ridiculed their habits of piety as well as their religious dress and questioned their apostolic techniques. If that isn't enough, they have given them Protestant hymns to sing along with an abrupt change in their manner of saying and hearing Mass. Little consideration has been given to their feelings, the members of the older generation feel, and little credit for their contributions to the Church. The youngsters clamor and the oldsters grumble, and today's religious superior is understandably strained in his effort to give an ear to both at the same time.

He wants to guide the Ship of Peter safely through the storms. But someone seems to have stolen his map and his compass isn't working well any more. He must get the older members of the crew safely to port without discouraging the young ones who want to head for the open sea. Is he sailing by the right stars? Is there really danger of mutiny? "How can I be the captain," he asks, "when I have to take care of so many other people and, at times, am not sure of myself?"

Rectors and religious superiors have to be strong and generous in carrying out their vocations in this age. They have to live with uncertainty, as mature men must. They have little time left for themselves, and, as far as they can see, no one seems even to try to understand their position; they are probably right. Changes must be made if the Church is to be a growing organism in the world, but how do you affect this growth prudently and surely? How do you keep from rocking the boat too much, they ponder, when there is such a terrible risk that, even with the best of intentions, you might steer it into a reef and send it to the bottom of the sea?

There are valid reasons for the anxieties that aggiornamento has brought into the lives of today's religious superiors. Some, at least, of the disturbing aspects of the age should be examined carefully, however, because they are not as fearful as they may at first seem.

We should be reassured, for example, by the fact that the problems of seminarians are not the problems of little children, but of grown-up men. The questions that are raised show a healthy concern for the salvation of the world, for the weightiest questions of human experience. These may be disturbing, but they show maturity. The strain arises only when superiors use solutions that were designed for the problems of children. That is to say, the paternalistic, omniscient and, at times, authoritarian attitude, which may be reassuring for the immature, is not effective with candidates who are growing up. It is disturbing to discover that the answers that may have satisfied us do not satisfy the students of today. It is a good kind of problem because it is a sign not of sickness but of health. The Church has the promise of a vital future when its new generation cannot be satisfied with an education that covers up, rather than opens up, the meaning of life for them. Today's student cannot be described as was yesterday's:

He is "finished," complete, in a sense. He is not likely to change much from now on. The prison walls have indeed closed entirely. The man who as a little boy loved to lie and roll in the snow, to look at the clouds and dream, will not be likely to do any of these things again. Nor will he question. The substance, the sensitive soul of youth, has been poured into the mold of convention . . . and the mold has hardened. His change is reflected in his very outward form. He has settled down. There is a kind of rigidity in his muscles, a slow pompousness in his stride. He will not question because he knows. He knows about this world and the next. . . . He knows about sin and salvation. If, for a time, he becomes a schoolmaster himself, he will teach exactly as he was taught, will beat and frighten and cow the children exactly as he was cowed and beaten. It is all quite simple.[3]

The challenge is to the responsibility of today's rector and religious superior. This is not in the sense of his performing his duty but in the literal meaning of the word: the ability to respond. Today's superior, "harried," as was St. Paul, "on every side," must be able to respond to this growing generation in a mature fashion. The questions of his subjects, some of them imprudently phrased or seemingly beyond their depth, are not occasions for panic as much as they are the healthy

[3] Agnes E. Benedict, "Glimpses of Colonial Schools" in *The History of American Education,* ed. by Carl H. Gross and Charles C. Chandler (Boston: Heath, 1964), p. 30.

signs of individuals who are growing up. They don't need milk any more but meat, and the superior must nourish them adequately. The rector or seminary professor may feel uncertain, but his task is surely not to quell a mutiny. An original meaning of authority is "to make able to grow"; those in authority are charged with being "increasers," not "restrainers." The superior should be reassured, not alarmed unduly, when he finds that his students are alive and growing. The full maturity of tomorrow's priests will depend on the fully mature response of today's superiors.

Another disturbing aspect of the superior's job today is concerned with increasing losses during the later years of training. Not only that, which can be upsetting enough, but, he notes, many of the personal problems of seminarians seem to arise because of the increased contact they have with the outside world. To the rector, conscientious about preserving vocations, the opening of the seminary may seem more like the opening of Pandora's box. Some of his students are entering the world, getting to know young ladies, and, to resume a previous analogy, are abandoning ship. Add to this the preoccupation many seminarians are beginning to display about their interpersonal needs and their desire for affection, and one can readily understand the uneasiness many superiors are experiencing. "What is going on?" they ask themselves when their candidates describe their "need to have a friend" to whom they can tell all their innermost secrets. This strikes the healthy superior as a little unusual, to say the least, and he begins to wonder whether the emphasis on personalism in much contemporary Catholic writing has not caused more trouble than anything else.

The repressions of the Victorian era are gone for good, but these kinds of difficulties make mature superiors wonder if they were so bad after all.

What is happening is, in fact, a blessing for the Church and for seminary education. The development of healthier atmospheres in religious houses is accomplishing what one should expect. The healthy candidates are thriving in more normal life situations. The unhealthy ones, long protected and rewarded by abnormal atmospheres, are beginning to stand out as they truly are. Those who are incapable of making mature personal relationships, a basic necessity for any priest or religious, are demonstrating their fundamental weaknesses. The opening of the seminaries has revealed their deep personal needs and inadequacies, facts that in a former age were manifested only after ordination or religious profession. These are the kind of students who will be able to discover that they cannot, in fact, live the priestly or religious life. It is much better, even if it is upsetting, both for them and for the Church, that this should become clear before they are ordained or professed. The suffering of this time cannot be compared to the amount of suffering that will be spared individuals and the Church as a result of the new atmosphere in seminaries. In other words, while things may look worse right now, they are actually much better.

The test of this all will be the ability of seminary superiors to understand what is really going on and to respond appropriately. Some of the responses, as evidenced by recent publicity, are complicating rather than clearing up the problem. The question of the meaning of freedom is the prime example.

It is very hard to be free, and it has meaning only in relationship to the genuine values of life. It is a sad thing, for example, to read headlines proclaiming seminary reform and greater freedom through mere modifications of the daily schedule. One seminary, according to *The New York Times*,[4] shut off its bells to let individuals regulate themselves with alarm clocks and watches and, after supper, the news item went on,

[4] February 28, 1965, p. 30.

the seminarians are free until 10 P.M. They can watch television, the superior proudly states, "until their eyes pop."

Can we seriously think that these kinds of changes are really significant in developing maturity in the growing generation? These are purely incidental aspects of life that no mature man thinks about twice. These are just the ordinary conditions of twentieth-century life; to celebrate these concessions as great steps forward is merely to advertise publicly how far we are still behind. After all, in our culture even a three- or four-year-old child has mastered the tuning of a television set, and by the time he is seven or eight he has learned to ignore it. He becomes remarkably discriminating in his tastes by the time he enters high school, and when he reaches college he has already put televison in its proper place in his life. To make a big deal out of unlimited television permissions, to think that it is a breakthrough to let men wake themselves up in the morning, suggests that our vision of freedom is myopic and picayune.

The fundamental aspects of responsible living should be built into our training systems but not heralded as great advances in the history of education. These are merely the normal healthy circumstances of any mature man's life, and it would be much better not to mention them at all than to proclaim them as the signs of our growing up. What can a responsible man in the world think when he reads that seminarians are now able to talk to one another during the day, that they can study without being supervised, that they can make phone calls without permission, that they can write letters that will not be inspected? He may shake his head and say, "It's about time." But he will never make the mistake of thinking that such permissions are even worth debating by men who really understand the meaning of life. While the world is preparing to launch men to the moon, one gets the impression that some seminaries are tooling up for life in the year 1900.

But centripetal forces are at work in the seminary world, and it is almost embarrassing to sense the self-congratulation we feel at finally letting men called to save the world have some contact with it. It is a minor tragedy to hear seminarians boasting about the freedom they have because now they can "go to the movies" or "buy a few beers." To hear them exulting like adolescents about these inconsequential occupations is to realize that their idea of freedom means to shed rather than to assume responsibility. It is difficult to believe we could be proud of the fact that our seminarians, in their twenties, prize these trivial experiences as "really living." What sense of values is operating when freedom has merely taken on the face of escaping regulations and supervision? It is not disturbing that the new breed wants freedom; it is disturbing if we and they think that just repealing rules is freedom. Seminarians deserve a better coat of arms than a golf club rampant on a TV screen with the motto *Quid pro quo* inscribed beneath.

Freedom is a far different thing. It centers on a man's being responsible for his own existence, for his own relevance to the adult world, for his pursuit of his full growth and true excellence as a human person. "Freedom," Camus says, "is not a reward or a decoration that is celebrated with champagne. Nor yet a gift, a box of dainties designed to make you lick your chops. Oh, no! It's a chore . . . and a long distance race quite solitary and very exhausting. No champagne, no friends raising their glasses as they look at you affectionately. Alone in a forbidding room, alone in the prisoner's box before the judges, and alone to decide in the face of one's self or in the face of other's judgments. At the end of all, freedom is a court sentence; that's why freedom is too heavy to bear, especially when you're down with a fever, or are distressed, or love nobody."[5]

[5] Albert Camus, *The Fall* (New York: Knopf, 1960), pp. 132–133.

Real freedom doesn't lead to selfish satisfactions but to the service of the human family. Man was made, Freud tells us, "to love and to work," and these are the values that illumine the meaning of freedom. It is not easily achieved or maintained and can only be realized by a man who has truly learned to love himself and his neighbor as himself. Freedom is doing the best we can, not just what we feel like, but we are in grave danger of misunderstanding it. It concerns life and death and responding to human needs in a mature and Christ-like fashion. It means we have to possess ourselves so genuinely that we can give of ourselves in the gift of love to others.

But this cannot be learned unless mature values predominate in the world of seminary training. Rectors and religious superiors must keep their hands on the tillers and not think that shore leave after a long journey is really the answer. The seminary is liable to become like Chesterton's celebrated sieve, "which stores the sand and lets the gold run free."

The superiors of today are under real pressure, but at least some of this arises because of healthy growth that is taking place. Some of it arises from the fact that the half-grown and those incapable of growth are making their lack of aptitude for the priesthood and religious life more obvious. Superiors must keep a strong and adult sense of Christian values if they are going to carry out their jobs effectively. Their responsibility to the Church rests on their ability to respond to the challenge of these times.

23 Filling the Void

> "To the full extent of my power, *because I am
> a priest,* I wish from now on to be the first
> to become conscious of all that the world loves,
> pursues and suffers; I want to be the first to
> seek, to sympathize and to suffer; the first to
> unfold and sacrifice myself—to become more
> widely human and more nobly of the earth
> than any of the world's servants. . . ."
> —Pierre Teilhard de Chardin[1]

Modern man has become painfully self-conscious in his search for the meaning of life. He has created a theater of the absurd to act out his gropings, visual arts that blind rather than illumine, a maddened modern music, paeans to alienation, non-heroes, non-books, and non-persons. If religion has proclaimed the meaning of life, it has failed to get a hearing with many of the thinkers, scientists, and men of letters who shape the anguished questions of the day. A void of meaning exists, but men are not looking to the Church to fill it, although She alone can do this. The scientists have been urged to show the way, to take the initiative in leading mankind to a better, if not braver, new world. So too a modern author says that the

[1] *The Divine Milieu* (New York: Harper, 1960), p. 80.

246

poet, rather than the scientist, technician, or statesman, will
have to lead man out of the chaos and bewilderment of modern
life because only the poet can "see around the unknown curve
to guess by means of intuitive wisdom what the unborn thing
we call our future will grow into."[2] And what of religion and
its leaders? Why are its Truth and their voices relatively un-
heeded by the forces that are shaping the future of the human
family?

A playwright's program notes reflect his thoughts about religion:

I suppose what is most distressing for me in reading history is the
way man constantly trivializes the immensity of his experience: the
way, for example, he canalizes the greatness of his spiritual awareness into the second-rate formula of a Church—any Church: how
he settles for a Church or a Shrine or Synagogue: how he demands
a voice, a law, an oracle, and over and over again puts into the
hands of other men the reins of repression and the whip of Sole
Interpretation.[3]

There is no point in saying that these mid-century seekers
are ignorant, ill-informed, or that they lack a true understanding of the meaning of religion. We have piped to them
and they have not danced. The void remains and a self-
righteous feeling that only we can do the job is far different
from actually doing it. Never before in history has the redemp-
tive role of the priests been more challenging or more uncer-
tainly charted. The priest is called to understand his suffering
brothers, to breathe on them the Spirit that alone can bring
them to life, to fill the painful void of meaning with Christ

2 Lillian Smith, quoted in *The New York Times,* March 21, 1965, p. 44.
3 Peter Shaffer, author of *The Royal Hunt of the Sun,* quoted in "New
York," *The New York Herald Tribune,* April 4, 1965, p. 25.

Himself. The great issues of the day are joined in the life that opens up for the priest who is mature enough to respond to his age and its anxieties.

The bright lexicon of modern spirituality might well be examined in the light of the times that must be ransomed. We are, we are reminded, to be "committed" to the Christian "encounter." At the root these words light up the pastoral relationship in dramatic fashion. *To commit oneself* means "to entrust oneself" to another, and *to encounter* means "to meet an enemy." This is the edge of realism for the priest called to love his fellow men. He must lower his defenses, let himself out, expose himself to hurt if "commitment" is to be wrested from the vague visionaries who use the word so often. The priest cannot love the world coldly, remotely, and maybe not even efficiently, but he must do it personally. He must be ready "to meet his enemies," to open himself up to all the painful confusion of modern man. He must turn his other cheek to men who will promptly reward him with another blow.

The priest of the era of Vatican II belongs to all men, and if the prospect is staggering, so too is the opportunity. "There is no such thing as seeking God," Martin Buber tells us, "for there is nothing in which he could not be found." Never before in history have the possibilities for Christianity been so great. It is not so much a situation where everything is against us as one where everything is open to us. It is not as though we have come to a tragic historical frustration of Christ's mission; it is, rather, that we are really just beginning to bring the good news to men.

The priest is involved in the history of salvation; his greatest failure would be to miss the meaning of his vocation, and its challenge to his growth, at this time. The priest, in Chenu's words, is in need of a mentality which, confident of the future, truly hungers after reality. He is in need of an authentic trust in himself, of a deep rooting in the present, of a reconciliation with his own time and his contemporaries.[4]

"When the Son of Man comes, will He find, do you think, faith on the earth?" The answer to that rests with this generation of apostles. For this generation must, in the most trying circumstances of change and confusion, existentially re-establish the relevance of the Church in the lives of men. We must read the signs of the times and respond maturely, or tragically miss the door that is evidently opening wide for us. The mass must be leavened now; the salt must not lose its tang.

Two words catch the burden of the challenge to today's priest: *bishop* and *pastor*. *Bishop* means "one who sees" and *pastor* means "one who feeds." The most unbishoplike thing that can be conceived, then, is to fail to see—to be blind, to lack vision. The most unpastoral thing that can be conceived is to want to be fed rather than to feed. The task for the Church's priests is to have a true vision of the world and its hungers and to have the courage to feed it generously.

[4] M. D. Chenu and Friedrich Heer in "Is the Modern World Atheist?" *Cross Currents* (Winter 1961), p. 24.

Appendix

The Psychological Assessment of Candidates

The purpose of this chapter is to give a concise yet comprehensive overview of what is going on today in the United States in the field of the psychological assessment of candidates for the priesthood and religious life.

The treatment will focus on the areas of greatest concern, i.e., the assessment of personality and of interests. The measurement of intellectual ability and of academic achievement through standardized tests and the collection of social and personal-history data through questionnaires, information sheets and autobiographies will not be considered. It is not that these are unimportant, but rather that they have become so commonly used and widely accepted that they can be taken for granted.

At the present time there is an unprecedented interest and receptivity to assessment on the part of religious superiors and of trained psychologists. There are many talks and published articles which have the aim of informing superiors on these questions. Four recent annual conventions of the American Catholic Psychological Association have devoted sections of their programs to assessment and have drawn unexpectedly large audiences. The A.C.P.A. has a Committee for the Study of Methods in the Psychological Assessment of Candidates for the Religious Life. The Chairman of this committee surveyed the membership of the A.C.P.A. in November 1960 to determine how many were involved in such assessment programs.[1] One hundred and fifty-three responded. A more detailed questionnaire was sent in the Spring of 1962 to those psychologists who had indicated involvement. Fifty-eight psychologists responded, which was 37% of the 157 to whom these questionnaires were sent. Twenty-four were female religious, 22 male religious, 4 secular priests, 3 laywomen and 15 laymen.

Thirty-four of the respondents described rather complete, regularly administered assessment programs. They provided services to 28 communities of male religious, 44 communities of female religious and 2 diocesan seminaries.

This receptivity by religious for scientific methods of selection has flourished in a milieu which is receptive to such approaches. The public has been subjected to selection procedures in the armed services, civilian employment, civil service and in education, has grown used to them and come to accept them. Personnel selection is an established field of specialization within American psychology. After World War II, the book *The Assessment of Men,* which chronicled the struggles of the O.S.S. to select recruits for its highly specialized organization, dramatized the necessity and value of selection methodology. Closer to home, the professions of clinical psychology[2] and of psychiatry[3] have grappled penetratingly with the problems of effectively selecting recruits for their fields. The Protestant[4] and Jewish clergy have likewise been concerned with the selection of clerical candidates, have contributed to research and methodology in this field, and have on-going screening programs.

The selection of religious personnel has its own peculiar problems. The typical problem of selection in the secular world involves choosing a set number of the best-qualified from an oversupply of applicants. There is no question of an oversupply of applicants for the priesthood or for the religious life. All who meet the requirements will be accepted. The problem is one of establishing adequate criteria and determining whether or not each applicant meets them.

While the present climate is one of enthusiasm, the response has not always been such. Initially there was strong opposition to such procedures because it seemed to many priests that there was something inappropriate and profane in applying scientific methodology, admittedly useful in the secular professions, to the discerning of a supernatural calling. Father William Bier,[5] in a number of papers and addresses, has devoted himself to the clarification of this question and to the development of the basic rationale for psychological assessment of candidates for the priesthood and religious life. He has pointed out that the selection of suitable candidates for the priesthood and the religious life and the organized observation of them through the period of probation and training has ever been one of the traditional responsibilities of an ecclesiastical superior. What has happened in our time has been that developments in the field of psychology have put at the disposal of superiors additional precise information which enables them to make a decision based on greater evidence. Any significant present opposition to assessment is not to its fundamental rationale, as previously, but to the effectiveness of the methods used.

The origin of these trends toward personality assessment can be traced to an article written by Father Thomas Verner Moore[6] in 1936 on the rate of serious mental disorder among priests and religious. It was his belief that later mental disorder was primarily due to the acceptance into communities of prepsychotic personalities. He proposed that programs of psychological assessment would be effective in locating such candidates at the time of application, and if they could at that time be eliminated, the rate of subsequent mental disorder would be lowered.

PURPOSES

The primary goal of personality assessment of aspirants is to identify those who are already emotionally disturbed or who are likely later on, under situations of stress, to suffer serious emotional difficulties. Some of the more common categories of unsatisfactory, or at least dubious, candidates are the following:

(1) The severely and chronically scrupulous. The obsessive-compulsive.
(2) The withdrawn, isolated, schizoid candidate.
(3) The impetuous, aggressive candidate with authority problems. The psychopath.
(4) The generally inadequate candidate.
(5) The chronic underachiever.
(6) The latent or overt homosexual and the person with chronic auto-erotic problems.
(7) The passive-dependent candidate.

These categories are not mutually exclusive, and to some extent overlap.

There are a large number of drop-outs from seminaries and religious communities. About 80% of the young men who enter the minor seminary in first-year high school and perhaps 50% who enter in first-year college withdraw before ordination. From the point of view of the individual candidate, improved selection and guidance will prevent many young men and women from making a needless vocational detour. From the point of view of the seminarians who are accepted, it will prevent the dilution of the training program by a large number of candidates who do not persevere. From the point of view of the diocese or community it will lessen the investment in personnel and in funds for so many who eventually leave. It has been the experience of seminary counselors that the lion's share of personal individual attention is given to those who eventually leave, rather than to the candidates who will go on to the goal of the priesthood.

This has led to the development of programs which add to expert diagnosis equally expert counseling and guidance. Such programs are positively oriented toward helping those who are successfully assessed get off to a good start in the seminary. Only an estimated 10% of priesthood candidates are rejected predominantly because of the personality assessment, and these too are helped to make their adjustment. Those candidates who are accepted with problems are helped to start working toward their resolution prior to entrance to the seminary and are referred to a skilled counselor on the seminary staff with whom they can make contact upon arrival. They are thus given the necessary help to start their development immediately and to keep growing through their training years. A necessary adjunct to such pre-seminary screening and counseling programs is effective follow-up work in the seminary in the form of a professionally trained psychological counselor who can give effective help to overcome difficulties located at the time of assessment which are not in themselves so severe as to be an obstacle to acceptance.

Programs, of which counseling is a part, can be of great help in clarifying vocational motivation. Many candidates who meet the criteria for acceptance and who are in no sense a psychological risk are confused and plagued with vocational doubts. This is true despite the fact that they have discussed their vocation with parish priest or vocational director. The skilled personal counselor performs a service to them and to the communities they are contemplating joining by helping them in the assessment interview to clarify, understand and resolve their own vocational motivation. As a result, some with the other necessary qualifications do not apply for the seminary or religious life after their counseling interview; others apply with much greater insight and security about their vocation.

Since emotional disturbance is motivational disturbance, it is not surprising that where assessment procedures identify personality problems there is also likely to be something wrong with the vocational motivation. Many candidates who respond to counseling while in the seminary and work through their previous emotional difficulties discover that, with the resolution of their problem, their vocation has disappeared. This implies that their desire, need or inclination to be a priest or religious was linked to their personality problem. The less mature the personality, the less stable the vocational motivation. There are thus two considerations about accepting candidates with lesser personality problems. There is not only the question of whether they will be able to resolve these problems during their training years but also the further question of the effect the resulting personality growth will have on their vocational motivation if they do so.

While personality tests, both of the inventory and of the projective variety, are the main instruments for personality assessment, the vocational interest test is the instrument for determining to what extent the individual has the pattern of likes and dislikes characteristic of successful members of various occupational groupings. These tests open up new dimensions of assessment. They make it possible to determine to what extent an individual has the characteristic pattern of interests of, for example, the diocesan priesthood or missionary priesthood, of teaching or nursing Sisters, or of teaching Brothers. This knowledge can help the individual in deciding between different types of religious life or between different communities, and can also assist in more satisfactory placement within the community of his choice.

An assessment report is especially helpful to the one responsible for acceptance, when it enables him to resolve a doubtful case. An example of this would be the case of a candidate who is very highly recommended but whose family background raises serious questions. Furthermore, the superior can accept candidates with dubious reports and act on these later when the reports from the houses of training confirm the initial doubt. Finally, such reports, and the fundamental data upon which they are based, provide material for later research and evaluation, which is an important part of any complete assessment program.

PROFESSIONAL QUALIFICATIONS

There is insistence by many workers and writers in this field that the assessment be done by a qualified person. There is a fear that, because of the availability of standardized personality tests, such assessment will be done by the amateur. The possibilities of harm to the individual's mental health and of injustice to a vocation are accentuated when such work is done by those who are not qualified. The precise qualifications needed by one who is to do assessment work have not yet been carefully thought through or agreed upon.

In the survey referred to earlier, of the fifty-eight involved in assessment work, forty-one had a doctoral and seventeen a master's degree. Sixteen had specialized in clinical psychology and six in educational psychology; thirty-two did not specify, other than that their training was in psychology. Four respondents were trained in a field other than psychology, one of them being in psychiatry.

Training in clinical psychology would appear to be the best preparation for the fundamental goal of these programs, which is the assessment of personality strengths and weaknesses. Other types of training within psychology give further desirable preparation in therapy and interviewing, for the problems of personnel selection, for placement, for vocational guidance and for the systematic design of research. There is need for the further refinement of the professional qualifications needed for this work. They may overlap the traditional professional divisions.

There is no single blueprint for an effective assessment program. Each program must be tailored to fit the needs and objectives of the community or diocese which it serves. It should be evaluated on its ability to achieve the goals and purposes for which it was set up. A program for assessing candidates for a teaching order of Sisters concentrated within a single diocese will be very different from a program for assessing candidates for the priesthood in a community devoted exclusively to the foreign missions which draws vocations from the entire country. Present assessment programs in the United States have one common characteristic: they confine themselves to evaluating candidates who are at least completing their high school education and are thus at least seventeen or eighteen years of age.

In terms of knowledge and skills, the following psychological competencies are relevant for one engaging in the psychological assessment of candidates for the priesthood and religious life. Depending on the type of program, certain qualifications will be more necessary than others:

(1) Psychopathology.

(2) Clinical diagnosis and prognosis, especially of late adolescents.

(3) Therapeutic counseling and interviewing.

(4) Psychology of personnel selection and placement.

(5) Psychology of vocational choice and development.

(6) Psychology and sociology of religious personnel.

(7) Psychology of the assessment of candidates for religious vocations.

In order to fulfill the need for specialized preparation over and above basic professional preparation, the previously mentioned Committee on Assessment of the A.C.P.A. has drawn up a proposal for a workshop of a week's duration, which would provide expert consultation for those specializing in this work. A foundation grant is being sought which would subsidize this pioneer venture.

TESTS EMPLOYED IN ASSESSMENT PROGRAMS

The above-mentioned survey discloses that a wide variety of instruments, both group and individual, are used in the thirty-four assessment programs, to evaluate intelligence, achievement, personality and interests. The single most commonly used measure of intellectual ability is the Wechsler Adult Intelligence Scale. The most commonly used personality measure is the MMPI. The Rorschach, TAT, Sentence Completion, and Draw-a-Person tests and the Guilford-Zimmerman Temperament Survey are also widely used. The Kuder Preference Record is the leading measure of vocational interests. The Strong Vocational Interest Blank is also used but necessitates machine scoring and is thus more costly. There are now available a number of special scoring scales for the Kuder and Strong.

A Kuder D scale has been developed for teaching Sisters and one for teaching Brothers. Scoring scales have been developed on the Strong Vocational Interest Blank for diocesan priest, missionary priest, teaching Brother and teaching Sister. Validity studies are in progress on some of these and look promising.

EVALUATION AND RESEARCH

An integral part of assessment work is systematic evaluation to determine whether the program has been effective in accomplishing its purposes. Assessment work has been in progress since shortly after World War II, and there is a realization and acceptance by many of the active workers in this field of the need and importance of evaluation. Several such studies have been published within the last year and others are in process. (Notes 7, 8, 9 and 10.)

There is a large body of research on the psychology and sociology of priests and religious, much of it unpublished material done for graduate theses at the universities. There is now a fairly complete bibliography available.[11] Much of this research gives a valuable background for the specialist in the assessment of religious candidates. This material falls into a few main categories:

(1) Environmental factors associated with a priestly or religious vocation.
(2) Psychology of vocational choice as it applies to religious vocations.
(3) Personality of priests and religious using personality inventories and projective tests.

(4) Vocational interests of priests and religious.
(5) Attitudes of priests and religious.
(6) Personality growth after entrance into religious life.

There are a number of important research needs:

(1) There is a need for an annotated bibliography and for more comprehensive reviews of the research already done. (Notes 12 and 13.) This is a great lack, especially since so much of the research is unpublished. This research has to be integrated with the extensive parallel studies on the clergy of other faiths.
(2) Since most research is by graduate students, there is a need for more research by older and more experienced specialists into all aspects of the problem.
(3) A pressing specific and basic research problem is the development of criteria for effectiveness in the priesthood or religious life.[14] Ordination and profession are not completely satisfactory, especially since the cause of the assessment movement itself was concern over the amount of mental disorder among the ordained and professed. Additional criteria must be explored, such as incidence of later mental disorder, number of changes of assignment, absence of disabling symptoms and later ratings in the priesthood and religious life by peers, superiors, and parishioners and by the individual himself.

Already it is apparent that assessment programs are not only achieving their goals of eliminating the unfit but are leading to significant developments in unexpected directions.

(1) There is an awareness of the need for more adequate follow-up counseling work after acceptance.
(2) There is awareness of needed improvements in training programs to meet the actual growth needs unearthed at

assessment. It is helping faculty and staff to have a clearer picture of the goals of training. They are becoming more aware of the role of feeling and emotion in the lives of candidates and of the conditions which are necessary for growth. There is an examination of whether the training is de facto providing the conditions for growth.

(3) As assessment provides a clearer picture of the type of candidate applying, it also discloses the types of effective youth who are not attracted to a religious vocation. This is raising questions, for those concerned with vocational recruitment, about the proper image of the priest and religious.

REFERENCES

[1] Walter J. Colville, "Psychologists and the Assessment of Candidates for Religious Life," *ACPA Newsletter Supplement* (1962), suppl. nos. 59 and 60.

[2] E. L. Kelly and D. W. Fiske, *The Prediction of Performance in Clinical Psychology* (Ann Arbor, Michigan: University of Michigan Press, 1951).

[3] Robert R. Holt and Lester Luborsky, *Personality Patterns of Psychiatrists* (New York: Basic Books, 1958).

[4] Molly Harrower, "Psychological Tests in the Unitarian Universalist Ministry," *Journal of Religion and Health*, 2 (1963), pp. 129–142.

[5] William C. Bier, S.J., "A Testimonial," *Catholic Psychological Record*, 1 (1963), pp. 3–5.

[6] Thomas V. Moore, O.S.B., "Insanity in Priests and Religious: I. The Rate of Insanity in Priests and Religious; II. The Detection of Prepsychotics Who Apply for Admission to the Priesthood or Religious Communities," *American Ecclesiastical Review*, 95 (1936), pp. 485–498, 601–603.

[7] Walter J. Colville, "Personality Assessment of Candidates to Seminaries: a study of Clinical and Psychometric Methods and Their Effectiveness as Predictors of Success in Major and Minor Seminaries," in S. W. Cook, ed., *The Research Planning Workshop* (New York: Religious Education Association, 1962), pp. 175–188.

[8] Petreolus Hispanicus, "Selecting Seminarians," in Arnold, B. Magda, *et al., Screening Candidates for the Priesthood and Religious Life* (Chicago: Loyola University Press, 1962), pp. 65–105.

[9] Richard P. Vaughan, S.J., "A Psychological Assessment Program for

Candidates to the Religious Life: Validation Study," *Catholic Psychological Record*, 1 (1963), pp. 65–70.

[10] Charles A. Weisgerber, S.J., "Survey of a Psychological Screening Program in a Clerical Order," in Arnold, Magda, *et al.*, *op. cit.*, pp. 107–146.

[11] Paul F. D'Arcy, M.M., *Bibliography of Psychological, Sociological, Literary and Related Studies on the Catholic Priesthood and the Religious Life* (New York: Committee for the Study of Methods in the Psychological Assessment of Candidates for the Religious Life, American Catholic Psychological Association, 1962).

[12] Paul F. D'Arcy, M.M., "Review of Research on the Vocational Interests of Priests, Brothers and Sisters," in Arnold, Magda, *et al.*, *op. cit.*, pp. 149–203.

[13] Vaughan, *op. cit.*

[14] Thomas N. McCarthy and E. Austin Dondero, F.S.C., "Predictor Variables and Criteria of Success in Religious Life: Needed Research," *Catholic Psychological Record*, 1 (1963), pp. 71–80.

Bibliography

PERSONALITY AND GROWTH:

Allport, Gordon, *Becoming*. New Haven: Yale University Press (paper), 1960.

———— *Pattern and Growth in Personality*. New York: Holt, Rinehart & Winston, 1961.

Cameron, Norman, *Personality Development and Psychopathology*. Boston: Houghton Mifflin Company, 1963.

Gardner, John. *Self-Renewal*. New York: Harper & Row, 1963.

McCurdy, Harold, *The Personal World*. New York: Harcourt, Brace & World, Inc., 1961.

Moustakas, Clark, ed., *The Self*. New York: Harper & Brothers, 1956.

———— *Loneliness*. Englewood Cliffs, N.J.: Prentice-Hall, Inc., 1961.

Pearce, Jane, and Newton, Saul, *The Conditions of Human Growth*. New York: The Citadel Press, 1963.

Peck, Robert, and Havighurst, Robert, *The Psychology of Character Development*. New York: John Wiley & Sons, Inc., 1962.

Rogers, Carl, *On Becoming a Person*. Boston: Houghton Mifflin Company, 1961.

Tillich, Paul, *The Courage To Be*. New Haven: Yale University Press, 1952.

PSYCHOLOGY OF YOUTH:

Bier, William, *The Adolescent: His Search for Understanding*. New York: Fordham University Press, 1963.

Blaine, Graham, and McArthur, Charles (with twelve collaborators), *Emotional Problems of the Student.* New York: Appleton-Century-Crofts, Inc., 1961.

Erikson, Erik, ed., *The Challenge of Youth.* Garden City, N.Y.: Anchor Books, 1965.

Sanford, Nevitt, ed., *College and Character.* New York: John Wiley & Sons, Inc., 1964.

Sutherland, Robert, Holtzman, Wayne, Koile, Earl, and Smith, Bert, eds., *Personality Factors on the College Campus*—Review of a Symposium. Austin, Texas: The Hogg Foundation for Mental Health, 1962.

PSYCHOLOGY OF THE LATER YEARS:

Birren, James, ed., *Handbook of Aging and the Individual.* Chicago: University of Chicago Press, 1959.

PERSONAL COUNSELING:

Brammer, Lawrence, and Shostrom, Everett, *Therapeutic Psychology.* Englewood Cliffs, N.J.: Prentice-Hall, Inc., 1960.

Curran, Charles, *Counseling in Catholic Life and Education.* New York: The Macmillan Company, 1952.

Frank, Jerome, *Persuasion and Healing.* New York: Schocken Books, 1963.

PSYCHOPATHOLOGY:

Arieti, Silvano, ed., *American Handbook of Psychiatry.* New York: Basic Books, Inc., 1959.

Kaplan, Bert, ed., *The Inner World of Mental Illness.* New York: Harper & Row, 1964.

Kisker, George W., *The Disorganized Personality.* New York: McGraw-Hill Book Company, 1964.

Landis, Carney, *Varieties of Psychopathological Experience,* F. A. Mettler, ed. New York: Holt, Rinehart & Winston, 1964.

Menninger, Karl, *Man against Himself.* New York: Harcourt, Brace & Company, 1938.

——— Mayman, Martin, and Pruyser, Paul, *The Vital Balance.* New York: Viking Press, Inc., 1964.

White, Robert, *The Abnormal Personality,* 3d ed. New York: Ronald Press Co., 1964.

RELIGIOUS PSYCHOLOGY:

Allport, Gordon, *The Individual and His Religion.* New York: The Macmillan Company, 1962.

Babin, Pierre, *Crisis of Faith.* New York: Herder & Herder, 1963.

Birmingham, William, *Cross Currents of Psychiatry and Catholic Morality,* Joseph Cunneen, ed. New York: Pantheon Books, 1964.

Clark, Walter H., *The Psychology of Religion.* New York: The Macmillan Company, 1958.

Meissner, William, *Annotated Bibliography in Religion and Psychology.* New York: Academy of Religion and Mental Health, 1961.

Oraison, Marc, *Illusion and Anxiety.* New York: The Macmillan Company, 1963.

———— *Love or Constraint?* New York: P. J. Kenedy & Sons, 1951.

VOCATION:

Bowers, Margaretta, *Conflicts of the Clergy.* New York: Thomas Nelson & Sons, 1963.

D'Arcy, Paul, *Bibliography of Psychological, Sociological, Literary and Related Studies on the Catholic Priesthood and the Religious Life.* New York: American Catholic Psychological Association, 1962.

Fichter, Joseph, *Priest and People.* New York: Sheed & Ward, 1965.

———— *Religion as an Occupation.* Notre Dame, Ind.: University of Notre Dame Press, 1961.

Hostie, Raymond, *The Discernment of Vocations.* New York: Sheed & Ward, 1962.

Merton, Robert, Reader, George, and Kendall, Patricia, eds., *The Student Physician.* Cambridge, Mass.: Harvard University Press, 1957.

Super, Donald, Crites, John, Hummel, Raymond, Moser, Helen, Overstreet, Phoebe, and Warnath, Charles, *Vocational Development*. (Columbia University Teachers College. Horace Mann-Lincoln Institute of School Experimentation. Career Pattern Study: Monograph 1.) New York: Teachers College, 1957.

────── *Vocational Maturity of Ninth Grade Boys*. (Columbia University Teachers College. Horace Mann-Lincoln Institute of School Experimentation. Career Pattern Study: Monograph 2.) New York: Teachers College, 1960.

────── Starishevsky, Reuben, Matlin, Norman, and Jordaan, Jean, *Career Development: Self-Concept Theory*. New York: College Entrance Examination Board, 1963.

Tiedeman, David, and O'Hara, Robert, *Career Development: Choice and Adjustment*. New York: College Entrance Examination Board, 1963.

SEMINARY:

Keller, James, and Armstrong, Richard, eds., *Apostolic Renewal in the Seminary in the Light of Vatican Council II*. New York: The Christophers, 1965.

Lee, James, and Putz, Louis, eds., *Seminary Education in a Time of Change*. Notre Dame, Ind.: Fides Press, 1965.

Poole, Stafford, *Seminary in Crisis*. New York: Herder & Herder, 1965.

AUTHORITY AND ADMINISTRATION:

Caplan, Gerald, *Principles of Preventive Psychiatry*. New York: Basic Books, Inc., 1964.

Crow, Lester, and Crow, Alice, eds., *Mental Hygiene for Teachers*. New York: The Macmillan Company, 1963.

Goffman, Erving, *Asylums*. Chicago: Aldine Publishing Company, 1962.

Likert, Rensis, *New Patterns of Management*. New York: McGraw-Hill Book Company, Inc., 1961.

O'Brien, Michael, and Steimel, Raymond, *Psychological Aspects of*

Spiritual Development. Washington, D.C.: Catholic University of America Press, 1964.

Simon, Yves, *Nature and the Functions of Authority*. Milwaukee: Marquette University Press, 1940.

Index of Names

Index of Subjects